Learning to Learn
Across the Life Span

*Robert M. Smith
and Associates*

Learning to Learn
Across the Life Span

 Jossey-Bass Publishers
San Francisco • Oxford • 1990

LEARNING TO LEARN ACROSS THE LIFE SPAN
by Robert M. Smith and Associates

Copyright © 1990 by: Jossey-Bass Inc., Publishers
                     350 Sansome Street
                     San Francisco, California 94104
                              &
                     Jossey-Bass Limited
                     Headington Hill Hall
                     Oxford OX3 0BW

Library of Congress Cataloging-in-Publication Data

Learning to learn across the life span / Robert M. Smith and
   associates. — 1st ed.
      p.   cm. (The Jossey-Bass higher education series)
   Includes bibliographical references and index.
   ISBN 1-55542-279-9
   1. Learning.   2. Learning, Psychology of.   3. Cognitive learning.
4. Continuing education.   I. Smith, Robert McCaughan, date.
II. Series.   III. Series: The Jossey-Bass higher education series.
LB1060.L428   1990
370.15′23—dc20   90-40145
CIP

Manufactured in the United States of America

JACKET DESIGN BY WILLI BAUM

FIRST EDITION

Code 9073

The Jossey-Bass
Higher Education Series

Contents

Preface

Learning to Learn Across the Life Span represents the most comprehensive treatment of its subject yet undertaken. It explains the principles, processes, and strategies involved in learning to learn, which is at the same time a multifaceted concept pregnant with implications; a goal for individuals, facilitators, and organizations; and a burgeoning area of inquiry and practice. This book encourages the reader to appreciate the power and potential of the learning-to-learn concept and to make applications that go far beyond study tips for learning how to be taught. The following questions are among those addressed:

1. How do people learn to learn?
2. How are teaching, learning, and learning to learn related?
3. To what extent does learning to learn represent a developmental process?
4. How can learning-to-learn components be incorporated into program and curriculum development, and instruction?
5. What principles and guidelines should inform the design and implementation of learning-to-learn activities?
6. How do context and setting affect learning to learn?
7. How can the electronic technologies contribute?
8. What can educators, educational systems, and policy

makers hope to gain from devoting energy and resources to the learning-to-learn idea?

These central issues emerged from conferences that were held at Northern Illinois University in 1986 and 1987, in which learning to learn was explored at length by a group of authorities from seven nations. As the second conference moved toward conclusion, conviction arose as to the feasibility and potential value of producing a comprehensive treatment of a subject previously treated somewhat atomistically. Some of the conference participants have contributed chapters to this resulting publication; they are joined by others who consented to add their experience and expertise. All in all, twenty-four persons have made major contributions to this book: the authors named on pages ix–xi and Ronald Cervero, Patricia Cross, Ravindra Dave, Virginia Griffin, Dai Hounsell, Alan Knox, Jim L'Allier, Roger Säljö, and Dusan Savicevic.

During the past two or three decades researchers and practitioners from various disciplines, fields, and settings have increasingly turned their attention to understanding what is involved in learning effectively and how people can be helped in the learning process. As a result, major contributions have come from research on metacognitive abilities and their enhancement by training interventions. The phenomenon of student learning, especially in secondary and higher education, has been explored in depth and important practical applications of the findings have been made. Much has been revealed about both self-directedness and collaboration in learning and their implications for learning to learn. These efforts have yielded such approaches and strategies as the reflective journal, the learning conversation, problem-based learning, learning style mapping, concept mapping, visualization, strategic teaching, Vee diagramming, participation training, Walkabout, intelligent tutorial systems, learning management, and double-loop learning, to name but a few.

Learning to Learn Across the Life Span synthesizes much of what we now know and can reasonably infer from research, theory building, and practice. It envisions a world in which learning to learn becomes a central purpose of education and an equal partner in the teaching-learning transaction. It links learning to learn and personal empowerment. It makes suggestions for better dissemination of information about learning to learn. It anticipates the implications of learning to learn for meeting the demands of an increasingly volatile and information-rich world in which people will assume greater control of their own learning. The emphasis is on practical applications of this intriguing concept. A major area of application is the facilitation of understandings, competencies, and strategies related to what, why, where, when, and how to learn.

Organization of the Book

The chapters in Part One, "The Concept and Meaning of 'Learning to Learn,'" provide the theoretical underpinnings for the book. Chapter One describes learning to learn as goal and process, demonstrates the centrality of context, and reveals something of the power and potential of the idea. Chapter Two reviews a considerable amount of the literature concerning learning to learn, identifies eleven outstanding characteristics of the concept, confronts issues of definition, and explains the importance of understanding how learners themselves construe learning opportunities and tasks. Chapter Three describes its author's personal journey of investigation into the meaning of the concept and presents a model to guide reflection, theory building, and practice. Chapter Four shows how people's nonrational capacities can be employed and fostered in learning and learning to learn. Chapter Five links theory and practice for fostering initiative and self-directedness in learning on the part of adults. Chapter Six presents guidelines for the design and facilitation of learning-to-learn activities.

Part Two, "Empowering Learners at All Levels," begins with Chapter Seven, which shows how to build and enhance children's strategies for reflecting on learning, connection making, and problem solving. Chapter Eight advocates a "thinking curriculum" for secondary education and presents models and strategies for teachers to use in implementing this curriculum.

Chapter Nine discusses a variety of successful learning-to-learn initiatives by colleges and universities, ranging from the entry-level course to the restructuring of institutional student support services. In Chapter Ten, the first comprehensive project to identify learning competencies and skills for participants in adult basic education is described. Chapter Eleven explores applications of learning to learn in the workplace and how they translate into an array of human resource development activities. In Chapter Twelve, self-planned learning as a universal, lifelong activity is discussed and suggestions are made for its encouragement and enhancement.

Part Three, "Challenges and Opportunities," explores trends, futures, and agendas for action. Chapter Thirteen relates learning to learn to the knowledge explosion and the new information technologies, describing the kind of learning and learning skills that will be required. Chapter Fourteen suggests centering research on learning to learn in the reflective domain of learning, describes appropriate methods for doing so, and presents some topics for investigation. Chapter Fifteen distills implications for programming and teaching from a learning-to-learn perspective, developing effective preservice and inservice education, and making dissemination more systematic.

Audience for the Book

This book is addressed to multiple audiences. People willing to consider the potential utility of the learning-to-learn idea can gain a comprehensive view of its dimensions and possibilities for implementation, while those already at work implementing the concept will find information about co-workers, together with useful principles, strategies, and tools. It is anticipated that the book can be utilized by curriculum and program developers, teacher trainers, educational design and media specialists, human resource managers and consultants, university faculty and students seeking research agendas, and people in remediation and student support centers in colleges and universities. There is also a wide spectrum of leaders and policy makers whom the book can help when they make decisions to further research and dissemination of the learning-to-learn idea.

Acknowledgments

Finally, I would like to thank the following persons for their encouragement and assistance: Denise Davis, Rick Kieltyka, John Niemi, Suzanne Royer, Ed Rund, L. Glenn Smith, and Patricia Wolf Smith.

DeKalb, Illinois Robert M. Smith
July 1990

The Authors

Frank P. Bazeli is professor and chair of the secondary education faculty, Northern Illinois University.

Stephen D. Brookfield is professor of higher and adult education, Teachers College, Columbia University.

Philip C. Candy is associate professor and director of academic staff development, Queensland University of Technology, Australia.

Mark Cheren is director of the adult degree program, Capital University, Cleveland, Ohio.

David J. Collett is professor of adult and vocational education, University of Alberta, Canada.

Mary E. Diez is chair of the division of education, Alverno College, Milwaukee, Wisconsin.

Maurice Gibbons is professor emeritus at Simon Fraser University, British Columbia, Canada.

Dennis D. Gooler is professor of education at Northern Illinois University.

David Hammond is president of Hammond and Associates Educational Software Developers, Belvedere, California.

Malcolm S. Knowles is professor emeritus of adult and community college education, North Carolina State University.

Ann Q. Lynch is associate professor of counselor education, Professional and Human Services Department, Florida Atlantic University.

Dana Maxfield is a doctoral candidate in adult continuing education, Northern Illinois University.

C. Jean Moon is associate director of the Center for Math/Science Education Research, University of Wisconsin, Milwaukee.

Robert M. Smith is professor of adult continuing education, Northern Illinois University.

Allen Tough is professor at the Ontario Institute for Studies in Education and the University of Toronto, Canada.

PART ONE

The Concept and Meaning of Learning to Learn

Chapter 1

The Promise
of Learning to Learn

Robert M. Smith

Knowledge about learning to learn far outstrips its dissemination, while few children or adults consistently learn with power, efficiency, and meaning. The personal and social costs run high: unfulfilled potential, dropout, poor educational and career decisions, inadequate responses to change, ineffective programming and instruction. Much of this waste is unnecessary. Three decades of research and development in North America and Europe have clarified the learning-to-learn concept and yielded strategies for implementing it.

In the post–World War II era, several forces have fueled the rapid expansion of interest and activity on behalf of learning to learn. During this period, the acceleration of social change has revealed the importance of lifelong learning. Breathtaking increases in available knowledge and technology have stimulated interest in making learning more efficient. New perspectives on teaching, learning, and the purposes of formal and nonformal education have emerged. Issues of "school reform," educational equity, and empowerment have come to the fore. A proliferation of institutional forms of education has occurred. And methodologies for investigating learning and learning-related activities have become more diverse and sophisticated.

Learning-to-learn activities take many forms, including the following: (1) increasing the individual's self-awareness and capacity for self-monitoring and reflection when engaged in educational activity; (2) helping people to become more active learners and to assume an appropriate amount of control of learning-related activity; (3) broadening the individual's repertoire of learning strategies; (4) preparing people to accommodate the requirements of different delivery systems, methods, and subject areas; (5) enhancing learner confidence and motivation; (6) compensating for metacognitive deficiencies (for example, improving adolescents' ability to think conceptually and analytically); (7) improving group inquiry and problem-solving skills; (8) helping people to make sound choices among the educational programs and resources available to them; and (9) fostering organizational learning.

Terminology

Those who write about the subject assign various labels: metacognitive training, metalearning, learning how to learn, learning to learn. Metacognitive training focuses on improving strategies people use in planning, monitoring, and revising instructional experience, while learning how to learn and learning to learn span a much larger territory. They are used more or less interchangeably to refer to knowledge, processes, and procedures by which people come to and are assisted to make appropriate educational decisions and carry out instrumental tasks associated with successful lifelong learning. These umbrella terms span such diverse concepts as school learning, self-directed learning, small-group learning, and transpersonal learning, as well as deliberate efforts to enhance one's own or others' capacities and skills in these domains. Metalearning also has plausible support as a relatively broad label (Biggs, 1987; Maudsley, 1979). All of these terms can be found in this book, but *learning to learn* predominates because it implies a continuing process as opposed to an attainment and conveys the meaning without implying that *how* to learn is necessarily more important than what, why, when, where, and whether to learn.

Not only is learning to learn a concept, but it represents a goal, a process, and an area of inquiry. As a goal, it challenges educators to foster and individuals to acquire the skills and understandings necessary to learn effectively in the various contexts or settings that they encounter. The process actually consists of a set of interrelated processes and activities, some *intrapersonal* (for example, self-monitoring and reflection), some *interpersonal,* such as those involved in deliberate efforts to facilitate the improvement of others' skills for learning. As an area of inquiry, learning to learn is experiencing rapid growth and yielding a body of subject matter with important implications for educational practice and policy.

A Worthy Goal

Learning to learn enjoys the endorsement of numerous authorities, who advocate it as a goal for educational systems and programs, for instruction, counseling, and consulting, and for incorporation into one's personal philosophy and intentions. It has even been identified as a national goal—an instrumental objective, central to plans for social and economic development. Early in the last decade, the Venezuelan government put the thinking skills improvement program of Edward de Bono into the nation's public school curriculum and exhorted educators to raise the intelligence of the entire population. The post-revolutionary Nicaraguan government identified learning to learn as one of five key national goals for education and development, the Director of Popular Education calling it "more important than learning subject matter" (Smith, 1988, p. 2). One reason for the appeal of the learning-to-learn concept in so-called underdeveloped or third world countries is disillusionment with the heritage of colonial era educational policies that overstressed the importance of formal education systems and proved to have little impact on the quality of life for the vast majority of the population (Blunt, 1988).

There is rapidly growing acceptance of learning to learn

as a fundamental goal for education in childhood and adolescence. In the midst of a rising tide of studies and reports calling for major reforms in elementary and secondary education, Patricia Cross, a respected examiner of issues and arguments, comes down heavily on the side of learning to learn: "How do we educate people to live in a world in which entire industries are created and wiped out in the short span of a single decade? The most important lessons that we can teach our children are the skills and attitudes that will be required of lifelong learners" (Cross, 1984, p. 172). Bruce Joyce, coauthor of the influential *Models of Teaching*, concurs: "The basic skills of learning how to learn should take their place with the basic skills of reading and arithmetic as the keys to a productive lifetime of personal growth" (1981, p. 26).

Maurice Gibbons and Gary Phillips (1982) similarly challenge the schools to join with parents and community agents to prepare children and youth for lifelong learning, especially for "self-education . . . that occurs outside of formal educational institutions." They introduce a description of a research-based program for implementation by saying, "Less than one percent of a person's life is spent in classrooms. Even the best educated adults have five decades or more still to live after they graduate. Yet the need for learning does not diminish. If anything, it becomes greater, more urgent, during adult life. How can this need be met? How can the educational potential of this huge and growing nonschool population be developed? A grand expansion of the educational empire would be impractical. The cost would be prohibitive, and many people would refuse to return to the classroom. But we can adapt the educational institutions we have to teach people how to teach themselves, how to design and pursue their own learning. And we can create community resources which help them to execute the self-educational programs they design" (p. 68). Donald Meichenbaum (1985) admits to a similar vision, asking, "Could one imbue the entire school curriculum and environment with the possibility of nurturing metacognitive skills? Our hope (or delusion) is to eventually develop a program to teach cognitive and metacognitive skills from kindergarten to graduate school. . . . In short, the entire study-skill process could become the focus of education" (pp. 421–422).

An example of one agency that has not left learning-to-learn applications for children and youth to classroom educators is the Cooperative Extension Service, a massive nonformal system with educational programs for people of all ages in every county in the United States. The agency's primary program for pre-adults (ages nine to nineteen) is the 4-H Club, a learn-by-doing organization in which members participate by means of the project method. In this approach, the participant selects and engages in several projects each year, with volunteer adult supervision. (Sample projects are animal science, child care, arts and crafts, water conservation, career planning, and leadership.) The leadership project is directed to skills development in communicating, decision making, participating in and leading groups, interpersonal relations, and learning to learn, each with a set of activities to be planned, carried out, and reflected on by participant and adult helper. Children as young as nine build learning skills by planning, conducting, and processing such activities as a field trip, teaching something to a friend, fantasizing, or describing a favorite teacher. They are assisted in developing habits of reflection on experience, information processing, the arts of questioning and listening, and self-understanding as learners. From 1987 to 1989, some eleven thousand young people participated in the leadership project in Illinois alone; elementary and secondary schools in that state and others now make use of the learning-to-learn materials developed for 4-H members and their leaders (conversations with Professor Mary Munson, University of Illinois-Urbana).

Learning to learn in colleges and universities has numerous advocates. The desired outcome is increasingly seen as far more than the enhancement of study or survival skills. Frequently mentioned results include helping students to develop more sophisticated conceptions of learning and knowledge itself, clarification of the demands and requirements of learning-related tasks, and deeper approaches to learning and study (Gibbs, 1981; Marton, Hounsel, and Entwistle, 1984). The college-educated person should be able to go forth to learn with understanding and critical reflectivity when the institution has taken seriously the responsibility for learning to learn: "If students can be exposed to concepts of how to learn, rather than just the content of learning, they will gain more from a college education than just facts. They will develop cognitive capacities that can never be taken away from them" (Schlossberg, Lynch, and Chickering, 1989, p. 204). Referring particularly to the older and more mature college student, Nancy Schlossberg and her colleagues link learning to learn to empowerment — enabling students to become more sophisticated and assertive consumers of education, even agents of change within the institution whenever that institution proves stagnant, complacent, or unresponsive to the needs of its clientele. They can "become advocates for their own learning process . . . [a] proactive process. . . . In fact, self-empowerment of adult learners through metalearning could revolutionize higher education" (p. 205).

Learning to learn has been proposed as a goal for adult education and the educators of adults since organized efforts at theory building and research in that field emerged after the first world war. Eduard Lindeman, variously termed the father, prophet, and architect of adult education as a modern movement and field of inquiry, described the educated person as one "to whom a valid learning method has become so natural and congenial as to be applicable to all experience." His interpretive biographer states that for Lindeman "learning how to learn and to continue learning is as important as learning a particular subject matter" (Stewart, 1987, p. 229).

The potential of adult education to enhance self-directedness in learning has often been stressed by authorities on the subject. Allen Tough (1971) has identified specific objectives for evaluating the extent to which participation in an educational program enhances capacities for self-planned learning. Malcolm Knowles, observing that in adult education "few objectives are program-wide," endorses only two in his influential *Modern Practice of Adult Education* (1980): to help bring about the maturing of the participant and to increase the participant's ability to engage in self-directed inquiry. He goes on to state that "every unit in every adult-education program, regardless of its particular goals, should contribute these two general objectives" (p. 209).

Learning to learn in the context of the organization has been central to the writings of Paul Bergevin and John McKinley. Their extensive research in adult religious education, for example, leads them to conclude that in this setting, effective learning (often collaborative) calls for participants who are skilled in the arts and attitudes of mutual support, face-to-face communication, self-examination, openness to change, and transfer skills. The role of the adult educator, the approach employed, and the educational outcomes should be focused on these objectives as much as on the acquisition of such content as theology and church history (Bergevin and McKinley, 1971). Bergevin emphasized learning to learn as a global goal for adult education in *A Philosophy for Adult Education* (1967).

In another organizational context, the workplace, mounting interest in learning to learn is evident. *Workplace Basics: The Skills Employers Want* identifies "knowing how to learn" as the foundation, the "most basic of all skills because it is the key that unlocks future success. . . . Equipped with this skill, an individual can achieve competency in all other basic workplace skills from reading through leadership" (Carnevale, 1988, p. 8). The authors urge employers and managers to create "learning organizations," capable of anticipating and responding to change, making flexible responses, and undertaking periodic renewal. In addition to participating in formal education and training activities, such organizations learn through (1) drawing lessons from previous experience, (2) observing other organizations, (3) experimenting, and (4) questioning their own assumptions and norms. Organizational learning requires people willing to acknowledge uncertainty, admit error, respond to the future, and acquire such skills as listening, problem posing, and nurturing (Bennis and Nanus, 1985). According to Alan Mumford (1986), the manager who has learned to learn knows the stages in the process and understands his or her own preferred approaches to it; he or she can identify and overcome blocks to learning and bring understandings from off-the-job learning to on-the-job situations.

This handful of examples typifies the learning-to-learn concept in the sense of a goal. Learning to learn emerges as a useful direction finder and outcome for education at all age levels and in a wide variety of contexts, with implications for instruction, program and curriculum development, and policy making. It represents a condition or set of understandings, attitudes, and skills that an individual can aspire to and an educator can seek to foster. The examples also convey the intense feeling of promise that the concept obviously evokes in its advocates—often the test of a goal worth pursuing.

A Complex Process

Learning to learn as *process* refers to both the acquisition and the fostering of attitudes, understandings, and skills associated with effective participation in education and the carrying out of learning-related tasks. A variety of interrelated intrapersonal and interpersonal processes are involved. The process dimension relates to how certain abilities and competencies are acquired and employed, ways of facilitating their acquisition and employment, and what happens when facilitation is undertaken. Two examples follow:

1. In order to enhance a group's effectiveness in collaborative learning, one might employ such activities as theory sessions, practice exercises, observation and feedback, and members' analysis of group performance. Facilitation, or training, can be viewed and understood as a process, as can what happens within individuals and to the group as they move through the overall experience—more specifically, what happens that is most directly relevant to group members' becoming more effective at *learning* in groups. Such concepts as developmental stages in groups and the establishing of group norms aid understanding of the process the group undergoes. Members of the group can be expected to experience a variety of negative and positive feelings if they are to deal successfully with the differing ideas, values, and behaviors of other group members as they explore together a problem or a topic or employ unfamiliar procedures. Research and experience provide theory

and strategies related to what to expect and how to work through these issues while moving toward improved performance (McKinley, 1983).

2. A history teacher accepts the challenge to enhance student learning skills and foster more meaningful learning as subject matter is imparted. The teacher might decide to focus on making the structure of the subject more available to the student. A variety of resources and strategies are available—for example, concept mapping and knowledge Vee diagramming, or exercises for finding the key ideas in a chapter or book or for generating meaningful questions. Thus, incorporating a learning-to-learn perspective into teaching is a process of identifying and employing certain strategies and supporting students in their adoption and use; the process will probably involve the teacher's examination of personal assumptions about the purposes of instruction, the students' experience of learning, the utilization of class time, and the evaluation of learning. As the teacher experiments with various activities, she or he develops personal knowledge about the utility of (and the optimum conditions for) employing intervention procedures and strategies where learning to learn becomes a goal of subject matter instruction. Information is available to guide the overall intervention process and shed light on the intrapersonal processes the student can be expected to experience (Gibbs, 1981; Marton, Hounsell, and Entwistle, 1984; Novak and Gowin, 1984; Smith, 1982).

A Developmental Matter. Viewed from the perspective of the life of an individual, learning to learn represents in part a developmental process. The ability to be aware of and reflect on one's own processes while undertaking to learn develops late in children, and it does not automatically increase with age (Schmitt and Newby, 1986). Such self-regulatory mechanisms as checking results, evaluating one's learning strategies, and planning one's next move may be present from early childhood, but they are more often used by older children and adults (Brown, 1987). Some people, in fact, reach adulthood without having acquired such crucial skills for learning (Campione, Brown, and Ferrara, 1982).

The developmental nature of learning to learn can be suggested through a description of an idealized condition, that of the person who has become an active, confident, flexible learner by the time full maturity is reached, one who possesses considerable insight into self-as-learner and a broad repertoire of learning-related understandings and strategies. This is a person who can learn effectively and meaningfully for a wide variety of purposes in a wide number of contexts.

The process of reaching this state obviously could not be the same for any two individuals, but anyone reaching it will probably have attained skills for critical thinking; basic communication and computational skills, including computer literacy; some subject matter mastery; and awareness of a great variety of resources for learning. She or he will know how to problem pose and problem solve, learn from peers and mentors, and conduct a personal learning project. The crucial abilities of self-monitoring while endeavoring to learn and reflecting on experience and learning-directed activity will be well developed. The process through which the individual attained this condition would have been a blend of more or less automatic concomitants of learning itself and of myriad experiences (the richer the better) in such settings as the home, the school, the voluntary association, and the workplace. For the individual, some of the experience will have been positive, insofar as it relates to becoming a successful learner; some will have been negative but converted to positive by the way it is responded to; some may have left wounds that have yet to heal—such as math or exam anxiety, difficulty in obtaining useful feedback, or a closed mind regarding certain topics. Some of the idealized learner's expertise will have resulted from deliberate facilitation by others of learning strategies, some from the residual effects of being taught subject matter, and some from observation and reflection on everyday experience.

A relationship between learning to learn and development is identified by Claudia Danis and Nicole Tremblay (1988). After an in-depth study of the learning processes of highly successful self-taught adults with recognized expertise in their fields, the investigators conclude that these subjects "transcend their own learning process" and are able to describe rules and principles pertaining to their own learning processes and the act of learning itself. Since these capacities increased with the age of the subjects, the authors suggest that "metalearning" may well be a developmental process. They also state that their findings reveal "evolution in the adult of his self-awareness as a learner" (pp. 176–177). Ericksen (1984, p. 96) refers to the "life-long process of learning how to learn independently."

It has even been suggested that learning to learn represents what might be termed a global evolutionary process and challenge. The anthropologist/sociologist Jules Henry concluded a quarter of a century ago that the human condition is not likely to improve until mankind (1) becomes more adept at confronting education with an unfettered mind, confidence, creativity, and intellectual curiosity and (2) unlearns various stereotypes that inhibit learning. After many years of research, much of which was centered in education and schooling, Henry, in *Culture Against Man* (1965, p. 283), stated that "the paradox of the human condition is expressed more in education than elsewhere in human culture, because learning to learn has been and continues to be *Homo Sapiens'* most formidable evolutionary task."

Understood as a goal and a developmental process that comprise a set of interrelated subprocesses, learning to learn clearly represents a complex matter. The complexities involved can be expected to bedevil the theorist and challenge the researcher; however, they preclude successful applications of the concept no more than the complexity of learning itself precludes learning by the individual or its facilitation by parent, instructor, or mentor.

The Importance of Context

Context impacts learning and learning to learn. It affects what, why, how, when, and where we learn, as well as the evaluation and application of what we learn. Context includes educational settings and environments for learning; subject matter or content; and the personal learning context, or orientation, of the individual. Perhaps as significant as context is the individual's interpretation of it: "Approaches to learning are highly context-dependent. That is they vary within the same student between different tasks and are functionally related to students' perceptions of teaching and assessment" (Martin and Ramsden, 1986, p. 150). To some extent learning in, for example, university and workplace require different competencies and strategies. Successful efforts on behalf of learning to learn take into account the relevant contextual realities and demands.

Institutional Settings as Context. The home, the school, the 4-H club, the university, the church, the hospital, the corporation — all clearly constitute different contexts for learning, and no organization in any one of the categories is exactly like another. The successful implementation of learning-to-learn activity in such settings is aided by identifying how the organization or institution itself affects the learning climate, the opportunities for learning, and the outcomes of learning.

Organizational goals, policies, norms, regulations, and practices impact the person who learns or considers the prospects for learning in the environment in question. In schools and colleges, student learning is influenced by overall policies and climate, departmental and course requirements, and the nature of the subject matter to be learned. In the home, norms, values, and climate also affect learning. In the middle-class home of a friend of mine, where the family gathered for at least two meals a day, the seven children were expected to remain silent at the table — not an ideal environment for the fostering of curiosity and inquiry. Some corporations go to great lengths to establish policies, procedures, and incentives that enable employees to take advantage of a wide variety of opportunities for academic instruction, in-house training, mentoring, and on-the-job problem solving. Other corporations pay little attention to these matters; in some the corporate values, norms, and policies favor only the education and development of management personnel (Cheren, 1987).

Some higher education institutions maintain multifaceted programs to enable the mature or returning student to make a smooth transition into an appropriate course of study, acquire or sharpen the necessary strategies, access various support services, and successfully link education to career planning and placement. Other colleges and universities exhibit little interest in such activity. Any comprehensive response to bridge this learning-to-learn gap would require examination and analysis of clientele needs to uncover appropriate modifications in policy and practice (for example, making various services available at night or on weekends), as well as appropriate programmatic responses by counselors and faculty (Schlossberg, Lynch, and Chickering, 1989).

Learning-to-learn advocates point to many aspects of the secondary school environment that stand in the way of learning for meaning and understanding and for acquiring attitudes and strategies likely to be useful in learning in adulthood. As with correctional education, in some secondary schools considerations of security and the maintenance of order contribute to a climate inimical to success by all but the more advantaged and determined. Even in more favorably situated schools, state and local policies and regulations seem to be increasingly driving instructional and evaluative practices that run counter to the acquisition of competence for self-planned learning that leads to collaborative learning and problem solving in adulthood (Resnick and Klopfer, 1989). As we shall see later in this book, demands on teachers to "teach to the test" and "cover" ever greater quantities of often ill-digested subject matter leave little time for attention to learning skills enhancement and the cultivation of attitudes and capacities for lifelong learning.

By examining a setting, we can identify learning competencies that are especially relevant for a particular institution or organization. For an organization that makes use of small groups for problem identification and problem solving, efforts to foster the acquisition of collaborative learning skills make sense. A university with a low completion rate in its distance education offerings can provide program participants with training for learning from text, self-questioning techniques, report writing, ways to relate a televiewing experience to course objectives, and so forth. High-achieving high school students bound for demanding university academic programs will have learning-to-learn needs different than marginally successful students entertaining the idea of entering a proprietary school or the job market. The latter should profit from coming to understand postsecondary options for job-related training and how to investigate the claims of providers. And even a perfunctory examination of the adult basic education environment reveals that confidence-building activity is probably in order for the entering student.

What about the home as environment for learning? A child who grows up in a resource-rich environment and is supported in efforts to utilize it obviously enjoys great advantages over one whose development of motivations, interests, and cognitive skills is largely left to outside influences. The home can become something of a laboratory for learning and (to the extent it constitutes a natural process) for learning to learn. The self-taught individuals studied by Danis and Tremblay (1988), highly successful at directing their own learning projects, are able to "create an environment for themselves which has educative potency" (p. 188).

Subject Matter as Context. A subject area often represents a challenging and sometimes forbidding context. Each has its characteristic modes of analysis and discourse. Academic disciplines and subject matter areas tend to reflect and assume the need for characteristic ways of thinking. Mathematics and science emphasize problem solving; economics and philosophy require analytical thinking; the arts stress imagination and creativity. "Models of teaching" represent modes of thinking that become part of the learned content. Teaching models reflect a wide variety of emphases: problem solving, inquiry, critical thinking, competition, negotiation, democratic process, experiential discovery, imaging, behavior modification, self-understanding. Content and the way it is presented convey not only a particular subject area but a way of reasoning (Joyce and Weil, 1986; Maxfield and Smith, 1987). In the context of a particular course or subject area, one needs to accommodate the nature of the subject matter, the methods employed, and the ways of demonstrating what has been learned. Also important is what Dai Hounsell (1988) calls the grammar of study. From his experience in researching university students' perceptions of what was expected of them when writing essays, and as a result of finding major discrepancies between student and faculty expectations, he states: "The first implication of the kind of research that we're talking about is that study skills in vacua . . . isolated from a disciplinary context — isolated from a course setting — can't actually make much headway. If we give students training in things like organizing their time, essay planning, style, punctuation and so on, all of those things won't make much of a difference. . . . Instead we might see the focal issue in cases like this as bound up with something that I want to call, perhaps rather grandly, 'the nature of academic discourse.' This refers to the 'grammar of study' [accompanying a] discipline — the norms, the principles, the rules by which academics, specialists within a particular discipline, communicate with one another . . . what they understand to be the nature of their discipline and its way of looking at the world as a form of inquiry" (p. 115).

Personal Learning as Context. Personal learning includes the values, goals, and assumptions one brings to an educational setting or a situation with potential for learning and learning to learn, together with one's learning style and repertoire of available strategies. This orientation is shaped by total life experience as well as experience in educational institutions. Culture and ethnicity influence that shaping, as they influence personality development. In secondary and higher education, the individual's values and goals affect responses to subject matter, instruction, assignments, and strategy choices. Qualitatively different results usually occur when the goal is merely to get by as opposed to competing for honors (Biggs, 1987). In literacy and English as a Second Language programs, institutional methods may be at variance with participants' culturally derived expectations and preferred ways of learning and being taught.

Learning style encompasses a person's characteristic ways

of information processing, feeling, and behaving in learning situations. Tendencies and preferences are involved—for example, tendencies to persist and persevere when seeking to learn or tendencies to rely on one or two of the senses more than others; preferences for the amount of external structure and affiliation present in the learning situation, as well as for time, place, and physical arrangements for learning. No person's learning style is identical to another's. Style plays an important role in determining choice of educational activities and response to situations in which one has little or no choice. Styles evolve and change over time—hence some educators' interest in enhancing or broadening styles through systematic exposure to new or unfamiliar methodologies, activities, or environments. Learning style profiling and collaborative analysis of the implications has proved to be an effective way to foster awareness and self-understanding as learner and ability to cope with obstacles to learning (Smith, 1982).

The competencies one possesses represent a component of personal learning context. Competencies for various modes of learning or educational settings have been identified in the literature (Cheren, 1987; Knowles, 1975; Smith, 1982) and are alluded to or discussed throughout this book. The participants in the 1986 conference at Northern Illinois University developed a set of generic competencies, which they labeled cognitive, personal, and interpersonal. The cognitive category included organizing and relating new information; retaining and recalling information; transfer skill; thinking convergently, divergently, critically; and understanding the nature of knowledge. The personal category included understanding of self as learner; confidence, persistence, openness, and flexibility; and awareness and sense of purpose in life and career. Finally, the interpersonal competencies included giving and receiving feedback; contextual analysis; collaborative inquiry; and using human resources (Smith, 1988, pp. 82–83).

Culture as Context. Culture and the enculturation process play an important role in the development of the individual's orientation to learning. Lack of experience in collaborative learning leaves the products of British schools and colleges ill equipped in that methodological context, according to an authority on learning to learn in the United Kingdom (Hounsell, 1988, p. 21). Of Laotian immigrants receiving English language instruction, Erika Lert (1980, p. 58) reports, "I observed an atmosphere of tension and disorientation in the classroom which . . . I felt to be symptomatic of a cultural clash . . . [resulting from] a lack of awareness Anglo teachers and administrators had regarding the students' preferred learning techniques. These included mimesis, identification with teacher, peer communication, and group cooperation and support." Even the term *learning* has different connotations from language to language. Some languages employ the same word for teaching and learning, with a suffix to convey an active meaning to the former term and a passive one to the latter.

Paulo Freire (1974) found Latin American peasants likely to believe that becoming literate represented an unrealistic personal goal—a condition reserved for the wealthy or influential—and that effective facilitation of literacy required instilling respect for previous life experience and previous learning as well as the modifying of negative self-images. The so-called dominant culture—through its definitions of learning, knowledge, and education—helps to shape the personal learning contexts of the members of a society. In an essay on learning to learn from experience, Phyllis Cunningham (1983, p. 68) states that "the most important learning for all learners is acquiring critical consciousness. The ability to analyze social structures will depend on the learner's understanding of power and how it works in the social system. When learners understand how gender, race, ethnicity, values, and culture are given or denied status or power by the dominant culture, then knowledge and schooling are demystified and learners are in charge of their own learning."

Clearly, context is central to understanding the learning-to-learn concept and acting on its implications. The chapters in Part Two of this book focus on contextual implications and applications.

Awareness, Reflection, and Self-Monitoring

Critical to effective learning and to helping others become more
effective learners are awareness and reflection, which exhibit an
interactive and mutually reinforcing relationship: "Awareness
and reflection are not merely symptoms of development in
learners, they bring about the development. It is through engaging students in reflecting upon the process and outcomes of
their studying that progress is made. . . . Above everything else,
it is the encouragement of students' active reflection about their
studying which is the cornerstone to their development" (Gibbs,
1981, pp. 90–91). Experience and research indicate that
Graham Gibbs's conclusions apply equally well to nonstudent
learning. Elsewhere I posited "self-understanding as learner" as
fundamental and stated: "Educational experience that involves
constructive self-examination stands to leave [any] learner better equipped for further learning because a central task of
learning how to learn is developing awareness of oneself as
learner" (1982, p. 57). Biggs (1987) stresses the importance of
becoming aware of one's own learning processes and increasingly gaining control over them.

People need to be (and therefore to become) aware of
their motives, purposes, and goals for learning; they need to
understand that different learning-related tasks make different
demands on them. Awareness, or understanding, of self-as-
learner includes preferred ways of intaking and processing
information or receiving instruction and undergoing evaluation, as well as preferred environments for learning. Awareness
of the distinction between learning and being taught can be
useful. This kind of awareness and self-understanding informs
reflection in learning, which Edward Cell (1984) defines as the
process of interpreting our experience. He distinguishes between ongoing reflection or "primary thinking" and secondary
reflection, in which from time to time "we remove ourselves
from the action to reflect more carefully and clearly on what has
been happening" (p. 58). The kinds of benefits that can result are
suggested by Alex Main (1985): "The student whose choice of
course was made by dominating parents or teachers . . . begins

to see his or her own potential for choosing and deciding; the student who chose a factual subject because it was easy to rote-learn . . . begins to realize that he or she gets so much more personal challenge from those subjects which use problem-solving skills; the adult learner who chose a university course for its prestige value . . . willingly transfers to a vocational college course with more direct feedback and personal guidance support services; and the housewife returning to study . . . develops greater awareness of the source of guilt feelings about changes in the household's standards. These benefits are not to be measured on any absolute scale, but in terms of the new (or renewed) freedom of choice experienced by the learner" (p. 98). Awareness and reflection can interact for positive impact in the rules we learn by. Sophisticated learners can identify and evaluate the personally meaningful rules and principles ("Avoid math-based subjects." "Study the difficult in the morning.") that govern their learning-related behavior. Being able to articulate these rules implies awareness as well as reflection on the individual's part of the process followed (Danis and Tremblay, 1988).

At first glance, taking control of one's learning would seem to be essential to learning to learn, and becoming self-directed in learning has often been endorsed as the central task of learning to learn. Closer examination of contexts for learning, however, reveals that many situations offer little room for learner control, nor is it always desirable to retain control. One important element in the art of learning to learn is learning to distinguish between elements that are outside of one's control; another is deciding when the relinquishing of control might be appropriate or suited to one's purposes (Smith, 1988, pp. 22–23). Some factors most likely to be subject to control are decisions to participate in an educational situation, whether or not to contribute verbally, and which learning and study strategies to employ. Awareness, reflection, and self-monitoring play critical roles in the making of such decisions.

Deliberate efforts to learn involve action, reflection, and self-monitoring. Choosing a course and carrying out an assignment for that course both require a series of activities, decisions, choices, strategies, and so on. The same holds true of what is often described as self-planned learning (or carrying out a personal learning project), as well as of learning through autonomous groups and mentors. We monitor ourselves for physical responses (fatigue, tension), psycho-sociological factors (anxiety, frustration, "blocks") and programmatic considerations (utility of a resource or strategy, rate of progress toward goals, adequacy of understanding or skills). We often feel pressured by external forces to make instantaneous responses to the data coming in from this monitoring. Our responses are sometimes dysfunctional—for example, substituting one inappropriate strategy for another or resorting to a resource even less useful than the previous one. Although there is a reflective dimension to monitoring, it is in periodic episodes of reflection that we are likely to gain the insights and understandings essential to the satisfactory outcome of a learning activity and to future efforts directed toward learning.

When we reflect on a specific learning event, we tend to extract instrumental inferences related to similar upcoming activity. ("I need to re-read the instructor's evaluative criteria before I submit a report.") We also reflect on larger blocks of educational experience—the first year of high school, college, or graduate school, for example. Here the quality of our reflection will often affect decisions with major implications for self-confidence, financial resources, career, as well as motivation and self-confidence in further learning. Placing reflection and learning in the larger context of life, Cheren (1987, p. 22) speaks of the value of acquiring "the ability-capacity to reflect about where you are in life—the forces in your life situation which inhibit and facilitate your learning and participation in education." Reflecting and acting on the implications early in an educational undertaking can mean the difference between an ordeal and a memorable learning experience.

Awareness, reflection, and self-monitoring, then, interact to make critical contributions in the learning process. They help us to identify and cope with barriers to learning and make satisfactory resolution of issues of self-direction and control. They allow us to extract meaning from everyday experience as well as from schooling and other deliberate efforts to learn.

They are essential to successful deployment of our personal repertoire of learning strategies. They play a part in making successful applications of what is learned, and they enable us to examine and modify the ingrained rules and principles that govern our learning. And they often produce insights that fuel the desire to become more effective at learning and the motivation for further learning.

The Power and the Potential

Applications of the learning-to-learn concept can result in a variety of benefits for educational institutions, agencies, and programs and for those whom they serve. Instructional applications of nonrational, transpersonal, and holistic learning are accelerating the rate at which people can acquire factual information and foreign language vocabulary words (Ostrander and Schroeder, 1979). People can also be helped to move away from the surface processing associated with rote learning to the deep processing associated with more meaningful learning (Biggs, 1987; Marton, Hounsell, and Entwistle, 1984). They can receive the necessary preparation and support to meet both personal and institutional goals in the often bewildering and threatening arenas of school, college, and adult basic education. Parents and potential adult students can save time, effort, and money by acquiring the information necessary to make sound choices among available educational institutions, agencies, and programs (Schlossberg, Lynch, and Chickering, 1989). The potential benefits to the individual and the larger society from expansion of sound, early-childhood intervention programs now appear to be clear to many parents as well as education policy makers (Schweinhart, 1985).

Empirical evidence of the impact of interventions is not lacking. At the University of Michigan, "Learning to Learn (Psychology 100)," an elective course for freshmen developed by Wilbert McKeachie and his associates, enrolls about two hundred students a year and has undergone rigorous evaluation. The results were assessed by pre- and postcourse scores on standardized tests of reading achievement; grades; measures of

personality, expectancy, and anxiety; perceptions of study strategies; and perceived self-improvement. Experimental groups
made greater changes than comparison groups in desired directions on almost all measures. Follow-up studies showed continued grade point improvement by learning-to-learn course participants in the ensuing semesters. Women, anxious students,
and high-aptitude students were among those who benefited
most (McKeachie, Pintrich, and Lin, 1985). By 1984 a thousand University of Texas (Austin) students were enrolling in a
semester-long learning strategies course designed for entry-level
high-risk students and underachieving advanced students. In
addition to rapidly increasing student demand, the positive
impact of this instruction has been verified by university data on
student retention, by student comments, and by experimental
research. A course module on "comprehension monitoring" has
been particularly useful (Weinstein and Rogers, 1985).

Stanford University offers a nine-week credit course for
students who are dissatisfied with their grades. Emphasis is on
personal goal setting, reflection on personal strategies, matching strategies with intentions, and understanding and remembering what is read. A study of one hundred participating
students in the 1981–1982 school year revealed average grade
point increases—and maintenance for at least one additional
term—of more than a full point on a four-point scale (Biggs,
1987). After studying high-risk students, Marcia Heiman, one of
the developers of "Learning to Learn," a widely used training
system for improving academic performance, reports that in
one New England community college employing the system,
students in the learning-to-learn program, who were able to read
at only a sixth grade level, were compared with students at the
same reading level receiving traditional remediation (tutoring
or basic skills support). The learning-to-learn students earned a
.7 higher grade point average and had only a 30 percent dropout
rate after three semesters, as opposed to 70 percent for students
receiving the contrasting treatment (Heiman, 1985).

Conclusion

New ways of looking at education, teaching, and learning are in
order. The shift in perspective that has almost brought learning

and the experience of learning to parity with teaching requires still further modification. Needed now is a paradigm that not only links teaching and learning in a reciprocal and collaborative manner—a transaction—but also links teaching and learning to learning to learn. Such a paradigm implies significant changes in perspective. Teaching becomes more learning-centered and consequently learning-to-learn-centered. Education becomes a process of not only arranging environments and conditions for learning to occur, but, equally important, for learning to learn to take place. And people begin to see their learning skills, capacities, and strategies as precious personal assets. They become more aware and knowledgeable partners in the teaching-learning transaction, and they become better equipped to hold accountable those who would presume to educate and teach them.

These changes will obviously not come easily. It is increasingly evident that implementing the learning-to-learn idea requires examination and modification of deeply ingrained assumptions, values, and habits. The notion that institutions have a responsibility to foster clients' learning capacities and competencies may seem unreasonable, impractical, or unprofitable to policy makers, administrators, and programmers. The most likely response, understandably, of instructors challenged to implement the concept goes something like this: "I don't have time enough now to cover the important material in the courses I teach." Implicit in the response are critical assumptions about the purposes and goals of education and instruction, the roles of instructor and those instructed. Implicit in a policy maker's statement that "what kids really need is more math and science if America is to remain competitive" is a set of assumptions about the role of schools in society. Finally, the individual usually possesses views of what education, knowledge, and learning "are" that can stand in the way of his or her development as a learner.

The means are available now for greatly accelerating the application of existing knowledge about learning-to-learn and for realizing the latent power of the concept. Potential payoffs loom large, as do implications of failure to seize the opportunities.

References

Bennis, W., and Nanus, B. *Leaders*. New York: Harper & Row, 1985.

Bergevin, P. E. *A Philosophy for Adult Education*. Greenwich, Conn.: Seabury, 1967.

Bergevin, P. E., and McKinley, J. *Participation Training for Adult Education*. St. Louis, Mo.: Bethany Press, 1965.

Bergevin, P. E., and McKinley, J. *Adult Education for the Church*. St. Louis, Mo.: Bethany Press, 1971.

Biggs, J. B. *Student Approaches to Learning and Studying*. Melbourne: Australian Council for Educational Research, 1987.

Blunt, A. "Education, Learning and Development." *Convergence*, 1988, *21* (1), 37–54.

Brown, A. "Metacognition, Executive Control, Self-Regulation and Other More Mysterious Mechanisms." In F. E. Weinert and R. H. Kluwe (eds.), *Metacognition, Motivation and Understanding*. Hillsdale, N.J.: Erlbaum, 1987.

Campione, J. C., Brown, A. L., and Ferrara, R. A. "Mental Retardation and Intelligence." In R. J. Sternberg (ed.), *Handbook of Human Intelligence*. New York: Cambridge University Press, 1982.

Carnevale, A. P., and others. *Workplace Basics: The Skills Employers Want*. Alexandria, Va.: American Society for Training and Development, 1988.

Cell, E. *Learning to Learn from Experience*. Albany: State University of New York Press, 1984.

Cheren, M. E. (ed.). *Learning Management: Emerging Directions for Learning to Learn in the Workplace*. Information Series no. 320. Columbus: National Center for Research in Vocational Education, Ohio State University, 1987.

Cross, K. P. "The Rising Tide of School Reform Reports." *Phi Delta Kappan*, 1984, *66* (3), 167–172.

Cunningham, P. C. "Helping Students Extract Meaning from

Experience." In R. M. Smith (ed.), *Helping Adults Learn How to Learn.* New Directions for Continuing Education, no. 19. San Francisco: Jossey-Bass, 1983.

Danis, C., and Tremblay, N. A. "Autodidactic Learning Experiences: Questioning Established Adult Learning Principles." In H. B. Long (ed.), *Self-Directed Learning: Research and Application.* Athens: Department of Adult Education, University of Georgia, 1988.

Ericksen, S. C. *The Essence of Good Teaching: Helping Students Learn and Remember What They Learn.* San Francisco: Jossey-Bass, 1984.

Freire, P. *The Pedagogy of the Oppressed.* New York: Seabury, 1974.

Gibbons, M., and Phillips, G. "Self-Education: The Process of Lifelong Learning." *Canadian Journal of Education,* 1982, 7 (4), 67–86.

Gibbs, G. *Teaching Students to Learn.* Milton Keynes, England: Open University Press, 1981.

Heiman, M. "Learning to Learn." *Educational Leadership,* Sept. 1985, *43,* 1, 20–24.

Henry, J. *Culture Against Man.* New York: Random House, 1965.

Hounsell, D. J. Edited transcript of conference participation. In R. M. Smith (ed.), *Theory Building for Learning How to Learn.* DeKalb, Ill.: Educational Studies Press, 1988.

Joyce, B. "Learning How to Learn." *Theory into Practice,* 1981, *19* (1), 15–27.

Joyce, B., and Weil, M. *Models of Teaching.* (3rd ed.) Englewood Cliffs, N.J.: Prentice-Hall, 1986.

Knowles, M. S. *Self-Directed Learning.* New York: Association Press, 1975.

Knowles, M. S. *The Modern Practice of Adult Education: From Pedagogy to Andragogy.* (Revised ed.) Chicago: Association Press, 1980.

Lert, E. N. "Adult Second Language Acquisition: Laotian Hmong in Southland." Master's thesis, Brown University, 1980.

McKeachie, W. J., Pintrich, P. R., and Lin, Y. "Teaching Learning Strategies." *Educational Psychologist,* 1985, *20* (3), 153–160.

McKenzie, L. (ed.). "Participation Training." *Viewpoints,* 1975, *51* (entire issue).

McKinley, J. "Training for Effective Collaboration Learning." In R. M. Smith (ed.), *Helping Adults Learn How to Learn.* New Directions for Continuing Education, no. 19. San Francisco: Jossey-Bass,1983.

Main, A. "Reflection and the Development of Learning Skills." In D. J. Boud, R. Keogh, and D. Walker. *Reflection: Turning Experience into Learning.* New York: Nichols, 1985.

Martin, E., and Ramsden, P. "Do Learning Skills Courses Improve Student Learning?" In J. A. Bowden (ed.), *Student Learning: Research into Practice.* Parkville, Australia: University of Melbourne, 1986.

Marton, F., Hounsell, D. J., and Entwistle, N. J. *The Experience of Learning.* Edinburgh: Scottish Academic Press, 1984.

Maudsley, D. B. "A Theory of Metalearning and Principles of Facilitation." Unpublished doctoral dissertation, University of Toronto, Canada, 1979.

Maxfield, D., and Smith, R. M. "Learning to Learn." In C. Klevins (ed.), *Materials and Methods in Adult Continuing Education.* Los Angeles: Klevins, 1987.

Meichenbaum, D. "Teaching Thinking: A Cognitive-Behavioral Perspective." In S. F. Chipman and J. W. Segal (eds.), *Thinking and Learning Skills.* Hillsdale, N.J.: Erlbaum, 1985.

Mumford, A. "Learning to Learn for Managers." *Journal of European Industrial Training,* 1986, *10* (2) (entire issue).

Novak, J. D., and Gowin, D. B. *Learning How to Learn.* New York: Cambridge University Press, 1984.

Ostrander, S., and Schroeder, L. *Superlearning.* New York: Dell, 1979.

Pfeiffer, J. W., and Jones, J. E. *A Handbook of Structured Experiences for Human Relations Training.* San Diego, Calif.: University Associates, published annually since 1972.

Resnick, L., and Klopfer, L. (eds.). *Toward the Thinking Curriculum: Current Cognitive Research Association for Supervision and Curriculum Development Yearbook.* Washington, D.C.: Association for Supervision and Curriculum Development, 1989.

Schlossberg, N. K., Lynch, A. Q., and Chickering, A. W. *Improv-*

ing Higher Education Environments for Adults: Responsive Programs and Services from Entry to Departure. San Francisco: Jossey-Bass, 1989.

Schmitt, M. C., and Newby, T. J. "Metacognition: Relevance to Instructional Design." *Journal of Instructional Development,* 1986, *9* (1), 29–33.

Schweinhart, L. J., and others. "The Promise of Early Childhood Education." *Phi Delta Kappan,* 1985, *66* (8), 548–553.

Smith, R. M. *Learning How to Learn: Applied Theory for Adults.* New York: Cambridge Book Company, 1982.

Smith, R. M. (ed.). *Theory Building for Learning How to Learn.* DeKalb, Ill.: Educational Studies Press, 1988.

Stewart, D. W. *Adult Learning in America: Eduard Lindeman and His Agenda for Lifelong Education.* Malabar, Fla.: Krieger, 1987.

Tough, A. *The Adult's Learning Projects.* Toronto, Canada: Ontario Institute for Studies in Education, 1971.

Weinstein, C. E., and Rogers, B. T. "Comprehension Monitoring as a Learning Strategy." In G. d'Ydewalle (ed.), *Proceedings of the Twenty-third International Congress of Psychology of the International Union of Psychological Science, Acapulco, Mexico, September 2–7, 1984,* Vol. 3: *Cognition, Information Processing, and Motivation.* Amsterdam, The Netherlands: North-Holland, 1985.

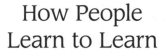

Chapter 2

How People
Learn to Learn

Philip C. Candy

With the exception of such physical necessities as breathing, learning is probably the most ubiquitous of all human activities. In all cultures and in all ages, people have had to adapt to changing, and often rapidly changing, circumstances. Throughout their lives, people learn to speak, to walk, to relate to one another, to perform complicated and demanding physical and intellectual tasks, and somehow to bring order to a range of experiences and stimuli of breathtaking complexity. To be sure, some of these accomplishments are developmental and may not properly be counted as learning, but the fact remains that learning is both a lifewide and a lifelong phenomenon—one of the defining characteristics of human existence.

A philosopher who was almost totally blind until his late teens, who was without a day of formal schooling in his life, and who developed his philosophy as a stevedore on the docks of San Francisco, Eric Hoffer (1973) writes: "People are perpetually unfinished. . . . It is this incurable unfinishedness which sets people apart from other living things. For in the attempt to finish themselves, people become creators. Moreover, the incurable unfinishedness keeps people perpetually capable of learning and growing." Hoffer's evocative image of "incurable unfinishedness" implies that all but the most severely disabled are not only capable of, but are ontologically called to, learning throughout life; and since this accomplishment is universal and occurs in all cultures without any special provision being made, the skills of learning must, in some sense, be innate. However, once we go beyond such universals, it is also clear that people differ widely in their ability to learn. Some are able to draw inspiration and insight from music or art, some from the natural world, some from the company of other people, and some from such abstract symbols as print, hieroglyphics, and formulas. For some people, sporting achievements or feats of dexterity, endurance, or strength reveal their particular capabilities as learners; others may master many languages, have prodigious memories for people and events in the past, or be able to apply algorithms to the solving of complex and unique problems. Finally, there are those people who succeed in formal learning situations where others fail. In a diversity of disciplinary areas, some people are able to undertake advanced study and even to contribute to the development of new knowledge and understandings, while others grapple unsuccessfully with the basic "code" inherent in the subject and end up being classed as failures. Given that there is some innate capability which all people seem to have to "learn" in the broadest sense of the word, how do people learn to learn in particular domains of human existence? Is this, too, an inborn facility, a natural endowment that some people have and others lack, or are the skills of learning themselves learned?

In this chapter, I will contend that, as in the nature/nurture debate, the question of when and how people learn about learning is partly a matter of aptitude and partly a matter of personal experience. I will examine some of the literature concerning learning to learn—both what it is and how it is accomplished—and explore the important, but often ignored, dimension of how learners themselves construe, or make sense of, learning tasks and learning opportunities. The chapter begins with a discussion of the definition of "learning to learn" and progresses to a consideration of the inherent capacities for learning possessed by most people. This is followed by an examination of how such capacities are extended, strengthened, and at times truncated or distorted by experience: the learning-to-learn effects of living! Since such adventitious acquisition of learning competence leaves much to be desired, a variety of programs have been developed—predicated on a diverse range of ideological assumptions and philosophical positions—to strengthen learning capacity. Such programs usually have one of two focuses (and occasionally a combination of these); either they seek to develop the independence of learners, or else they attempt to improve the quality or depth of learning outcomes. Strategies aimed at the development of independence may be limited to specific skills of learning, or may go beyond this to address such higher-order skills as problem solving and critical thinking or to encourage self-awareness and self-responsibility. Although programs like these are often conducted as if learning competence and confidence are generic, evidence suggests that they tend to be context-specific.

Approaches that aim to increase the depth of learning, or to move learners along a continuum from rote toward meaningful learning, are usually embedded within the teaching/learning situation and again may take one of two forms: those that try to increase the learner's understanding of what it means to learn, and those that strengthen an understanding of what knowledge is and how it is created. Overall, proponents contend that the development of more competent, sophisticated, flexible, and self-responsible learners is a complex and demanding enterprise, which affects all facets and all stages of education—formal and nonformal—and which has important and inescapable ramifications for teaching and learning.

Some Characteristics of Learning to Learn

Like its close relations, *metacognition* and *self-direction,* learning to learn is a phrase recruited to serve the objectives of widely differing educational ideologies. It is extolled by some as the true purpose of education and the highest outcome of the educative process, and by others as the only responsible reaction to the need for a better trained and more versatile work force. For some, learning to learn is the prerogative of elementary schooling, others see it as the mandate of adult education, and still others as a lifelong endeavor. For some people it is a process; for others it is a product. While some view learning to learn as a relatively applied, instrumental concept for use in formal education settings — perhaps even limited to a particular subject or topic — others view it as an integrated and unified development of the whole person, leading to (or at least accompanying) such lofty goals as self-actualization and self-fulfillment.

It is hardly surprising that a concept at once so attractive and yet imprecise has generated an abundance of literature. Few, if any, people seem opposed to learning to learn, yet an absence of opposition is not enough to ensure consensus; and views about what it is, its potential importance, and how it can be brought about are remarkably diverse. Systematic research into the phenomenon is relatively rare and what there is tends to be uncoordinated. It has this in common with metacognition, which, as Reynolds and Wade (1986) point out, "has remained a concept that is both difficult to define and to put into operation" (p. 307).

There is, as yet, no wholly satisfactory definition of learning to learn, certainly none that is widely agreed to. It is possible, however, to gain a sense of the scope of the idea from a selection of writings by various authors who have, directly or incidentally, dealt with the concept. For instance, Smith (1982) states that "learning-how-to-learn involves possessing, or acquiring, the knowledge and skill to learn effectively in whatever learning situation one encounters" (p. 19). Kolb, renowned for his work on learning styles, states that "continuous, lifelong learning requires learning how to learn, and this involves appreciation of and competence in diverse approaches to creating, manipulating and communicating knowledge" (1981, p. 8). Brown, Campione, and Day (1981) address the skills of learning in these terms: "In order to become expert learners, students must develop some of the same insights as the psychologist into the demands of the learning situation. They must learn about their own cognitive characteristics, their available learning strategies, the demands of the various learning tasks and the inherent structure of the material. They must tailor their activities finely to the competing demands of all these forces in order to become flexible and effective learners" (p. 16).

Säljö (1979a) takes up the issue of learning to learn as a developmental process when he writes: "From our interviews, it was clear that for some of the participants *the phenomenon of learning in itself has become an object of reflection*, while for others this is not the case. For some, learning is something which can be explicitly talked about and discussed and can be the object of conscious planning and analysis . . . when people become aware of their own learning in different respects, they will be better . . . at handling learning and reading problems of the kinds encountered in everyday life, or at least, in everyday studying" (pp. 446, 451). This is not to say, however, that learning to learn is a static accomplishment which, once achieved, applies to all conceivable domains of learning encountered thereafter. Like autonomy, which is situation-specific, "learning-how-to-learn is a lifelong process; I don't think one reaches at any point the current state-of-the-art of learning-how-to-learn" (Knowles, 1988, p. viii).

Putting aside the issues of definition, the following features of the learning-to-learn concept are apparent.

- It is a lifelong process.
- It is a developmental process in which people's conceptions of learning evolve and become consciously available to systematic analysis and review.
- It involves the acquisition of a repertoire of attitudes, understandings, and skills that allow people to become more effective, flexible, and self-organized learners in a variety of contexts.
- It occurs both prior to, and coincidental with, learning endeavors.
- It may be enhanced through processes of formal schooling and the way in which the curriculum is constructed and is therefore a viable—perhaps crucial—objective for educational systems at all levels.

- It involves entering into the deep meaning structures of material to be learned and, in its most advanced forms, may lead to critical awareness of assumptions, rules, conventions, and social expectations that influence how people perceive knowledge and how they think, feel, and act when learning.
- It has both generic and context-specific components.
- It is a multidimensional entity whose meaning varies according to the meaning given to the word *learning*.

This last point is one of the least well explored with respect to understanding and implementing the concept of learning to learn.

Learning to Learn and the Concept of Learning

Some years ago, Säljö (1979b) decided to find out what people meant when they used the word *learning*. He approached the issue directly, simply by asking them: "What do you actually mean by learning?" Their answers revealed five different conceptions, which reflect varying levels of complexity or sophistication:

1. *Learning as the increase of knowledge.* Answers in this category tended to be vague, describing learning in terms of its outcome rather than its essence, based on a view of knowledge as a "quantum" that can be accumulated.
2. *Learning as memorizing.* Although this response reveals something about the cognitive processes of learning, it rests on the assumption that learning involves transferring units of information or pieces of knowledge from a source outside the learner—a teacher or a book or an experiment—into the learner's head.
3. *Learning as the acquisition of knowledge that can be retrained and/ or utilized in practice.* The main difference between this conception of learning and the one before it is the notion of application. The implication is that items of information or experiences might be scanned for their practical utility or applicability and hence that some sort of valuing or

judging is also involved in learning. In turn it is implied that
some sort of cognitive mechanism exists whereby new information is compared with what is already known and is
stored according to its similarity to other items of knowledge already held.

4. *Learning as the abstraction of meaning.* This conception moves
    away from a view of learning as primarily a matter of
    reproducing aspects of an outside reality, to one of abstract-
    ing meaning from what is seen and heard. The reproductive
    conception is replaced with a reconstructive one, and learn-
    ing events and materials are seen not as ready-made knowl-
    edge but as the raw material from which learning can be
    extracted.

5. *Learning as an interpretive process, aimed at understanding reality.*
    This is by far the most sophisticated conception of learning
    because it emphasizes the interpretive nature of learning,
    and the relationship between the learner's valuation system
    and the outside world.

In commenting on these different conceptions of learning, Säljö highlights a fundamental difference between the first
two and the last two. The first, he argues, are based on the idea
that knowledge is external to individuals and that learning,
accordingly, consists of a more or less *verbatim transfer* of knowledge from an external source into the head of the learner. The
last two conceptions, on the other hand, stress that knowledge
is *constructed* by individuals through active efforts to abstract
meaning and to relate it to an internal explanatory system.

It is important to recognize that these are not textbook
but commonsense definitions of learning. In other words, they
are the working beliefs that people actually have about their own
learning, and as such they influence the approach people take
toward the acquisition of learning skills. Clearly, each conception carries with it a quite different view of learning to learn,
because any proposed definition of learning needs to be complex enough to embrace the process of acquiring the skills of
learning themselves. Thus, "if learning is thought of as 'an increase in knowledge' or 'memorizing,' then the phrase 'learning-

to-learn' must mean 'learning to increase knowledge,' or 'learning to memorize,' yet clearly it means much more than this. What is more, the word 'learning' must have at least two quite different meanings, or else the phrase translates into 'memorizing how to memorize' or 'increasing knowledge about how to increase knowledge.' [However,] if learning means roughly 'an interpretive process aimed at the understanding of reality,' then 'learning-how-to-learn' means something like 'an interpretive process aimed at understanding how to interpret and understand reality'" (Candy, 1988, p. 134).

This represents a much richer definition of what it means to learn, but rather than dismissing the first two notions as wrong or inadequate, it may be preferable to see them as extremes representing paradigms for success in different contexts. The distinction is frequently made, especially in adult education, between learning in "formal instructional settings" and learning in "natural societal settings" (Jensen, 1960). Unfortunately, learning within instructional settings is often associated with rote memorization — of facts, formulas, and figures — whereas the more heuristic and unpredictable nature of learning in the "real world" tends to emphasize the search for meaning. Based on this distinction, learning to learn in schools, colleges, and universities might involve a narrower and more restricted set of competencies than those called for in learning for life.

Many readers at this point (if not earlier) might throw up their hands in horror at the suggestion that schools and colleges are centers of mindless and meaningless rote learning. Surely educational institutions — particularly higher education institutions — are concerned with critical thinking, not conformity? And don't they deliberately seek to develop and pursue the quest for meaning? While such a negative portrayal may be a caricature, unfortunately the evidence against traditional educational institutions is damaging. Whether in the outspoken and radical criticisms of deschoolers like Freire (1972), Goodman (1962), Holt (1964), Illich (1971), and Reimer (1971), or the more measured but no less telling critiques of Becker, Geer, and Hughes (1968), Entwistle and Percy (1974), and Miller and Parlett (1974), the fact is that traditional formal schooling, including higher education, tends to emphasize rote learning and regurgitation of isolated pieces of information. Recognizing this, students adapt themselves to the requirements for success within the institution, developing study habits that exemplify reproductive (or surface) as opposed to transformational (or deep-level) learning outcomes (Biggs, 1987). Hounsell sums up the difference in these words: "Like Roger Säljö, I'm interested in the distinction between learning and studying. We can look at most educational situations and define learning as something like a quest for meaning and define studying as something like what is necessary in order to survive and do what the institution requires. We find very often that those two are in conflict with one another. If we actually train or help students to learn-how-to-learn, this may be dysfunctional in terms of their educational achievement. So if we are intervening, somehow or other we've got to teach students how to study as well as how to learn, if they're to both grow and survive." (1988, p. 17)

This clear-cut distinction between learning and studying, although it has intuitive face validity, is deceptively simple. It implies that there are certain objective features of a situation that would allow an outsider—such as a counselor, trainer, or teacher—to identify whether skills involved in a particular situation were those of studying or of learning. In fact, the critically important distinction is not whether the activity looks like studying or learning from a third-person perspective, but rather the learner's perception of the requirements of the situation.

In an article published over two decades ago, Thomas (1967) identified a similar difference when he drew a distinction between "studentship" and "membership." Studentship is the familiar mode of learning within formal educational contexts. It is characterized by a considerable degree of dependence on the teacher or instructor; individualism in learning endeavor and outcome; a market orientation, in the sense that there is an identifiable transaction between the teacher and the taught; and, above all, a conscious awareness of being a student and behaving in a student-like way. The membership role is almost the opposite: "The member is neither dependent upon institutional authority nor particularly self-conscious about the engagement in learning. It is the collective goal that is important, not individual enhancement, and thus the learning is merely a means . . . to an end. The member does not, for the most part, become a member to learn something of advantage to himself, but to do something" (p. 71).

As Thomas comments, "there is some psychological quality in each role that is of very great consequence to learning" (p. 68). He argues here that the psychological quality is primarily the learner's conception of the dimensions and demands of the learning task to which he or she must make a "situational adjustment" in order to succeed (Ramsden, Beswick, and Bowden, 1987, p. 174). It seems reasonable to assume that there would be a significant difference in the learner's eyes between, for instance, learning tasks that are personally defined and those that are externally mediated, and that such differences would influence the learner's approaches to widely differing contexts. In turn, both their perceptions of the demands of the situation and the learning approaches they employ will depend, at least in part, on their reservoir of previous experiences.

The Role of Experience in Learning to Learn

How then do people learn to learn? For almost all, the answer seems to be: haphazardly. As previously mentioned, all humans have a latent potential for learning; indeed this may be counted as one of the defining characteristics of humankind (Rogers, 1969). This capacity or propensity for learning is basic to most humanistic psychologies of education. For example, Kelly, author and architect of *The Psychology of Personal Constructs* (1955), maintained that from the time of their birth people are embarked on a continuing voyage of enquiry and exploration, and that "instead of buying the prior assumption of [the human being as] an inert object . . . we propose [that] . . . the organism is delivered fresh into the psychological world, alive and struggling" (Kelly, 1966, p. 37). Kelly and others take as axiomatic that people "have two basic attributes, an innate and powerful drive to relate to others, and a continuing attempt to make sense of their experiences" (Ryle, 1975, p. 1). These are the wellsprings of all learning and, since they are innate, the capacity for learning must also be innate, at least at some elemental level. But people's experience of life rapidly teaches them not just about the content but also about the process of learning.

To take a simple example, while children are learning to catch a ball, they will also learn other incidentals as well. They might learn the requirements for hand/eye coordination, for practice, for the help of others, and for positive feedback. They might learn that they lack the manual dexterity or the perseverance necessary to master such a learning activity and this, in turn, might influence their attitudes toward such sports as tennis, baseball, and football. In other words, alongside the acquisition of content, children develop learning strategies, and they also develop concepts of themselves *as learners.* These self-concepts cover a broad range of preferences and predispositions in learning. In discussing their research, Thomas and Harri-Augstein (1985) write that there are a wide variety of personal learning myths that guide learners in all sorts of situations, both formal and informal: "The most easily related myths were usually about what students felt to be the necessary physical or social conditions of learning. Many described how they must have coffee or snacks on hand all the time. . . . Some students knew that they had to sit up 'properly' at a desk if they were to read something and really remember it, whilst others were equally convinced that they could only really concentrate if they were comfortably stretched out on the carpet. Personal beliefs about being 'a morning person' or only being able to work effectively between 10 P.M. and 3 A.M. . . . were held equally strongly by different learners; so were ideas about the optimal length of personal study sessions. Preferences varied from 20 to 30 minutes to 6 or 8 hours" (p. 11).

In addition to beliefs about the conditions of learning, people develop views about their own innate capacities: "They have come to a firm belief about their talents for math or dancing, for writing, athletics, chess, house repairs or embroidery. Everybody into or beyond their teens already 'seems to know' that they lack a whole range of special aptitudes or talents"

(p. 11). According to Thomas and Harri-Augstein, these personal myths about learning are often deeply held so that the learner may not even be consciously aware of them; yet they profoundly influence how people approach learning tasks and, to the extent that they are negative, they may inhibit people's approaches to learning and disable their performance. Not all incidental learning about learning is negative, of course, but in all learning situations the same basic mechanism is operating; as people learn specific contents, they also develop their repertoire of approaches to new learning. The implication of this is that when they approach a new learning task, they cast around for some analogous situation from the past to give guidance as to how to approach this new situation.

Some of the most obvious examples are in the domain of reading. On the surface, reading appears to be a single undifferentiated skill. It is expected to be mastered in elementary school; indeed, it is so fundamental that, as Goodman says, given the amount of exposure that any urban child gets to it, "the puzzle is not how to teach reading, but why some children fail to learn to read" (1962, p. 27). Yet in secondary schools, in universities and colleges, and in the workplace, people's inability to read at the level and pace required of them suggests the need for more conscious training in skills and strategies of reading (Harri-Augstein, Smith, and Thomas, 1982, p. x). It is not that people lack the ability to decipher the marks on the page, or even to relate these to words whose individual meanings they recognize (Säljö, 1984, p. 71). The problem is that they must invest the words with some significance. As Anderson (1977) puts it, "Text is gobbledygook unless the reader possesses an interpretive framework to breathe meaning into it" (p. 423). This perspective differs sharply from the impression most people have, that the message is implicit in the written word. On the contrary, "it is our background knowledge of language structures, word meanings and sound, *together with our background knowledge of the particular topic described,* which helps us make predictions about what we are reading. The more we are able to predict what a particular piece of text will be about, the more we are likely to be able to read it with understanding" (Morris and Stewart-Dore, 1984, p. 17, emphasis added).

Thus it seems that learning from reading may represent an ideal example of the skills of learning generally. There is certainly a generic or context-free component to the skill of reading, but to read with *understanding*, to read for *meaning*, necessitates some content-specific knowledge as well. In the same way, all learning involves the attribution of meaning and the subsumption of new skills and information into existing cognitive structures. Accordingly, learning competence is to some degree content-specific, and it is this content-specific aspect that perhaps more than anything else, has bedeviled attempts at developing general all-purpose learning-to-learn skills (Gibbs, 1983, p. 84; Ramsden, Beswick, and Bowden, 1987, p. 174).

From the foregoing, it is apparent that some learning skills are innate, and many others are refined on the basis of experience and reflection on that experience (Candy, Harri-Augstein, and Thomas, 1985; Main, 1985). This is, however, a rather hit-and-miss way of acquiring learning competence and may result in dysfunctional learning strategies and the emergence of "personal learning myths." Accordingly, there is a long-established tradition of attempting to actively increase learning competence by direct intervention. According to Bowden (1986), there are five basic types of intervention strategies: "[Firstly, there are] the well-known study skills packages and learning skills counselling. As well, there are co-operative research programmes in which student learning researchers join with subject teachers to investigate how students learn in that subject and to consider better ways of teaching the particular discipline. Subject-related learning skills activities comprise the fourth; these are programmes in which learning advisors share teaching sessions with subject teachers or provide special classes where the processes of learning the subject are emphasised. The fifth strategy, a complete change in the way a course is structured, taught and assessed, occurs least often" (pp. 14–15).

Almost all efforts to increase learning competence have one of two basic purposes (and occasionally a combination of both): Either they are aimed at increasing capabilities for self-management (Bagnall, 1987), or they seek to increase the quality of learning outcomes. Although in practice these two domains are intimately linked, in the discussion that follows, the distinction will be maintained as an aid to understanding the methods and primary focus of various learning-to-learn programs.

Increasing Self-Management Capabilities

If learners can function only in the presence of teachers, their ability to acquire information in noninstructional settings is severely limited: although they might have learned to be taught, they have not yet learned to learn. Major objectives of learning-to-learn programs, therefore, must be to enhance the independence of learners, and this seems to comprise two components, namely (1) the development of specific skills of learning and (2) the development of the ability to use such skills appropriately (Kirschenbaum and Perri, 1982, p. 91). It must be emphasized that independence does not necessarily imply solitude, but rather self-regulation: much learning both in formal instructional settings and in everyday situations occurs in the context of group membership.

There are many versions of what the skills of learning are, but most theorists agree that they include certain research and library skills, time management, goal setting, reading, listening, note taking and questioning, and, since at least some learning derives from nonrational sources, the ability to disengage. Since a large proportion of learning occurs within social settings, learning skills might also include certain interpersonal and group-oriented competencies as well. However, programs of learning skill development in formal educational settings have tended to undervalue this aspect of learning (Slavin, 1980).

It is not my intention here to review either the extent or the nature of programs designed to develop such competencies. But I would like to highlight a potential problem if training to develop or enhance these skills is offered in isolation, in the form of advice or tools to be used as a formula for success in learning. I am inclined to agree with Gibbs: "The assumption underlying almost all attempts to improve student learning is that studying consists primarily of techniques, and that to increase skill in using specific techniques is therefore to increase learning outcomes. I believe that this assumption, and the approach to advising and training students in study skills that follows from it, is fundamentally misguided" (1983, p. 85). In a paper entitled "Understanding Why Students Don't Learn," Gibbs, Morgan, and Taylor (1980) demonstrate the limitation of simply conducting study skills or learning-to-learn courses which focus on doing particular things, or even doing things in particular ways. Although it is certainly possible to identify the differences between successful and unsuccessful learners, it is very difficult to attribute these differences simply to particular patterns of behavior.

These observations do not completely invalidate advice on learning skills. There is evidence to suggest that some practices are more effective than others *for specific learning purposes,* and that the learning competence of particular individuals can be enhanced if their repertoire of skills is increased (Kirschenbaum and Perri, 1982, pp. 90–91). But simplistic assumptions about *behaviors* that are alleged to relate to effective learning are called into question. As Gibbs and others state, it is often very unclear what people are actually *doing* when they are studying: "It may be possible to record some aspects of the observable behaviour of studying, but this is unlikely to tell you very much about the underlying cognitive processes—the purposes, plans and thoughts which direct and make use of this behaviour" (1980, p. 3). This statement directs attention to the higher-order aspects of learning-to-learn programs, namely those that develop the ability to use the learning skills appropriately, to reflect on personal purposes (Thomas and Harri-Augstein, 1985), and to have a sense of potency or control in the learning situation (Kirschenbaum and Perri, 1982; Wang, 1983).

The more elaborate and sophisticated aspects of developing learning competence can perhaps be subdivided into those typified as higher-order skills (problem solving, critical thinking, planning of learning purposes) and those that rest on increased self-awareness and self-control (clarity of personal goals, understanding of personal structures of meaning and preferred learning styles, and self-efficacy). Once again, these dimensions are not mutually exclusive but, for the purpose of analyzing and discussing learning to learn, it is desirable to consider them as independent goals. It is worth pointing out that the term *higher-order skills* is somewhat misleading, because it implies "that there is a sequence from lower level activities that do not require much independent thinking or judgment to higher level ones that do. . . [In fact] cognitive research on the nature of basic skills such as reading and mathematics provides a fundamental challenge to this assumption" (Resnick, 1987a, p. 8).

Each of the skills mentioned above (problem solving, critical thinking, and planning) is, in fact, not simply a skill but a disposition. Critical thinking, for instance, does not consist merely of raising questions or of indiscriminate skepticism (Furedy and Furedy, 1985, p. 55), but instead it comprises "certain attitudes, dispositions, habits, and character traits which together may be labelled the *critical spirit* or *critical attitude*" (Seigel, 1980, p. 10). This distinction between mere question raising and the possession of a critical attitude is reminiscent of the earlier distinction between learning and studying: whereas learning may necessitate a "critical attitude," in Seigel's terms, studying might demand only a questioning approach. According to Furedy and Furedy (1985), it is possible to encourage critical thinking through certain styles of assignments and course structures, but "if critical thinking is to be truly promoted in an essay examination, the exam questions must be formulated so as to require genuine discussion of the relevant issues. . . [and] students must be confident that they will not be penalized for a sound but independent approach to the issues" (p. 65). It seems, then, that those interested in the development of critical thinking must be prepared, in order to be congruent, to have their views challenged, even to the extent of challenging their views on critical thinking itself (Millar, Morphett, and Saddington, 1986; Torbert, 1978). Also, a critical approach to learning involves calling into question established views of knowledge; it therefore presupposes a degree of intellectual

sophistication and an orientation to knowledge that is associated with the higher levels of Perry's developmental continuum
(1970). In this respect, at least, there is a conceptual convergence
between the domain I have labeled independence in learning,
and that which I have called depth of processing, to be dealt with
later in this chapter.

There is a parallel here between critical thinking and the
development of learning competence generally. Although the
skills of critical thinking can, to some extent, be developed in a
content-free way, it is only possible to say whether or not someone is thinking critically when he or she applies this orientation
to a particular field. It is not possible to be a critical thinker
without something to think about. In the same way, it is not
possible to be a learner without something to learn. Critical
thinking, then, like learning to learn, has a generic and a content-specific aspect to it: "We think that critical thinkers would be
inclined to question and assess, even when discussing issues
outside their own particular areas of expertise. Obviously,
though, one will not be so proficient in specialized evaluation in
an unfamiliar field" (Furedy and Furedy, 1985, p. 56). For a
discussion of the content-specific nature of autonomy in learning, see Candy (1988), "On the Attainment of Subject-Matter
Autonomy."

Likewise, the development of independent learners is
predicated on at least a redefinition of the teacher's role, and
perhaps even the ultimate redundancy or obsolescence of the
teacher altogether, and this necessitates a degree of ego strength
and commitment to learning, in preference to teaching, that
many educators may find difficult to attain. Wang (1983) states
as follows: "The implementation of instructional programs that
encourage the development of self-management skills requires
fundamental changes in the traditional classroom authority
structure and instructional-learning process. The conventional
role of the teacher as the manager of students needs to be
modified so that a greater amount of routine classroom management and management of student learning is transferred to the
students. The teacher . . . to use Bloom's terms, should become

more a 'manager of instruction' and less a 'manager of students'" (p. 219).

The ability to use one's learning skills appropriately involves, in addition to the mastery of techniques (both higher-order and lower-order; generic and specific), the development of a reflective self-awareness, which Mezirow (1985), among others, has identified as part of "emancipatory education." There are several levels or layers to such self-awareness, extending from knowledge about one's learning style to the development of a sense of personal control and a robust self-concept as a learner.

Learning Style. The literature on the assessment of learning styles is voluminous and complex. Instruments designed for the purpose, which rest on a range of theoretical perspectives, purport to identify, often on the basis of self-report questionnaires, preferences for structure, environment, climate, complexity, sensory modality, philosophical orientation, cognitive organization, and so on (Smith, 1982). Broadly speaking, the assessment of learning styles is usually aimed either at modifying the delivery of instruction (matching) or at developing the learner's range or repertoire of learning approaches. This latter is achieved in one of two main ways, either via direct instruction or practice or through "metacognitive awareness," wherein it is assumed that a knowledge of one's strengths and preferences (and hence, by implication, of one's weaknesses) is a vital step toward enhanced competence across a range of learning situations.

Once again, we confront the generic/content-specific issue. Many learning style theorists have been seduced by the psychometric tradition and have accordingly sought to identify consistent personal preferences in learning that hold across a range of learning situations. Recent work by Biggs (1987), Ramsden (1987), and others, however, has shown that learners pay attention to a wide variety of contextual clues, see themselves as more or less competent in various subject areas, and utilize a range of learning approaches according to their individual "reading" of each situation. It is apparent, therefore, that more useful than a multipurpose, content-free learning style instrument is a detailed individual study, using naturalistic research methods, of the learner's approach in particular subject areas or learning domains. Such data are then reflected back to the learner as a basis on which he or she might make considered adjustments (Candy, Harri-Augstein, and Thomas, 1985; Gibbs, 1983; Main, 1985). Such approaches, however, have proved to be relatively easier to implement in the case of students in formal instructional settings than for people seeking to increase their learning competence in natural societal settings.

Related to the idea of learning styles is that of mental models, conceptual frameworks, or schemata. In a thoughtful and provocative presidential address to the Adult Education Research Association, Resnick (1987b) makes the point that, in an increasingly technological society, people must be educated "to do exactly what machines cannot: step outside the system and reason about it" (p. 18). In order to do this, they need to develop a mental model of the system (Gentner and Stevens, 1983), that is, "an idea of all its parts, what each does and how they work together, how changes in one part of the system cause changes in other parts" (Resnick, 1987b, p. 18). Elsewhere (Candy, 1988, p. 69) I have argued that the development of such "anticipatory schemes" (Kuhn, 1981) is essential to successful autonomous learning and, as Resnick (1987b) notes, "One important function of schooling is to develop the knowledge and mental skills students will need to construct appropriate mental models of systems with which they will eventually work" (p. 18). Two techniques deserve particular mention: repertory grids and concept maps.

Repertory grids owe their existence to Kelly's *The Psychology of Personal Constructs* (1955) and to considerable subsequent work which builds on Kelly's ideas. Repertory grids represent an attempt to sample part of a person's frame of reference selectively with respect to some domain of human existence. The technique, in its simplest form, consists of presenting the respondent with three items from an array of qualitatively similar elements (for example, "situations from which I have learned"; "books I have read"; "teaching methods I have experienced") and asking him or her to say in what way two of the items are similar and thereby different from the third.

This process, when repeated a number of times with differing combinations of trigger items (that is, different triads), produces a series of bipolar descriptors (for example, "interesting-boring," "threatening-safe," "easy to understand-difficult," "useful-irrelevant") which can then be used by the respondent to differentiate all the items in the array—not just the three used to generate it. This process yields a two-way matrix, with the "constructs" down one side and the "elements" or items down the other, and each element can be given a score or rating on each construct dimension. The resulting data are susceptible to various forms of statistical analysis—more or less sophisticated depending on the purpose—and the results may be given back to the respondent in a diagram or other pictorial way for reflection and personal analysis. An extension of the basic repertory grid technique is to program a computer, which can interactively question a respondent and provide him or her with immediate feedback on his or her view of the world, privately and without the intervention of another person. This is a particularly powerful device for learning to learn (Thomas and Harri-Augstein, 1985).

The concept map affords another approach to externalizing and understanding how individual people structure meaning. The map depicts, in a diagrammatic form, ideas, examples, relationships, and implications about a particular concept (for example, feudalism, marketing, art). Usually the central or core idea is placed at the center or top of the page, and radiating from it are a number of spokes or lines leading to other concepts related to, or indicative of, the central idea. These are then linked to other notions, which in turn may be further linked both to one another and to even more nodes on the network in complex and multidimensional ways. There is no inherent limit to the number of concepts that may be included in a single map, although common sense dictates that it would be impractical to depict more than a fraction of the total connections a normal adult has available in understanding any particular domain of human discourse, so rich and complex are our cognitive schemata (Novak and Gowin, 1984).

Concept maps (by a variety of names) have proved useful in helping learners to visualize their patterns of understanding and to make explicit assumptions and relationships that are usually implicit and unarticulated (Buzan, 1978). It is argued that an appreciation of one's own tacit network of concepts is a vital prerequisite to learning, and an essential corollary of learning about one's own learning. Like repertory grids, concept maps may be created using a paper and pencil or computer software (Fisher and others, 1987). However, unlike the repertory grid, no formal orientation or training is required, and a concept map might consist of as little as a hasty diagram scrawled on the back of an envelope. The map's strengths as a learning-to-learn device are, as Novak and Gowin (1984) point out, its remarkable flexibility and ease of use, as well as its idiosyncratic and relatively unstructured form.

Self-Concepts and Personal Control. Approaches to increased learning competence that go beyond these cognitive elements begin to address aspects of learners' belief systems, including their self-concepts. Although both the repertory grid and the concept map have the capacity to reflect strength of relationships, preferences, beliefs, and attitudes, they do not do so as explicitly as exercises in values clarification, personal goal setting, or questionnaires and inventories that assess the learner's self-concept or feelings of self-efficacy.

Several people have recognized that the ability to exert effective control over one's learning demands, in addition to acquiring certain technical skills, involves both an attitudinal disposition and a self-concept of potency and self-efficacy. The issue has been approached from different perspectives, ranging from the more behaviorally oriented work of Bandura (1981), Kirschenbaum and Perri (1982), and Wang (1983) through the radical humanism of such emancipatory educators as Freire (1972), Gibbons and Phillips (1982), Mezirow (1985), and Torbert (1978). Although these authors differ sharply from one another in their philosophical orientations and therefore in their recommendations about how such competence might be developed, they all recognize that the competent adult learner is able to give direction to, and take responsibility for, the pattern of his or her own learning activities.

It seems to me that no comprehensive program of learning to learn can be complete if it fails to address issues of personal empowerment, including limitations imposed by society on such empowerment.

Increasing the Quality of Learning Outcomes

Approaches that aim to increase the quality of learning, as opposed, perhaps, to increasing its quantity (Säljö, 1975, p. 14) have at least two major components: (1) developing a more elaborate and complex conception of learning and (2) moving along a continuum of epistemological sophistication—that is, coming to realize what knowledge is, its relatively tentative nature, and how knowledge claims are made and supported.

Earlier in this chapter, the discussion of Säljö's work on conceptions of learning indicated that these conceptions are, in a sense, cumulative; that is, the more advanced notions about the nature of learning tend to subsume and to go beyond the less developed ones. People develop their ideas about learning at least in part from their exposure to teaching, and they identify certain contextual clues as to the demands of the instructional situation (Becker and others, 1968; Miller and Parlett, 1974). If, for instance, their experience has emphasized the need for uncritical memorization as a precondition for success, then in all probability they will adapt themselves to that expectation and develop a strong capability for rote learning. If, on the other hand, their experience has led them to value more critical, analytical, and interpretive strategies, it is likely that their definition of learning will be correspondingly more elaborate and sophisticated. One of the hallmarks of more successful learners is that learning is not simply something that happens to them, nor even the application of particular procedures and strategies, but is itself an object of reflection. In other words, learning can be explicitly talked about, planned, and analyzed, and learners can make a conscious adjustment of their strategies to the purposes they have in mind (Novak and Gowin, 1984, pp. 1–11; Säljö, 1979a, p. 446; Thomas and Harri-Augstein, 1985).

In the past decade or so, several researchers have studied learners who restrict themselves to memorizing or rote learning. Rote learning has been long recognized as an indispensable aid to "getting on" in formal educational settings, but it has been found to have limitations because it fails to address underlying principles and focuses instead on superficial characteristics of material to be learned. Rote learning, of course, has its place. In many instances, mastering certain bodies of knowledge depends, at least in the first instance, on the acquisition of certain basic building blocks, more or less without detailed understanding. However, if a learner's intentions and strategies are limited to what has been called surface or reproductive learning, his or her ability to function at more advanced levels, to solve problems, to apply principles, and to deal with novel or unanticipated situations is severely limited. On the other hand, it has been found that learners who seem to do well, to grasp underlying concepts, to integrate new learning within their existing frames of reference, and to ask "what if" questions (Baird and Mitchell, 1986) are generally more successful, especially in situations that demand problem solving or critical analysis.

Since a large proportion of adult learning is directed toward problem situations, it is to be expected that adult learners would, on the whole, value deep-level or transformational learning in preference to its shallower and less meaningful counterpart. However, this is not universally true and, as Häyrynen (1980) points out, "in new tasks, a person decides whether to penetrate deeper into the subject context or to reproduce the task in mastery" (p. 10). In short, there is an important distinction between surface-level and deep-level learning, and while learners may actively choose between these alternatives, it is the latter which is usually more highly regarded, sought after by teachers, and valued in real-life learning situations.

The way in which teaching and learning are carried out tends to emphasize one of these approaches rather than the other. Conventionally, formal education has tended to strengthen and reinforce the tendency toward surface learning. Most school learning is "arbitrary, verbatim, non-substantive. . .; no effort [is made] to integrate new knowledge with existing concepts in cognitive structure; [and] learning is not related to [real-life] experience with events or objects" (Novak and Gowin, 1984, p. 167). The net effect of such an educational system is to repress strategies of nonverbatim learning, to emphasize and reward the reproduction of "approved" responses rather than creative or critical thinking. Moreover, concerned that some students "fail" in the educational system, a number of counselors and study skills advisers have put together programs whose aim is to help students be better surface learners—emphasizing skills such as note taking, listening, essay writing, and even exam techniques—a process Knox has likened to "trying to help people learn to breathe during a nuclear winter" (Knox, 1988, p. viii). Although there is both a demand and some justification for these programs, it is also apparent that learning to learn calls for more meaningful, transformational learning outcomes, and that these may be encouraged both in the way education is conducted (for instance, Barrows and Tamblyn, *Problem-Based Learning*, 1980), and through various strategies such as Gowin's Vee, which reveal the nature and structure of knowledge (Novak and Gowin, 1984, p. 9).

Developing More Sophisticated Concepts of Knowledge

Alongside a richer and more comprehensive conception of learning, it is possible—indeed, I believe, essential—for people to develop a fuller and more elaborate idea about knowledge, what it is, and how it is created. One person who has devoted considerable attention to a developmental continuum of understandings of knowledge is Perry who, on the basis of more than thirty years working with the Bureau of Study Counsel at Harvard University, proposed a nine-stage developmental scheme with respect to students' views of knowledge. He typifies three of these positions as follows:

Let us suppose that a lecturer announces that today he will consider three theories explanatory of (whatever his topic may be). Student A has always taken it for granted that knowledge consists of correct answers, that there is one right answer per problem, and that teachers explain these answers for students to learn. He therefore listens for the lecturer to state which theory he is to learn.

Student B makes the same general assumption but with an elaboration to the effect that teachers sometimes present problems and procedures, rather than answers "so that we can learn to find the right answer on our own." He therefore perceives the lecture as a kind of guessing game in which he is to "figure out" which theory is correct. . . .

Student C assumes that an answer can be called "right" only in the light of its context, and that contexts or "frames of reference" differ. He assumes that several interpretations of a poem, explanations of a historical development, or even theories of a class of events in physics, may be legitimate "depending on how you look at it." . . . He supposes that the lecturer may be about to present three legitimate theories which can be examined for their internal coherence, their scope, their fit with various data, their predictive power, etc. [Perry, 1970, pp. 1–2]

Although Perry's work was limited to college students (and a rarefied group of students at that), further research in formal learning situations and with adult learners in general has vindicated his suspicion that adults generally are spread out along a developmental continuum with respect to knowledge. Accordingly, people will approach learning situations with quite different expectations about what learning entails (memorizing the "right" answer; figuring out the "right" answer; or recognizing the relativity of various explanatory systems). To the extent that learning-to-learn programs aim at enhancing the capacity for deep-level learning, then they must also address the relative and tentative nature of knowledge, bring into question simplistic and absolutist views, and engage learners in critical reflection with respect to the object of their learning. As Gibbs, Morgan, and Taylor put it, "A goal of the whole of education should be to encourage the development of increasingly sophisticated conceptions of the learning process and of the nature of knowledge, and this should clearly be the central goal of any direct attempt to influence student learning" (1980, p. 18).

Several observations about the issue of epistemological sophistication are in order. The first is that, since the continuum is developmental, it is natural and applies to everyone. Although it may be possible to accelerate people's development, although some people may be prodigies and may at an early age demonstrate more complex understandings than others, it is to be expected that, at different times, individuals will be at different points along the continuum. The implication of this is that learning-to-learn programs will always suffer from an inherent limitation: learners cannot go beyond the capability that is defined by their particular point in the spectrum of views about knowledge.

The second observation is that it is possible for a person to be at different stages of development in different subject areas or domains (Feldman, 1980; Gibbs, Morgan, and Taylor, 1980, p. 14). A recurring theme in this chapter has been that learning competence has a generic and a content-specific aspect, epitomized by the fact that a learner may think relativistically about some area or domain of knowledge and yet be much more absolute in his or her view of some other topic area (Weinstein and Rogers, 1985, p. 621). To the extent that learning competence is inhibited by less developed views of knowledge, a person may be simultaneously at different levels of learning ability in various aspects of life.

Third, although it is possible to foster movement along Perry's continuum with respect to particular subjects, such interventions must be embedded within the teaching and learning of the subject concerned. Baird and Mitchell, in *Improving the Quality of Teaching and Learning* (1986), make it clear that there is little if any transfer of metacognitive competence from one subject area to another. Therefore, increased knowledge about knowledge, to the extent that it can be developed in formal instructional settings, cannot be achieved purely via exercises, workshops, courses, or textbooks but must flow from the way in which particular subject matter is taught and learned.

Conclusion

This chapter has ranged widely over a number of issues bearing on the subject of learning to learn. Although an emphasis has been placed on adulthood, it has argued that the development of learning competence is a lifelong pursuit and that programs designed to develop or enhance learning competence—either directly or indirectly—are the concern of all educators in both formal and informal contexts. It has been shown that, in addition to the innate capacity all people have for learning at some level, different people have or develop learning competence in particular subject areas or domains. Sometimes this occurs without any special provision being made, often incidental to some other activity. Since the process, however, is somewhat haphazard in terms of the development of "anticipatory" lifelong learners (Botkin, Elmandjra, and Malitza, 1979), a variety of programs have evolved that are aimed explicitly at enhancing learning competence.

These programs vary along several dimensions. Some focus on the acquisition of specific skills, while others seek to develop metacognitive awareness. Some approach learning to learn as if it represents a universal accomplishment that applies to all domains, while others recognize the highly content-specific nature of people's approaches to learning tasks. Some programs try to teach learning skills as a subject in its own right; others involve an approach to education that weaves a learning-to-learn perspective into both the method and the content of instruction. Some view the attainment of learning competence as limited to formal instructional settings; others view it as a preparation for a lifetime of adaptation to a kaleidoscope of changing circumstances.

In this chapter, I have assumed one principle to be axiomatic: in matters of learning, especially adult learning, it is the perspective of the learner that counts (Boud and Griffin, 1987; Stanage, 1987). Such a perspective may be faulty and biased, in which case it is the responsibility of the educator to help the learner achieve a more balanced and functional point of view. But it is the perspective of the learner that determines what is learned and what is not, influences the value that is placed on various aspects of any given subject or topic, dictates how new information and insights are integrated into existing frames of reference (Candy, 1982), and directs the learner's approach and strategy in any given learning context. Therefore, any program to develop, enhance, modify, or reorient someone's learning skills and strategies must start with the learner's perspective. Moreover, it is apparent that even learning the skills of learning will be approached within the constraints, and using the techniques, applied to other learning tasks. Ironically, therefore, a person who has come to define himself or herself as lacking ability will bring the same mind-set and self-image to bear in acquiring new learning approaches, which may further reinforce a sense of inadequacy and failure. One of the greatest challenges confronting those with an interest in learning to learn is to transcend such self-imposed limitations and to give learners, as Archimedes put it, a new place to stand from which they can move their respective worlds.

Although "learning to learn" has become a slogan and may be in danger of losing some of its power through overuse, it is nevertheless, along with reform of the education system itself, arguably the most urgent agenda item for the development of people who "can make wise choices from among the many learning options that will confront them as adults in the learning society" (Cross, 1984, p. 172).

References

Anderson, R. C. "The Notion of Schemata and the Educational Enterprise." In R. C. Anderson, R. J. Spiro, and W. E. Montague (eds.), *Schooling and the Acquisition of Knowledge.* Hillsdale, N.J.: Erlbaum, 1977.

Bagnall, R. G. "Enhancing Self-Direction in Adult Education: A Possible Trap for Enthusiasts." *The Australian Journal of Educational Studies,* 1987, *8* (1), 90–100.

Baird, J. R., and Mitchell, I. J. *Improving the Quality of Teaching and Learning: An Australian Case Study — The PEEL Project.* Melbourne, Australia: The PEEL Group, Monash University Printery, 1987.

Bandura, A. "Self-Referent Thought: A Developmental Analysis of Self-Efficacy." In J. H. Flavell and L. R. Ross (eds.), *Cognitive Social Development: Frontiers and Possible Futures.* New York: Cambridge University Press, 1981.

Barrows, H. S., and Tamblyn, R. M. *Problem-Based Learning: An Approach to Medical Education.* New York: Springer, 1980.

Becker, H. S., Geer, B., and Hughes, E. C. *Making the Grade: The Academic Side of Academic Life.* New York: Wiley, 1968.

Biggs, J. B. *Student Approaches to Learning and Studying.* Melbourne: Australian Council for Educational Research, 1987.

Botkin, J. W., Elmandjra, M., and Malitza, M. *No Limits to Learning: Bridging the Human Gap.* Elmsford, N.Y.: Pergamon, 1979.

Boud, D. J., and Griffin, V. *Appreciating Adults Learning: From the Learners' Perspective.* Toronto, Canada: Ontario Institute for Studies in Education, 1987.

Bowden, J. A. "Educational Development and Phenomenology." In J. A. Bowden (ed.), *Student Learning: Research into Practice — The Marysville Symposium.* Melbourne, Australia: Centre for the Study of Higher Education, University of Melbourne, 1986.

Brown, A. L., Campione, J. C., and Day, J. D. "Learning to Learn: On Training Students to Learn from Texts." *Educational Researcher,* 1981, *10* (2), 14–21.

Buzan, T. *Use Your Head.* London: BBC Publications, 1978.

Candy, P. C. "Personal Constructs and Personal Paradigms: Elaboration, Modification and Transformation." *Interchange: A Journal of Educational Policy,* 1982, *13* (4), 56–69.

Candy, P. C. Edited transcript of conference participation. In R. M. Smith (ed.), *Theory Building for Learning How to Learn.* DeKalb, Ill.: Educational Studies Press, 1988.

Candy, P. C., Harri-Augstein, E. S., and Thomas, L. F. "Reflection and the Self-Organised Learner: A Model of Learning Conversations." In D. J. Boud, R. Keogh, and D. Walker (eds.), *Reflection: Turning Experience into Learning*. London: Kogan Page, 1985.

Cross, K. P. "The Rising Tide of School Reform Reports." *Phi Delta Kappan*, 1984, *66* (3), 167–172.

Cross, K. P. Edited transcript of conference participation. In R. M. Smith (ed.), *Theory Building for Learning How to Learn*. DeKalb, Ill.: Educational Studies Press, 1988.

Edfeldt, A. W. "Ar Det Meningsfullt med Studieteknisk Traning?" (Is There a Meaningful Study Skill Training?) *Forskning om Utbildning*, 1976, *3*, 15–24.

Entwistle, N. J., and Percy, K. A. "Critical Thinking or Conformity? An Investigation of the Aims and Outcomes of Higher Education." Research into Higher Education—1973. London: Society for Research into Higher Education, 1974.

Feldman, D. H. *Beyond Universals in Cognitive Development*. Norwood, N.J.: Ablex Publishing, 1980.

Fisher, K. M., and others. "Computer-Based Knowledge Representation as a Tool for Students and Teachers." Working paper, University of California, Davis, 1987.

Freire, P. *Pedagogy of the Oppressed*. Harmondsworth, England: Penguin Books, 1972.

Furedy, C., and Furedy, J. J. "Critical Thinking: Toward Research and Dialogue." In J. G. Donald and A. M. Sullivan (eds.), *Using Research to Improve Teaching*. New Directions for Teaching and Learning, no. 23. San Francisco: Jossey-Bass, 1985.

Gentner, D., and Stevens, A. L. (eds.). *Mental Models*. Hillsdale, N.J.: Erlbaum, 1983.

Gibbons, M., and Phillips, G. "Self-Education: The Process of Lifelong Learning." *Canadian Journal of Education*, 1982, 7 (4), 67–86.

Gibbs, G. "Changing Students' Approaches to Study Through Classroom Exercises." In R. M. Smith (ed.), *Helping Adults Learn How to Learn*. New Directions for Continuing Education, no. 19. San Francisco: Jossey-Bass, 1983.

Gibbs, G., Morgan, A., and Taylor, E. "Understanding Why Students Don't Learn." Study Methods Group Report no. 5. Milton Keynes, England: Open University Press, 1980.

Goodman, P. *Compulsory Miseducation.* Harmondsworth, England: Penguin Books, 1962.

Harri-Augstein, E. S., Smith, M., and Thomas, L. F. *Reading to Learn.* London: Methuen, 1982.

Häyrynen, Y. P. "Aesthetic Activity and Cognitive Learning: Creativity and Orientation in New Problem Situations." *Adult Education in Finland,* 1980, *17* (3), 5–16.

Hoffer, E. *Reflections on the Human Condition.* New York: Harper & Row, 1973.

Holt, J. *How Children Fail.* New York: Pitman, 1964.

Hounsell, D. J. Edited transcript of conference participation. In R. M. Smith (ed.), *Theory Building for Learning How to Learn.* DeKalb, Ill.: Educational Studies Press, 1988.

Illich, I. *Deschooling Society.* Harmondsworth, England: Penguin Books, 1971.

Jensen, G. E. "The Nature of Education as a Discipline." In G. E. Jensen (ed.), *Readings for Educational Researchers.* Ann Arbor, Mich.: Ann Arbor Publishers, 1960.

Kelly, G. A. *The Psychology of Personal Constructs.* 2 vols. New York: Norton, Inc., 1955.

Kelly, G. A. "A Brief Introduction to Personal Construct Theory." Unpublished paper, Brandeis University, 1966.

Kirschenbaum, D. S., and Perri, M. G. "Improving Academic Competence in Adults: A Review of Recent Research." *Journal of Counseling Psychology,* 1982, *29* (1), 76–94.

Knowles, M. S. Edited transcript of conference participation. In R. M. Smith (ed.), *Theory Building for Learning How to Learn.* DeKalb, Ill.: Educational Studies Press, 1988.

Knox, A. B. Edited transcript of conference participation. In R. M. Smith (ed.), *Theory Building for Learning How to Learn.* DeKalb, Ill.: Educational Studies Press, 1988.

Kolb, D. A. "Learning Styles and Disciplinary Differences." In A. W. Chickering (ed.), *The Modern American College: Responding to the New Realities of Diverse Students and a Changing Society.* San Francisco: Jossey-Bass, 1981.

Kuhn, D. "The Role of Self-Directed Activity in Cognitive Development." In I. E. Sigel, D. M. Brodzinsky, and R. M. Golinkoff (eds.), *New Directions in Piagetian Theory and Practice.* Hillsdale, N.J.: Erlbaum, 1981.

Main, A. "Reflection and the Development of Learning Skills." In D. J. Boud, R. Keogh, and D. Walker (eds.), *Reflection: Turning Experience into Learning.* London: Kogan Page, 1985.

Mezirow, J. D. "A Critical Theory of Self-Directed Learning." In S. D. Brookfield (ed.), *Self-Directed Learning: From Theory to Practice.* New Directions for Continuing Education, no. 25. San Francisco: Jossey-Bass, 1985.

Millar, C. J., Morphett, T., and Saddington, T. "Curriculum Negotiation in Professional Adult Education." *Journal of Curriculum Studies,* 1986, *18* (4), 429–443.

Miller, C.M.L., and Parlett, M. *Up to the Mark: A Study of the Examination Game.* London: Society for Research into Higher Education, 1974.

Morris, A., and Stewart-Dore, N. *Learning to Learn from Text: Effective Reading in the Content Areas.* North Ryde, Australia: Addison-Wesley, 1984.

Novak, J. D., and Gowin, D. B. *Learning How to Learn.* New York: Cambridge University Press, 1984.

Perry, W. G. *Forms of Intellectual and Ethical Development in the College Years: A Scheme.* New York: Holt, Rinehart and Winston, 1970.

Ramsden, P. (ed.). *Improving Learning: New Perspectives.* London: Kogan Page, 1988.

Ramsden, P., Beswick, D. G., and Bowden, J. A. "Learning Processes and Learning Skills." In J.T.E. Richardson, M. W. Eysenck, and D. Warren Piper (eds.), *Student Learning: Research in Education and Cognitive Psychology.* London: Society for Research into Higher Education, 1987.

Reimer, E. *School Is Dead.* Harmondsworth, England: Penguin Books, 1971.

Resnick, L. B. *Education and Learning to Think.* Washington, D.C.: National Academy Press, 1987a.

Resnick, L. B. "Learning in School and Out." *Educational Researcher,* 1987b, *16* (9), 13–20.

Reynolds, R. E., and Wade, S. E. "Thinking About Thinking

About Thinking: Reflections on Metacognition." *Harvard Educational Review,* 1986, *56* (3), 307–317.

Rogers, C. R. *Freedom to Learn: A View of What Education Might Become.* Columbus, Ohio: Merrill, 1969.

Ryle, A. *Frames and Cages: The Repertory Grid Approach to Human Understanding.* London: University of Sussex Press, 1975.

Säljö, R. "Qualitative Differences in Learning as a Function of the Learner's Conception of the Task." Gothenburg Studies in Educational Sciences, no. 14. Gothenburg, Sweden: University of Gothenburg, 1975.

Säljö, R. "Learning About Learning." *Higher Education,* 1979a, *8,* 443–451.

Säljö, R. "Learning in the Learner's Perspective. I — Some Commonsense Conceptions." Reports from the Institute of Education, University of Gothenburg, no. 76, 1979b.

Säljö, R. "Learning from Reading." In F. Marton, D. J. Hounsell, and N. J. Entwistle (eds.), *The Experience of Learning.* Edinburgh: Scottish Academic Press, 1984.

Seigel, H. "Critical Thinking as an Educational Ideal." *The Educational Forum,* 1980, *45,* 7–23.

Slavin, R. E. "Co-operative Learning." *Review of Educational Research,* 1980, *50* (2), 315–342.

Smith, R. M. *Learning How to Learn: Applied Theory for Adults.* New York: Cambridge Book Company, 1982.

Smith, R. M. Edited transcript of conference participation. In R. M. Smith (ed.), *Theory Building for Learning How to Learn.* DeKalb, Ill.: Educational Studies Press, 1988.

Stanage, S. M. *Adult Education and Phenomenological Research: New Directions for Theory, Practice and Research.* Malabar, Florida: Krieger, 1987.

Thomas, A. M. "Studentship and Membership: A Study of Roles in Learning." *The Journal of Educational Thought,* 1967, *1* (1), 65–76.

Thomas, L. F., and Harri-Augstein, E. S. *Self-Organised Learning: Foundations of a Conversational Science for Psychology.* London: Routledge and Kegan Paul, 1985.

Torbert, W. R. "Educating Towards Shared Purpose, Self-Direction and Quality Work: The Theory and Practice of

Liberating Structure." *Journal of Higher Education,* 1978, *49* (2), 109–135.

Wang, M. C. "Development and Consequences of Students' Sense of Personal Control." In J. M. Levine and M. C. Wang (eds.), *Teacher and Student Perceptions: Implications for Learning.* Hillsdale, N.J.: Erlbaum, 1983.

Weinstein, C. E., and Rogers, B. T. "Comprehension Monitoring as a Learning Strategy." In G. d'Ydewalle (ed.), *Proceedings of the Twenty-third International Congress of Psychology of the International Union of Psychological Science, Acapulco, Mexico, September 2–7, 1984, Vol. 3: Cognition, Information Processing, and Motivation.* Amsterdam, The Netherlands: North-Holland, 1985.

Chapter 3

A Working Model
of the
Learning-How-to-Learn Process

Maurice Gibbons

Let me invite you on a journey of investigation into the meaning of the term *learning how to learn* (LHTL)—what it is, what practices it involves, how we learn those practices, and how they apply to our lives. When I examine an educational process like LHTL, I imagine a universe containing all the phenomena that the practice may involve and then begin to organize those phenomena into categories dictated by the dynamics that drive them. The final step is to integrate the categories into a model that illuminates the relationships among them.

I pursue this process of expansion and reduction, generation and classification, for three main reasons. First, I am convinced that implicit in any such area as LHTL there is a vision of a model in which it is fully developed and excellently applied, and that a description of the model is a useful guide to any application of the practice in the field. Second, I think that practice means process and process spells complexity, and that models can concisely represent complexity. Too often I have worked with educational processes that promised much, attempted little, and achieved almost nothing. We have seen individualized learning in which students are all studying the same material at the same time; independent learning in which the only independence is in the rate at which students work their way through a stack of mimeographed sheets; experiential learning in which students do not leave the premises or even their classrooms, and so on. With a fully developed model on hand, it becomes more difficult to apply a piece of the practice and pretend it is the whole by, for instance, teaching students how to follow instructions and calling that a program in LHTL. Finally, I will try to build a model of LHTL because that is the way I learned how to learn, or taught myself how to learn, about such matters. Building the model will force me to think about the concepts and the relationships among them, and once the model is built, I will have a structural framework that will help me to remember the elements of the practice and how to apply them. It will be a tool for thinking about LHTL, and a construction to remodel as that thinking leads to further insight. The search also reminds me how personal learning is—how idiosyncratic—and how often, in the most compelling learning, the curriculum or content is unknown. It may also remind you that this is a fallible human construct upon which you can readily improve.

Let us begin by operationally defining LHTL so that we can use that definition as a guide to describe the universe of events we are investigating. Any meaning we give to LHTL depends on the meaning we give to learning. What, therefore, do we mean by learning? The most familiar definitions, either explicitly described in educational literature or implicit in traditional educational practices, are concerned with a student's absorption of a curriculum of content outlined by some authority and presented by a teacher. But that doesn't account for infant or adult learning, or for critical learning that occurs beyond the classroom either during or after the years of formal education. I have asked hundreds of people, "What learning experience had the greatest impact on your life?" and I cannot remember more than a handful citing a classroom incident. It is more realistic and productive to open up our definitions so that learning becomes any increase in a person's knowledge, skills, capacities, or tendencies by any means at any age in any circumstances, and LHTL becomes any increase in a person's *ability to increase* his or her knowledge, skills, or capacities.

Assuming that these definitions offer an acceptable beginning, we can probe deeper. It seems that any human experience is potentially a learning experience, and, therefore, any experience is a challenge to learn how to learn from it. But we do not learn from all our experiences, and we usually learn only a portion of what is potential in each of them. If we imagine a diagram in which the larger circle representing all potential learning events—all of life's experiences—contains a smaller circle representing those from which we actually learn, then we can say that LHTL is the influence that urges and enables us to derive learning both by widening our circle of learning experiences and by deepening each learning experience we encounter. But the potential for learning in any one experience, or during the collective experiences of a lifetime, is far more vast than anyone can absorb. LHTL, therefore, must also include discrimination: learning how to choose what to learn to manage it for use.

But since learning and LHTL can both be involved in any experience, and since both are forms of learning, how do we clearly distinguish between the two? "Learning how" suggests a process and "learning that" suggests a content, but when the content is a process the distinction blurs. We may, for instance, learn *that* Moscow has a certain latitude and longitude, or we may learn the process of *how* to employ latitude and longitude to locate Moscow or any other city. But when we learn that "the scientific method involves the following steps," the content is a process that enables us to learn; learning is LHTL. It is more discriminating to consider *learning* to be the more particular term and *LHTL* the more general term. Thus, when one learns the location of Moscow and one also learns how to find the location of cities like Moscow in the same instance, then the location is the particular or learning term and the process of finding the city is the more general or LHTL term. But should the particular learning be finding cities systematically, then a suitable general or LHTL term would be reading maps or drawing them accurately. From this perspective any learning can be, at some level, LHTL, and any LHTL can be learning.

Learning, therefore, can be thought of as the operational function and LHTL as the executive function. We *do* learning, and in LHTL, we learn more about *how* to do it. From these perspectives, LHTL is a relative relationship to learning that results in an increase in the individual's general ability to manage the more specific operations of learning. We can visualize a continuum of learning that stretches from the most specific kind of learning to the most general, from facts to complex processes that generate knowledge, for instance. On this continuum we can see that for each specific task, such as learning the location of a city, there is a more general task (such as learning how to find cities) that represents LHTL.

The criteria of appropriate and successful LHTL are generalizability, control, and autonomy. The greater the generalizability of the LHTL term, so that it enables the individual to succeed in more specific instances of learning, the more useful it is. Similarly, the more control such generalizability gives a person over the learning experience and the more autonomy that results, the more fully LHTL is realized and applied. LHTL, therefore, is an executive function of learning that serves to increase one's ability to manage the specifics of learning so that one is empowered to control more and more of the educational experience in one's own way, time, and place.

What are the dynamics of that empowerment? If, as I proceed with the exploration of an answer to this question, I seem to be ignoring the massive work on metacognition, thinking about one's own thinking, it is because that approach has accumulated a framework of assumptions that constrain the free-wheeling investigation I wish to conduct. While the results of metacognitive studies are important, they tend to formalize learning and imply that what is found to be generally true about metalearning across a population is specifically true and appropriate for individuals. I suspect that LHTL has profound natural and personal dimensions, as well as a formal one, and that all three dimensions require different forms of cultivation. Similarly, metacognitive studies often assume that all learning, and therefore all metalearning, is cognitive, a function of conscious thought. While reason is obviously a critical aspect, it seems most likely that learning and LHTL are often appropriately intuitive and preconscious and are always inseparable from the emotive and intentional dynamics that drive them. While even these can be described as rationalized functions, my experience is that metaphor, passion, and energy are often equally critical factors to include. Finally, studies in metacognition emphasize school-related skills required to learn a curriculum of content, while I regard LHTL as a part of all life experience, and I suspect that we learn and learn to learn quite differently when the focus is on technical or social or personal development issues. For these reasons I have chosen to consider three kinds of learning and LHTL, three aspects of learning essential to success in each of them, and three domains of life experience in which the way we learn how to learn is unique.

Three Kinds of Learning and Three Kinds of Learning How to Learn

I propose to examine the universe of human learning experiences in order to tease out distinctive categories of learning represented in it. Then I will examine each category in turn to determine the unique features of LHTL it represents. With the arenas of learning and LHTL described, the quality issue can then be explored by considering the dynamics that drive learning toward excellence in each area. Finally, I will try to identify basic domains of human activity so that the unique features of LHTL in each domain can be clarified. When this analyzing and classifying are complete, we should have a model of LHTL, as a fully developed field of human activity—a model that should not only be a guide to programs in LHTL but should also provoke a reexamination of educational practice.

I need touchstones in my own experience to ground my thinking or I find the language taking on a life and reality of its own, no matter how rational I attempt to be. Perhaps this is because my attempt to be rational lifts me away from the reality of experience into the logical unrealities the language makes possible. Three critical incidents stand out in my learning life, and each seems to represent a distinctive kind of learning.

When I finished high school and entered university, I had the most disastrous educational year imaginable. I had no purpose, no discipline; I became socially hyperactive and I failed half my courses. I left, entered a one-year teacher training program, taught for two years, and then returned to the university. There was no comparison between the two experiences. The second time I was there to become an English teacher and shaped most of my courses to that end. I had learned to work in a disciplined way with goals, a schedule, and high output in a short time span. I learned how to prepare for lectures, find key concepts, and follow them up. I took an accelerated reading course and set up a study group with bright students in my most difficult subjects. I developed my diagramming and model-building study method, and I found that I could project exam essay topics with considerable accuracy. The difference in my disastrous first year and my much more successful second year was the LHTL skills and strategies I had learned and developed.

The second learning incident began about fifteen years later when, sitting on a beach supervising my children while they rowed on the bay, I picked up a piece of wood and began to whittle absent-mindedly. Suddenly I realized that the figure of a woman was emerging from the wood, and that with each cut the pattern of the grain changed. I began consciously to carve the figure and to work the patterns in the wood. To my children's peril, I became completely absorbed in this shaping process: the feel of it, the smell of the wood, and the sight of the emerging sculpture. That was the first wood carving of many. Learning mostly by working with the wood, I tried out designs from my own imagination until I was ready to begin exhibiting. Later, I consulted others, read books, traveled to view sculpture and to work with an African tribe and a Balinese master carver. I continue to learn my art by following the route of instinct and pleasure, and somehow I am also learning how to learn it in ways that particularly suit me and the activity.

The third incident happened during my early years as a

teacher, when I was appointed to a provincial curriculum committee set up to revise a high school English program that had existed unchanged for a very long time. I knew nothing about the curriculum development process on such a scale so I began an education in it. I called the university, consulted with curriculum experts, and took books away to read. The established pattern was to lay out goals, purchase textbooks, and circulate them to schools with a curriculum guide. Although both seemed essential, there were neither plans nor funds for consulting interested parties such as teachers and for field testing our design before it was implemented in every school. In these circumstances, I began studying two new themes. First, I explored the structure of English so that I could design and recommend patterns for the proposed curriculum to my colleagues. Second, I tried to learn about political strategy so that I could influence the process by which the curriculum would be developed. We did develop a radically different program but, although I informally surveyed a few teachers and won a token field trial, I was far from successful in changing the traditional process. Success in political influence has continued to elude me despite my efforts to become skillful; I suspect the impediment is in my nature rather than in a failure of technique.

These three touchstones suggest three distinctive forms of learning that I conclude are ways of categorizing the realm of learning events. The carving incident represents a *natural* or spontaneous form of learning, an unexpected collusion between inner readiness and environmental opportunity. Like Blake's grain of sand, the piece of wood contained the universe, in my case the universe of wood carving, once I could see it. And in my encounter with the wood I discovered in myself a talent and passion for wood carving that had remained hidden during all my efforts to learn what my talents were and how I should be using them. My university studies, by contrast, represented *formal* or directed learning events in which a structured sequence of content is presented to us in some way designed to help us learn. What stands out in my mind is that in the university experience I confronted another kind of incredibly rich environment whose potential I could see only when I made a passionate connection with it, developed the skills I required, and took the initiative to find my own ways to master the situation. In my failure, education was happening to me; in my success, I was in active pursuit of it.

The curriculum development incident represents *personal,* self-directed learning events in which we consciously pursue a course of study and action following a pattern of our own choice and design, usually in response to a personal interest or necessity. Like anyone who must make a personal change, solve a problem, master a new field, or accomplish a task, I had to learn not only new concepts and skills, but also how to apply them and how to solve the problems that arise during their application in situations that were often difficult. Once again I realize that my own drive to find the best possible English program—for personal as well as professional reasons—pressed me into the search and guided me through many obstacles. I also realize that I had to learn and develop ways to proceed successfully and that I was drawn on by an emerging vision of a program in which students would become informed and dedicated humanists, and teachers would have choices and support in shaping their own programs to help students accomplish this task. It is noteworthy also that while general knowledge in such fields as curriculum development was helpful, the program I needed was a unique one; that is, learning in this situation included generating concepts and procedures that were not available from sources. I am struck by how often learning is a unique personal search for knowledge, skills, and procedures that seem unavailable at the time, leaving the learner to find or create them and then make them work.

Can we consolidate descriptions of these three kinds of learning—natural, formal, and personal—and derive from them some of the basic kinds of LHTL that enable us to perform successful acts of learning in each of them? We can try; see Table 3.1.

Natural Learning. Natural learning can occur at any time throughout life and whether we want it or not, accidentally and spontaneously. It is potential in the material world, presses upon

Table 3.1. A Comparison of Aspects of a Learning Act in the Three Basic Kinds of Learning

	Natural	*Formal*	*Personal*
Type of Learning	Interactive: Individual interacts spontaneously with environment	Directed: Individual is directed through learning procedure	Self-Initiated: Individual designs desired learning procedure
Source of Content	Available: Content selected by interest from available environment	Assigned: Content assigned by educational authority	Chosen: Content selected and organized by learner
Method of Instruction	Transactional: Process occurs between accidental influence and inner state	Presented: Content presented systematically to student for learning	Enacted: Individual enacts and monitors own learning procedure

us in every medium of our burgeoning information world from breakfast cereal boxes to complex computer programs, and is urged upon us by people in our social world anxious to tell us what they know and what they think we should do. Natural learning is most obvious and observable in the preschool years, during which children learn to walk, talk, relate, differentiate, explore, experiment, play, and generally lay the foundation for the kind of people and learners they will become. Each infant, for instance, must learn the process of human speech, without a teacher or a curriculum, and it must be learned during a brief window of psycho-physical opportunity or it will never be so readily learned again. As in most spontaneous learning, the child observes, practices, and initiates; but the results will be determined both by the richness and tone of the surrounding environment and by the quality of processing and inner drive he or she brings to the task. Every child on the planet learns for his or her language roughly the same sounds in the same sequence until each becomes shaped into the utterances of the language environment; there is a kind of unfolding inner program. The competence level of that program will be limited by the quality of language spoken within the child's environment, and by the number of times the child is directly engaged in the process of sound making. It will also be limited or enhanced by the child's desire to learn, the level of skill she or he develops in learning and practicing language, and the confidence developed during the language encounters. The intensity, nature, and success of this natural learning process and other sequences like it will help to shape the life of the child.

A number of themes seem evident among natural learning events. One is a developmental curriculum that unfolds throughout life, presenting each of us with a similar pattern of opportunities, crises and challenges. As our minds, bodies, and personalities mature, our transformative upheavals seethe for resolution within us during our passage through childhood, adolescence, mid-life, or old age. Similarly, our emerging capacities and talents press to be used. There seems to be a species-wide as well as an individual desire to know the world, understand it, and either function successfully in it or bring it under control. As curiosity and capacity combine with the possibilities of our surroundings and the nurturing provided by those around us, we begin to accumulate our understanding of the world and our place in it, which gradually develops into our world view. In a parallel fashion, our capacity to construct alternate realities through imagination, creativity, intuition, and play also develop, leading us to visionary views of the world.

There are also themes in natural learning events that pertain to the development of our personal characteristics, three of the most basic being our nature, values, and competence. Each situation teaches us something about ourselves— who we are, our strengths and weaknesses, our male and female features, what is expected of us, and what we can expect of ourselves. Each situation we experience also has a value valence, teaching us first what is painful and what is pleasant, and then what is good and worthy or what is bad and unacceptable. Similarly, each experience has a competence valence, teaching us what we do well and with pleasure and what we do poorly and with discomfort. While formal education will reveal to us the accepted truths about the world, natural learning will be the chief influence on our maturation, our general knowledge, our imagination, our character, and our talent. These will unfurl through the accumulated life experiences each of us has and what we make of them.

In this form of learning, what is LHTL? What are the executive learning operations that govern learning spontaneously from experience? If natural learning depends upon responsiveness to the potential of the available environment, what operations can be distinguished from the specifics, the substance to be learned, which, if mastered, will result in success? I find at least five basic processes.

1. *Learning how to learn from interaction with others.* It is essential, especially in the infant years, to learn to trust others and oneself; to feel one belongs but is a distinctive, separate person; and to feel that the person one becomes is worthy and capable. In later years, it is essential to maintain and enhance these feelings. They underlie the confidence in individuals that they can learn, relate, and act successfully. Without that confidence, learning can be severely restrained.

2. *Learning how to learn from the stimulation of the environment.* In the early years, learning to develop one's sensory, cognitive, and performative capacities depends upon appropriate, available stimulation, especially at the critical period of development for each ability in the maturation sequence. Active interaction with a stimulating physical and human environment is irreplaceable in infancy and is a basic source of learning throughout life.

3. *Learning how to learn from exploring the environment.* In the early years it is essential for individuals to develop, and fulfill, curiosity through rewarding explorations of the environment, and from these explorations to develop intention and initiative. For the active pursuit of learning to continue to develop throughout life, these drives must be nurtured regularly, and success must often be achieved.

4. *Learning how to learn from practice.* Whether infants are learning to speak, walk, or think, they must learn the rewards of achievement attained through practice. Imitation, repetition, and rehearsal—often learned through play—are the foundations of competence and essential for both learning and development throughout life.

5. *Learning how to learn from the teacher within.* Children are natural, autonomous learners. To progress beyond reaction to reflection, they must develop an inner dialogue in which the child as reflective learner mediates—with reason, intuition, and creativity—between the influences of the environment and collective experience in order to generate insight, decision, and invention. The teacher within has several possible forms: children's natural ability to absorb, abstract, hypothesize, construct, and revise impressions and ideas about what they confront in the environment; the pattern of growth in their readiness for certain kinds of learning that seems to be time tabled within; the recapitulation of human history in their development of such expressions as language and art that seem to have a natural pattern of unfolding; and the press of their accumulating knowledge and skill shaped by their individual interests and talents and guided by the encouragement and success they experience in their efforts.

The way in which these LHTL processes develop depends upon what the environment provides, the individual's nature, and the interaction that occurs between the two. If the environment is rich in opportunity; if the individual is healthy, confident, curious, developmentally ready, and has inherent capacity; and if the interaction between the two is active rather than passive, nurturing rather than destructive, and leading regularly to the individual's success rather than failure, learning will be increased, and over time, the "increase will be increased." Natural learning is not serial or additive but cumulative and integrative, each achievement enriching the base from which the next learning can occur. It is also clear that this form of learning provides a foundation for formal and personal learning.

Formal Learning. In formal learning situations, the content is usually chosen by others and presented to the individual for learning. In addition, the order, pace, and manner in which this content will be learned are also predetermined, together with the criteria for success and the way success will be measured. Although formal learning nearly always includes content to be learned, it seldom includes instruction or training on how to accomplish the task. Through most of my education, the most critical task was to remember the course content, especially for tests and exams, but no one ever taught me how to remember or how to organize concepts into a comprehensive structure for longer-range recall. The crisis created by not knowing how to learn in this context came to me in my first attempt at university study where professors offered content and made assignments, which we either comprehended and mastered on our own or did not do and slipped irretrievably behind. In this classic reaction to the experience of entering the university, the basic categories of LHTL in formal educational situations are starkly revealed: knowing how to prepare for learning, how to learn from a lesson or lecture, how to conduct exercises and assignments, how to find and summarize important information, how to organize for comprehension and recall, and how to perform well on tests and exams.

My experience demonstrated to me that it is important, especially from a long-range perspective on education, to learn to make a connection between a passionate personal purpose and the content to be mastered. It is also important to "learn how to learn how to learn"; that is, one must also begin to consciously equip oneself to be successful at learning, which may mean creating a personal style of learning, developing new learning techniques, and learning the politics of successful course achievement. This also includes mastering basics that impact all learning, such as remembering, speed reading, logical argument, problem solving, and thinking aggressively, critically, and creatively about the issues involved. And it may mean a critical self-examination of oneself as a learner, even returning to such basic questions as What does it all mean? What am I going to do? and What do I value? Above all, LHTL in formal situations requires initiative, the determination to be successful, and the confidence that one can be. Keeping these other issues in mind, consider the following five basic aspects of LHTL in formal situations:

1. *Learning how to learn from instruction.* Students learn to listen actively to a lesson and to question, observe, summarize, record, visualize, apply, and review what is presented.
2. *Learning how to learn to perform assigned learning tasks.* Students learn to perceive the purpose of a task, to follow instructions, to anticipate the kind of response expected, and to verify their answers.
3. *Learning how to learn from an assigned learning task.* Students learn to relate the practice activity to the lesson taught, to consciously practice that lesson, and to relate what they are learning to their own experience.
4. *Learning basic learning skills.* Students learn skills basic to all formal learning, such as how to find the information needed; read for understanding; summarize, organize, and review; and memorize and recall.
5. *Learning how to generalize from a learning activity.* Students learn to apply what has been learned from one task to a similar task and to new and different tasks, and they learn to make the transfer from hypothetical exercises to real situations. What is learned becomes integrated with their personal knowledge and part of their repertoire of responses to learning situations.

Formal learning usually dominates any other form of learning in our minds and seems to be the only legitimate method of education. It is encapsulated, its value often limited to further experience in school or other educational institutions. These methods of LHTL act as a bridge to three kinds of learning, and they make formal learning portable so that it is more applicable to other dimensions of our lives. It is also a reasonable hypothesis that knowing the skills of LHTL significantly increases the accessibility of formal learning to students, especially those who have not absorbed them intuitively.

Personal Learning. When I began my personal learning project as a member of the English revision committee, I had none of the support structures evident in the formal situations in schools and other educational situations: no teacher, no curriculum, no texts, and no timetable. In fact, it seems to me now that I learned to do what teachers and educational authorities had formerly done for me. Although the overall task of deciding on the curriculum was given, I still had to decide what my purpose and goals would be, how I could learn the skills of curriculum development, the concepts involved in the structure of English, the way to generate and present new ideas, and how to present them with political effectiveness. But an additional problem that I had which my teachers didn't have was taking the risk to apply my learning in a real and critical situation where a great deal was at stake for me, my committee colleagues, and those who would teach and study the curriculum. And I had to motivate and mobilize myself to take that risk and keep up the pursuit in the face of difficulties and opposition.

All of these are typical LHTL tasks involved in personal or self-directed, intentional learning activities. The scope of such activities is not limited to adulthood or to professional concerns. Many children of school age have already become active and skilled in personal learning by involving themselves in an array of activities from sports, the arts, and hobbies to highly technical fields such as automobiles and computers. But it is most evident in adulthood where people are regularly confronted with needs and opportunities to learn and act in a great variety of fields, including occupations, social relationships, self-development, leisure activities, service and politics, creative expression, current events, and so on. The most critical activities in these times of great change are often in the field of work. Whatever the application, the following skills will be essential:

1. *Learning to decide what to learn.* Individuals learn to focus on goals and purposes, consider a range of options, make choices, and design plans for their own learning.
2. *Learning how to manage one's own learning.* Without an institutional framework for study, people must organize the sub-

ject matter or tasks they have selected, gather the resources they need, secure the necessary contacts and opportunities, and then manage themselves—their own attention, time, and effort.

3. *Learning how to learn from experience.* In live situations there are many opportunities for people to learn from the experiences they observe, those that happen to them, and those they themselves initiate. A new and inexperienced sales manager, for instance, will learn from watching a successful motivator, from the experiences he has while attempting to motivate others, and the experiences he creates, such as coaching a team, interviewing his staff, or consulting others in situations like his own.

4. *Learning to be an intentional learner.* Learning in life situations is a holistic experience; it engages all aspects of our behavior—thinking, sensing, feeling, and acting. The more perceptive we are, the more skilled, motivated, and intentional, the better we are able to absorb and pursue learning from experience. LHTL is learning to become a healthier, more aware person capable of the executive, reflective management of one's own learning and growth.

5. *Learning to take action.* While formal learning situations are usually hypothetical and abstract, life experiences are real and concrete. Few life-learning episodes are complete until our behavior has changed or we have applied what we have learned through action. This involves forming new attitudes toward taking initiatives, formulating strategies, facing risks, and coping with unpredictable circumstances.

The Educational Issues. All three kinds of learning can occur throughout our lives, in close proximity at any particular time, perhaps even in the same situation. It may be axiomatic that ideal formal educational situations strategically involve our tripartite learning capacities. In my own experience, I see that I could easily have been taking a course in sculpture, during which I also spontaneously discovered an interest and a talent for wood carving and personally began planning an exhibition.

Just as easily, I could have, in close proximity, been planning an English curriculum, taking a night course in theater, and discovering an interest in wood sculpture on a weekend outing. If we are concerned about people's learning lives, we must be concerned about all three forms and how they interact with each other. The basic issues come first from the acknowledgment of these learning forms and their importance, and then from commitment to cultivating them appropriately. How can we ensure that the early years, the most dynamic and shaping years of learning, are appropriately stimulated? How can we increase an individual's desire for, capacity in, and control over formal learning? And how can we equip and empower people to deal skillfully with the learning necessities and opportunities they confront throughout their lives?

I cannot think of a more important goal of education than to ensure that every child has an equal opportunity to develop his or her natural learning capacities in those early years in which the individual's learning future is so critically shaped—years in which one has such an amazing capacity to learn. Parent training, and perhaps training for everyone, in cultivating natural learning seems essential, as does the provision of preschool experiences that enrich children and encourage them to pursue their interests and abilities confidently. Moving from natural to formal learning presents an abrupt interface. Schooling for LHTL would begin with a transitional curriculum that fosters and enhances natural learning before gradually leading to more formal experiences, following such processes as those developed by Maria Montessori, John Dewey, and Sylvia Ashton-Warner. Similarly, it seems critical that school-age students learn not only the curriculum of content but also a curriculum of LHTL that parallels it and is designed to give students greater and greater skill, both in formal learning and in taking control over their own learning processes. Finally, it seems clear from this exploration that any plan for lifelong learning must include preparing people of all ages to meet the demands of personal learning successfully. This goal basically means teaching them the functional equivalents of direct instruction so that they can do for themselves what a teacher has formally done for them: set goals, plan sequences of learning experiences, assemble resources, evaluate progress, and review programs.

My three touchstone experiences remind me again that there is much more to learning a curriculum than mastering the content. It is possible to focus on *thinking* under the formal conditions of a formal classroom learning situation. However, the importance of *feeling* and *action* in the less controlled life conditions in which natural and personal learning occur cannot be eliminated from the learner's experience either within or beyond the classroom, even though the authorities of formal education may define them as outside their responsibility. As a human experience, learning involves reason, emotion, and action; all three must be considered as dimensions of LHTL. Indeed, in life situations, effective performance is often the *raison d'être* of learning, and achieving healthy emotional states is often the primary goal. Any strategic intervention designed to enhance people's skill in LHTL must therefore include strategies for the development of the appropriate inner emotional states and performance abilities that accompany knowing and understanding. Otherwise, all learning and life are circumscribed with limitations.

What are the main characteristics of reason, emotion, and action in the three forms of learning, and what are those characteristics directly associated with LHTL?

Reason. In general, reason is the executive operation in LHTL, more concerned with the management of our thinking than with the thinking itself. It is concerned with our decisions to perceive, analyze, propose, imagine, and reflect, and to do so actively rather than passively, consciously rather than accidentally. It is concerned with our decisions about what to focus our attention on, how we go about our examination, what we make of what we see, and how we integrate our observations and conclusions with what we think we already know. It is the deliberation that leads us from such acts of reasoning to projects involving more extended thinking about an issue, and even further into life missions of devoted exploration. It is ultimately the executive capacity to determine the reality in which we live, what it all means to us, and the way we will live in it.

Drawing on the touchstones and the outlines of the three forms of learning already described, we can begin to note what the key elements of the role of reason in LHTL include.

1. *Perceiving.* Learning how to observe, listen, sense, and otherwise take in and make sense of the environment. Learning to see more—more details, more connections, more interactions—and to bring more knowledge to perceiving.
2. *Analyzing.* Learning how to comprehend the nature of events and situations, to understand the elements and principles that compose them, and the greater structures of which they are a part. Learning to understand how the world works and why. Not just perceiving things but comprehending them as functioning wholes—their relationships to the greater scheme of things, the parts that compose them, and the casual relationships among them.
3. *Proposing.* Learning how to think our own thoughts, to weigh evidence, and to form propositions about reality. Learning to form our own generalizations from perception and analysis and to think critically about the propositions and generalizations of others in light of our own knowledge.
4. *Imagining.* Learning how to create new ideas, solutions, images, processes, and realities. Learning to think original thoughts, imagine new possibilities, see new solutions visually in our minds and create visions of our worlds and ourselves in ideal states. Learning to generate alternative choices in all aspects of our lives.
5. *Reflecting.* Learning how to consider, weigh, and manipulate perceptions, proposals, analyses, ideas, and visions and to make reasonable judgments about revising and extending them. Developing an inner discussion that moves us toward clearer thinking, consideration of a broader range of possibilities, and the formation of new enterprises moving in new directions and following ever more effective plans.

Reason is receptive, generative, and ruminative. LHTL in this aspect involves learning how to heighten and focus awareness through observation and analysis; how to probe and question in order to hypothesize and demonstrate; and how to debate and dramatize inwardly in order to understand and revise. Institutions emphasize the receptive characteristic, occasionally touch the generative, but seldom approach the ruminative. The reasoning skills—LHT reason—are required and exercised but seldom explained and taught.

Emotion. While the central thrusts of reason in LHTL are taking in, processing, and then putting out information and ideas, the central thrusts of emotion are responding with feeling, developing commitment, and acting with confidence. In its simplest, most direct form, this means learning to "feel our feelings" and to understand the relationship between our experience and our feeling response to it. If feelings are repressed, and especially if those repressed feelings are having a deleterious effect on our thinking and actions, then we must be able to manage the overcoming of these effects, either by removing the cause in the environment or reassessing the inner experience from which they arise. In a more positive way, we must also learn both to trust our authentic feelings as guides to action and to gather feeling support—or self-motivation—for those enterprises we choose to pursue. Through the successes we accumulate, we must also ensure that we increase our sense of well-being and self-worth, knowing that self-esteem is the most enabling of our feelings about ourselves. Success in the management of our emotional lives will be determined primarily by the number of learning experiences from which we can derive self-esteem, even including those in which we do not achieve material or public success.

The second issue is self-control. Our ability to learn and to accomplish our goals depends greatly upon our ability to focus our energies and to maintain that focus despite distractions from within or without. This capacity to maintain effort until a task is complete, often referred to as will or determination, governs our effectiveness in the world, especially in the realm of work. To accomplish this, we need to be able to control and adapt our emotions to the situation we are facing, and that is especially important in our interaction with others where we want to establish relationships based upon rapport. This requires the ability both to communicate our feelings to others and to feel what they are feeling, and to be guided by our processing of both. Above all, control should enable us to establish a life experience in which satisfaction is the prevailing emotion, regularly accentuated with contentment, joy, and sometimes even ecstasy. The key elements in the emotional aspect of LHTL are as follows:

1. *Feeling.* Learning how to experience one's own authentic emotional response to situations and understanding the causes of such a response
2. *Clarity.* Learning how to express feeling as interest in ourselves and the world; how to discover who we are, where we are going, and what we want to do; how to develop commitment and passion for what we are doing or are about to do
3. *Confidence.* Learning how to feel worthy and capable; how to become confident that what we plan we can make happen; how to develop a capacity and appetite for success
4. *Determination.* Learning how to develop drive and toughness — the drive to take risks, solve problems, and overcome opposition whether the difficulties arise within oneself or originate in the situation
5. *Intuition.* Learning how to trust our own unarticulated feeling of rightness about ideas, decisions, or actions; responding confidently to our instinctive inner voices

LHTL in the realm of emotion is threefold. The first goal is learning how to identify and eliminate those inner states that are inhibitory to learning, such as emotional numbness or artificiality, personal confusion, insecurity, helplessness, and self-doubt. The second is learning how to establish those inner states that are enabling, such as authentic feeling, clarity, confidence, determination, and trust in our own judgment. The third is learning how to access or build the intensity of caring, pleasure, and power that are involved in passionate pursuit.

Action. If thought is the language of the mind, action is the language of the body. We must understand and integrate both languages to achieve informed action. The paradox of these inner states is that we need them in order to reason and to act, and yet we can develop them only through reasoning and taking action. We can feel successful, for instance, only by being successful, and yet our chances of success are greatly increased when a pattern of achievement has already taught us to expect success and how it can best be achieved. This interconnectedness of reason, emotion, and action leads me to the conclusion that no learning is complete until it has led to action that is in some way meaningful in our lives. Without this stage, part of the model implicit in the term *learning* is masquerading as the fulfillment of the whole vision—something untranslated into the fabric of our active lives, unintegrated with our general knowledge, and unfinished in the sense that we have not mastered the unique complexities of its use.

Action involves its own unique form of knowing. Taking action is a gesture in which body sense provides what intellect alone cannot. Think of dance, karate, surgery, flying, or sculpture. We can know all that reason can know about the actions involved and still be incapable of the appropriate actions themselves. Successful performance requires learning to act almost without thinking. And only when the body has learned these skills can we be successful in them. And achieving excellence requires finding ways to release the body into its own higher state of grace, for which we can often be coached but not taught. In every field of action there is a form of appropriate measure of success, a manner, style, grace, presence, or skill that makes a difference, a difference that we can ultimately learn only by teaching it to ourselves, by feeling it in ourselves. The unique features of learning to take action also include learning how to apply what we know by making decisions, designing action plans, taking the risk to act, anticipating the action skills required and practicing them, securing feedback and modifying our course of action, and recognizing and acknowledging success. These essential learning functions are learnable, but only if significant action itself is included. LHTL in this realm means learning how to coach ourselves. When we act, the following aspects are critical to LHTL:

1. *Decision making.* Learning how to consider a range of choices of action in a situation, to make a promising decision about a course of action to take
2. *Initiative.* Learning how to generate the energy and drive to be an active rather than passive element in the equation that determines outcomes in situations
3. *Practice.* Learning how to perform the mental and physical rehearsal required for improving the ability to perform well
4. *Problem solving.* Learning how to assess an ongoing event based on feedback; how to recognize inadequacies and devise and execute more promising courses of action
5. *Influence.* Learning how to persuade, lead, or otherwise shape the course of events in a situation; how to develop skill in the politics of action

The only way we can learn to act skillfully is by taking action. Much can be learned in the classroom and on the practice field, but in the end we can master the performance only in the game itself. Knowing we are going to perform gives meaning to practice; performing tells us what practice is needed. Through performance we learn from both success and failure, finding out what we do well and how to do it better.

In summary, we see that reason, emotion, and action together play a coordinated part in the successful pursuit of each of the three kinds of learning. Each kind involves increasing initiative by the individual. Feeling and attitude are the forces that energize the searching, shaping mind into the journey of discovery, whether in spontaneous, directed, or personally managed learning.

Educational Issues. If we contrast the prevailing model of schooling with the model of LHTL emerging in this exploration, three key issues arise: reflection, control, and initiative. Learning how *not* to learn represents educational helplessness, a state that is both learnable and teachable. LHTL is taking charge of our education and our lives, which is also learnable and teachable if we can master the three keys to action.

LHTL is a reflective act; reflection and reason make up the executive function of LHTL. Stepping back from a task, stepping outside ourselves, enables us to consider how it can best be accomplished and to examine and shape our thoughts, feelings, and actions. We pay dearly in loss of direct innocent experience for the reflective power we gain from such detachment, but it does enable us to examine, imagine, choose, design, and manage the experiences we have, to shape our own evolution through many transformations in one lifetime. Despite its critical importance in learning and living, however, reflection is seldom acknowledged, encouraged, or taught in schools. It seems either unnecessary for the curriculum or undesirable for the anarchic diversity of individual thinking that could result. There must, of course, be more than a fixed question with a fixed answer for reflection to become important. There must be a reason to reflect, time for reflection, and skill in conducting an inner dialogue. It must be made clear that a variety of outcomes of the reflective process are expected and potentially acceptable. This means greater control by the individual and guidance in utilizing that control successfully.

Control is a critical issue for both individuals and institutions. LHTL suggests that the focus of educational control should be within the individual. Knowing how to learn is knowing how to decide and manage one's learning inside or outside of educational institutions. But should the focus of control be in the individual from the beginning, as in a completely permissive situation, or should the task of the institution be to educate for control and to confer it as the individual is able to manage it? The message of this exploration is that LHTL is a complex process and that it may be more respectful and productive to cultivate a capacity for control rather than to grant autonomy at the outset. Freedom to be a "law unto oneself" without the competence to exercise it is empty, and without the responsibility to guide it, it is dangerous.

Learning to get answers to assigned questions does not cultivate initiative, which requires time and opportunity at least and flourishes when people feel confident, competent, and compelled. The challenge of schooling is to ensure competence by teaching students to employ the functional equivalents of teaching involved in self-teaching, namely, to set appropriate learning goals and design workable plans for achieving them. It means cultivating the emotional equivalents required for successful self-direction, which are obviated by the consequences of a directed learning system, namely clarity, confidence, and determination. Finally, it means encouraging the initiative required for successful action, namely, providing students with the opportunity for responsible and informed action in challenging real-life situations and coaching them to meet those challenges successfully. LHTL means knowing how to reflect purposefully, how to take control responsibly, and how to take initiative courageously.

The Domains of Learning How to Learn

Equally important in our search are the critical domains in which each of us must learn in order to achieve a full life. The three endeavors that most concern us are our interactions with the environment, with each other, and with ourselves. Influenced by the work of Jurgen Habermas, I call these the technical, social, and developmental domains of LHTL. The quality and nature of our lives depend upon our ability to deal with the practical demands, interpersonal relationships, and personal growth that are the main themes interwoven to make up the fabric of our lives. Each theme is a lifelong sequence of challenges not only to learn but to learn how to learn from engagement in experiences in reflections on these challenges. The quality of our lives — our work, our interactions with others, and our own becoming — will depend upon our ability to derive sufficient understanding from one experience to guide our improved performance in the next. What will establish these domains as necessary elements in our model is the demonstration that each involves an essential and unique manner of LHTL.

The Technical Domain. The technical domain embodies all of our efforts to achieve instrumental control over our environment, with the result that we can make predictable results occur in it. The range of these efforts spans all of our attempts to apprehend the world, to comprehend how it works, to understand how we can intervene to make things happen, and to become skillful in making things happen that we choose to make happen. They include such practical activities as learning to grasp and walk, using tools and engaging in work, conducting research and changing normal practice, and effecting policy and practice in the management of the world's affairs, whether in microcosm or macrocosm. Learning in this domain is any increase in understanding the causal relationships among conditions or events and in the skill to manage or direct those relationships to produce predictable accomplishments. LHTL in the technical domain is any increase in the executive ability to identify important outcomes, the skills and steps necessary to achieve them, and the program that will organize the learning effort successfully. In this domain doing is learning, and learning how to do is LHTL.

1. *Focus.* How to be productive in the realm of work and other practical affairs and activities
2. *Mode of inquiry.* Logical analysis to determine the relationships between predictive proposals and productive action to yield intended outcomes
3. *Means.* The pursuit of competence through study, experiment, and practice in the accomplishment of goals
4. *Outcome.* Productive effectiveness enabling us to control outcomes in practical tasks, whether in the realms of work, life circumstances, or the environment

It is interesting, in retrospect, that all three of my touchstone experiences, spanning the three kinds of LHTL, are in this domain. Each involved gaining the capacity to manage events, with the result that I became more productively effective.

The Social Domain. The social domain embodies all aspects of our diverse interactions with others. The range of those interactions is vast, including intimate relationships, child rearing, and family life. It includes all of our casual, friendly, and leisure contacts; our meetings in clubs, groups, teams, committees, and squads; and our community, business, political, and service activities. It includes disagreement and conflict as well as understanding and cooperation, frustration and chaos as well as resolution and order. What we seek in the maelstrom of conflicting individual feelings, needs, and dreams is a rapprochement in which the opportunities for each individual are maximized and the dangers are minimized. The range of activities involved in this pursuit includes our communicative exchanges, relationships in which we act cooperatively to achieve shared goals, and our negotiations to achieve agreements and function together with mutual benefit and safety. It is the development of communicative skill in creating shared meaning, regard, and intent, which requires learning the capacity both to generate and communicate our own feelings, understandings, and desires and to interpret and respond to the feelings, understandings, and desires of others.

LHTL, therefore, involves learning from social interactions how to improve our ability to communicate so that we achieve deeper mutual understanding and forge agreements that extend the freedoms we can exercise without infringing on our responsibilities to others. It means learning to interact openly, cooperate, negotiate fairly, and decide democratically. In this domain relating is learning and learning how to relate is LHTL.

1. *Focus.* Learning how to relate to others for mutual benefit
2. *Mode of inquiry.* Negotiated interaction to discover how to reduce individual subjectivity and interpersonal conflict in order to achieve mutual understanding and contractual agreement

3. *Means.* Active communication in pursuit of understanding oneself, the other, and the forces that impede and enhance interactions that lead to mutually beneficial agreements
4. *Outcome.* Social integration; moving toward greater interconnection and interdependence with others, with increased clarity, agreement, and affection; and moving away from confusion, conflict, and hostility

The importance of this domain is indicated by the influence of social competence on so many aspects of our lives. Our personalities are shaped by it, the quality of our existence depends on it, our success in every interaction is enhanced by it, and the future of our communities and our planet will be determined by it. With this recognition of the social domain in LHTL, it becomes clear that interconnectedness and interdependence are as important as autonomy and control, which seemed so central to LHTL in the beginning of this exploration. We may also add that the openness and risk of the personal domain are necessary to complete a holistic description of the dynamics of LHTL. So much of my own life is concerned with social interaction. To match my three themes of experience in the technical domain, I need to add my struggles as a parent and partner, the challenge to teach people how to interact and work in teams, and my efforts to master the complexities of political action as touchstones in the social domain.

The Developmental Domain. The developmental domain embodies all of our efforts to achieve personal control over our own experiences, with the result that we can freely choose those that cultivate our growth as individuals. These efforts include all of our attempts to free ourselves from forces and influences that limit our control over our lives, as well as those in which we take opportunities to increase our power to choose and act. They include, for instance, our efforts to overcome self-doubt and the interpretations of us by others who control us, as well as our efforts to reach out to new experiences and to achieve goals that demand new or higher levels of performance from us.

The range of such efforts includes all the stages through

which our personality develops, the distinctive choices we make as an expression of our emerging selves, and the expanding arena of opportunity we create for exercising those choices. That means becoming distinctive persons free from dependency on others, identification with them, and the control of their expectations. It means becoming autonomous: taking initiative and making our own choices. And it means shaping our lives with an expanding sense of possibilities and an increasing capacity to realize those possibilities unfettered by inhibition or constrained by opposition. In this freeing process, we learn how to recognize and resolve the limitations created by trauma, anxiety, depression, self-doubt, misconceptions about reality, counterproductive behavior, self-destructive attitudes and habits, and other impediments accumulated from our past. We also learn how to deal with our present circumstances so that we live most of the time in a state of contentment and hope, and so that we are continually developing new dimensions of ourselves, exploring new possibilities for the future, and moving toward an expanding vision of what our lives might become. Learning in this domain is becoming ourselves. LHTL is generating the power to become ourselves by learning how to free ourselves to pursue ever greater possibilities in our lives.

1. *Focus.* Learning how to achieve the freedom and the means to develop fully as a person
2. *Mode of inquiry.* Critical reflection about ourselves and our circumstances in order to identify the forces within us and around us that limit our ability to function; and positive projection that enables us to see possibilities and envision transformations that result from taking them
3. *Means.* Developmental change in which we eliminate impediments, expand our options, and increase our capacity to pursue choices
4. *Outcome.* Fully functioning adulthood in which we are capable of fulfilling our needs, interests, and purposes free from misconceptions about ourselves, illusions about reality, or intimidation

All classifications are lies in the sense that they overlap in some way, as all of the classifications in this emerging model do. We learn about ourselves, for instance, from our practical performances and from our relationships with others, just as who we are influences our relationships and what we do. But the developmental domain is distinctive in both intent and means from the others, and the distinction is important because our ability to influence our own development has such a powerful impact on the rest of our lives. As in the technical and social domains, my experience is significant. In my own life, in my personal struggle to be free, I consider that my struggle with anger as a young man, meeting a challenge of risky opportunity that was life-disrupting, and coping with fear when authority threatened my job and reputation are my touchstones in the developmental realm.

Educational Issues. If we agree that these three domains are critical for a full life and if we agree that they represent the three most important kinds of life-shaping competence in how to learn, then we must address the most significant issue of all — that traditional schooling all but disregards them. While the importance of these areas would not be denied, little concentrated effort is devoted to ensure that students are in command of them by the time they graduate. It is amazing, from a LHTL perspective, that most students graduate from school without any competence in a field of practical productivity that can be traced to their school experience, and they often leave without any plan of what they will become competent in, or even of how to go about choosing such a field. But developing practical and productive competence in a field is essential for many reasons, and the only known way to learn how to become competent in any field is to become competent first in one field. The challenge to schooling is, "Why does not every child graduate from school not only with a breadth of knowledge and skill, but also with a depth of experience and competence that makes him expert in at least one field of his own choice?"

It is equally true that in schooling the social domain is

treated as peripheral, and that classroom conditions are not only socially alienating to many individuals but also act as obstacles to social interaction. As an institution, school disen-franchises its constituents and, offering few opportunities for social responsibility, immobilizes their social development. Al-though group methods are being used increasingly as instru-ments of instruction, I know of no programs designed to pro-duce graduates competent in participatory control over personal relationships, contractual negotiations, cooperative productivity, community participation, social management, family life, child rearing, and politics, even though these will be essential activities throughout their lives and the life of their communities. The educational challenge is, "Why does not schooling model and cultivate the highest possible level of social competence among students so that they will grow socially as individuals and that they will learn collectively how to commu-nicate, share, negotiate, learn, decide, plan, cooperate, and contribute?"

Finally, we must note that while there is much concern about individual students in schools, there is little focused effort devoted to cultivating them as individuals or to equipping them to shape and maintain a healthy personal life of growth and development. When personal issues influence a student's ability to learn content, they become school issues; but the school issue is seldom how to nurture the child's fullest possible development as a person, or to teach ways to self-manage that development. It seems an incontrovertible truth that mass education, both by what it does and what it does not do, is largely destructive to personal development as outlined by the dimensions of our emergent model. There are many reasons why the ultimate challenge of helping students learn how to manage their own lives, and the practical and social challenges mentioned above, are not addressed. School people are frozen between their own familiar practices and the expectation of the familiar from the community; and while many within the schools and in the community are pursuing reform, the mainstream flows on much as before. The reformation so urgently needed could well begin with a response to the challenges presented by the technical,

Figure 3.1. The Kinds, Aspects, and Domains of Learning and Learning
How to Learn.

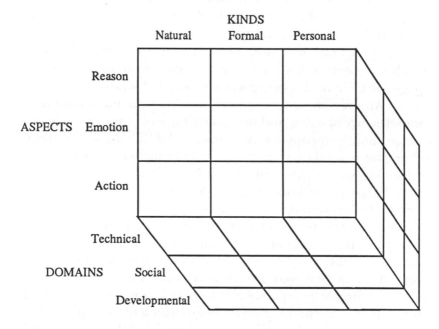

social, and developmental domains of LHTL. The burgeoning cost of remediation, therapy, counseling, social assistance, and other services required to repair the damage done and ignored may finally spur such a reformation.

These brief sketches of the domains complete a shadowy outline of the fully developed model implicit in the term *learning how to learn* (see Figure 3.1). If the model is an acceptable derivation from the term, it serves as the beginning for a fuller, more careful examination of its parts. The model also serves as a guide to remind us of its full implications, especially when we are considering programs for lifelong education and a full learning life.

As I consider the importance of the completed model of LHTL, I am struck by three major implications. The first is that it outlines an important pattern of learning that is seldom included in public schooling. This pattern of principles, skills, and processes about how to learn is as profound and significant, as valuable and applicable, as the curriculum of content on which the great majority of school programs are still based. As such, LHTL should be included in all future developments in education, at least as a companion curriculum to the subject-matter programs in place. The learning processes not only enable students to learn content, they constitute superior equipage for a life of successful learning beyond school.

An even stronger implication is that the model outlines the structure of a new and promising form of schooling that is a much more appropriate preparation for life in our rapidly changing times than a great majority of existing programs. The education we provide is always an implicit answer to the question, "What is the knowledge most worth having?" A process-oriented education that adds the power of natural and personal learning to the power of formal learning, an education that integrates the development of character and the capacity for action with the cultivation of reason, and an education as concerned about personal growth and social interaction as it is about technical competence is a compelling answer to that question. Such schooling would begin with a smooth transition between the natural learning of childhood and the more formal learning of the middle school years. Natural and formal learning, especially their LHTL features, would help to prepare students for the transformation to personal learning in which they would take major responsibility for the final stages of their education. All prior experience would prepare them for success in the final year during which they prepare to demonstrate their competence, confidence, and productivity in the technical, social, and developmental domains. On this occasion they would demonstrate their capacity to manage their own progress toward a vision of excellence, their readiness for adulthood.

Finally, the principles implicit in the model provide a guide for those who wish to empower themselves to learn. These individuals can devise their own programs for mastering basic skills in the three kinds of LHTL—natural, formal, and personal; employing three aspects of LHTL—reason, emotion, and action; and pursuing progress in the technical, social, and developmental domains of lifelong experience. Taken in its entirety, the model may be seen as a guide to the pursuit of the examined life, which Socrates valued above all else and without which he assumed life is not worth living.

For my part, with the completion of this sentence, I also conclude this personal voyage, trying to make what I am doing a demonstration of what I am saying, and trying to construct with it a platform from which to launch the next exploration— perhaps into the spiritual domain of learning how to learn. Learning is always about what comes next.

Chapter 4

Learning
with the Whole Mind

Dana G. Maxfield

In recent years researchers in the cognitive sciences have done much to expand our knowledge and perceptions concerning mind processes and their implications for learning. If nothing else, this information confirms what humans have always seemed to sense: we have capacities and abilities for knowing and learning far greater than we are always able to explain and understand.

Some cultures have traditionally been quite comfortable using and crediting vaguely-attended mind processes such as insight, intuition, visions, and dreams (Colorado, 1988; Gardner, 1983; Highwater, 1981; Samples, 1976; Sternberg, 1988b). Modern technological societies, however, have been more comfortable with emphasizing rational, logical, analytical, and linear processes, which are easier to reduce, isolate, analyze, explain, and control, and ignoring nonrational processes of knowing and learning.

Almost a decade ago Ferguson (1980) noted that what Michael Polanyi called tacit knowing—inner urgings, hunches, intuitions—does not contradict reason but represents "transcendent reasoning, the brain's capacity for simultaneous analysis we cannot consciously track and comprehend" (p. 107). Empirical

studies on reasoning and nonconsciously acquired knowledge
tend to support this statement. For example, in a series of studies
designed to investigate logical, rational thought processes,
Johnson-Laird and Wason (cited in Gardner, 1987) presented
subjects with a problem concerning the correctness of a rule.
Participants were given four cards, each of which displayed a
number on one side and a letter on the other. The problem
involved the use of a mental logic in testing whether the rule that
was given accurately described the relationship between the
numbers and letters. Ninety percent of the subjects (including
many logicians) were not able to solve the problem correctly.
However, the same reasoning processes were later explored with
similar testing procedures and conditions, except that the problem was stated in terms of a journey and numbers and letters
were replaced with names of destinations and modes of transportation. Only 20 percent of the subjects were unable to solve
the problem correctly when presented in this manner. Johnson-
Laird concluded that there can be reasoning without mental
logic and that people, when problem solving, do employ processes other than the rational-logical that are more dependent
on the actual content of a problem than on formal rules of
inference.

In another area involving tacit knowledge, researchers
have investigated processes used when information is acquired
without conscious awareness or control. Many automatic processes that an individual puts to use are initially acquired consciously and controlled, for example, driving a car, various
motor skills, and rules governing use of language. Some studies,
however, demonstrate a process whereby individuals acquire
and use knowledge that they never consciously recognize, articulate, or control. In one such study (Lewicki, Hill, and Bizot,
1988), subjects in the investigation were faculty members from a
university department of psychology who knew they were participating in an experiment involving nonconscious processing
of information. Nevertheless, the results revealed that while
performances of all subjects were influenced by a pattern of
stimuli presented to them during the experiment, and some
admitted to attempting to detect the manipulation and its

meaning, none of the participants noticed anything "even remotely similar to the actual nature of the manipulation (that is, the pattern)" (p. 24). The process is considered nonconscious because participants were never aware they were learning, nor were they aware that the information they had acquired facilitated their performance. In fact, the investigators state, "Subjects in this experiment were found to have very little choice or influence over whether or not they learned the pattern, and after they acquired some knowledge, whether or not to use this knowledge" (p. 34). The significance of this study is to demonstrate a "ubiquitous process" that the researchers conclude is used in the development of both elementary and high-level cognitive skills, enabling individuals to process and use much more information than can be handled by consciously controlled processes.

The Brain-Body-Mind Connection

Brain-Mind Functions and Learning. During the last two decades, neuroscientists have explored a lateralized model of brain-mind function, dividing the brain into right and left hemispheres. Research findings demonstrate that the two hemispheres seem to specialize in different processes: the left hemisphere in most people specializes in logical, rational, linear, sequential, and time-ordered functions such as language and analytical thinking, while the right hemisphere specializes in analogic, metaphoric, holistic, visual-spatial, and synthesizing functions such as map reading, drawing, and other creative capacities. Popular understanding of this information has tended to endow the two hemispheres with exclusive dominance of their respective specializations. New studies of brain activity (Sperry, 1989), however, indicate that both hemispheres of the brain are involved in even the simplest task and that hemisphere specializations operate in a complementary fashion. The significance of these findings for learning is that while asymmetries in function do exist, the brain operates in an integrated way, processing and storing information in multiple modes. Education practices that emphasize only the rational, logical, linear modalities leave much of what we know untapped.

Another way of looking at brain-mind function is from an evolutionary point of view. Scientists with this perspective propose a triune model reflecting a structure of activity from top to bottom (MacLean, cited in Houston, 1982). The earliest level to have evolved is associated with survival and self-preservation functions. The middle layer evolved next and involves emotions and particular memory functions. The third layer is the most recent to develop, and descriptions concerning this layer are consistent with those used to describe the lateralized brain. Several researchers have postulated that stages of human development are linked to an evolutionary sequence associated with the different brain layers. Houston (1982) notes that "normal development appears to be linked to the full expression of these developmental stages" (p. 101). The two earlier levels of the brain are not easily accessible and represent preverbal areas not usually reached by verbal processes or suggestions. Houston has worked to develop nonverbal, nonlogical techniques and strategies for accessing what the mind knows and stores at these levels.

Perhaps the most holistic model of mind processes to be influenced by neuroscientific research is that proposed by Karl Pribram (1971). In Pribram's view, brain-mind activity is more like a holographic process than dichotomous or triune functioning. A hologram is an optical record of an object in which all information is stored and distributed throughout the entire hologram in frequencies of light-wave patterns rather than in images. However, when an organizing kind of light (usually laser) is shined onto any part of the hologram, a three-dimensional image of the whole is reproduced. Pribram speculates that every part of the brain experiences and stores information that every other part experiences, but each does so in a different way. For brain-damaged individuals such as those Pribram worked with, the real task is to develop appropriate ways for retrieving information, from undamaged parts of the brain, that has been lost to damaged areas. The implication for those without brain damage is that the brain-mind processes and stores information in a holistic fashion; therefore, to most effectively retrieve what is known, one must use holistic approaches employing a variety of modalities and techniques.

Brain-Body-Mind Functions and Learning. Perhaps some of the most provocative of recent research findings are those that suggest mind is not just brain-mind but, more accurately, brain-body-mind. The placebo effect of mind over bodily performance has long been acknowledged even by those who believe mind and body to be both separate and fundamentally different. New discoveries, however, are suggesting a mind-body connection that has convinced some researchers that consciousness is not restricted to the head—the brain—but is active throughout the body as well.

In one such study, investigators set out to conduct a relatively simple taste-aversion experiment (Borysenko, 1987). Rats were given a saccharine solution to drink followed by an injection of cyclophosphamide, a drug that causes nausea and is known to suppress immune functioning. Usually one injection was enough for the rats to associate the nausea-producing symptoms with the saccharine, and further injections were not given. Several weeks into the study, however, the researchers discovered the rats seemed to be falling ill with just a taste of the saccharine alone. Further tests confirmed that the rats' immune systems, indeed, seemed to be conditioned to reduced functioning in response to the saccharine alone. Other researchers, working with humans, discovered that immune reactions in research volunteers could be inhibited by the individual's expectations (Borysenko, 1987).

In another area of study, epidemiologists investigated a small town in Pennsylvania whose residents had a very low rate of death from coronary heart disease (Wolf cited in Padus, Gottlieb, and Bricklin, 1986). Expecting to find exemplary health practices, researchers discovered, instead, that these residents had terrible health habits: cigarette smoking, fat consumption, a sedentary lifestyle, and being overweight. What they also had, however, was a close-knit community and extended family networks that offered a great deal of emotional support and cohesiveness: no one was ever abandoned. Statistics revealed that when residents left this community their rate of heart attack rose to the predicted level. One of the investigators concluded that "the experience clearly demonstrates that most important factors in health are the intangibles. . . . In terms of preventing heart disease, it's just possible that morale is more important than jogging or not eating butter" (p. 81).

The findings of these studies are significant for learning because of what they suggest about mind–body interaction: the body does not seem to distinguish between actual events that threaten and the threat of events that are present in thought alone. The body affects the mind and the mind affects the body (Green and Green, 1986). Many attitudes, beliefs, and expectations conditioned so that they are no longer consciously perceived or controlled. Learning to become aware and to take control of these nonconscious processes will necessitate not only learning and employing new techniques and strategies, but may also require unlearning attitudes, beliefs, and expectations that inhibit a full and effective use of the whole brain-body-mind.

Holistic Learning. Bob Samples, a psychologist and educator dedicated to a holistic approach to learning (1977, 1983, 1987), reacting to the recent discoveries concerning whole mind processes, suggests (1987) that the implications impact on learning in several ways, including the following:

> "Wholeness is reality—fragmentation is a deviation from that reality." Isolating and reducing experiences to parts and subjects without relating them to the whole as well does disservice to both part and whole and a larger inclusive perspective is lost.

> Experience and knowledge can be recovered in a wide variety of forms and ways. If not successful in accessing what the brain-mind "knows" in one way, another should be tried.

> "Consciousness is what we pay attention to." In schools we have learned to pay attention to a narrow range of mind activity. Expanding our ways of paying attention increases our flexibility and fluency in learning.

> We cannot avoid using our body-brain-mind system. What is at issue is not whether the whole mind is *on*, but whether or not we are *paying attention* to

what is *on*. The task in learning more effectively is to determine the most appropriate ways to recover more of what we know.

Culture has a profound influence on defining credible expressions of knowing. Logic and rationality are only two of the mind's valid forms of thought. Scientists have determined that humans have more than five senses available for experiencing and possibly as many different modalities as senses for accessing and expressing our experience. This suggests we are capable of learning in many ways as yet not fully understood or explainable but still employable.

If logical, rational approaches are insufficient for the most holistic, effective learning, then what is appropriate? What follows is a look at some of the alternative strategies and technologies that have been developed and used for accessing knowledge and information that is stored but not usually available through rational, logical, analytical modes. The techniques and methods explored are not meant to be a complete list but, rather, to represent methods that have been researched and applied in a variety of instructional settings: schools, nonformal educational programs, self-guided learning projects, and training programs in health care, business, and industry.

Holistic Techniques and Applications

Biofeedback. Before biofeedback was developed, it was considered impossible to consciously control the central nervous system (CNS) and the normally hidden processes it directs (for example, pulse rate, muscle tension, body temperature, and blood pressure). Biofeedback literature, which now includes several thousand research and clinical reports (Green and Green, 1986), indicates that self-regulation of these processes can be learned.

In biofeedback training, specially designed machines gather biological information while simultaneously feeding this information back in a form that can be seen (for example, a flashing light) or heard (for example, the sound of a beeper). The trainee learns to associate the signal with how he or she feels within. The person is taught to regulate the process being monitored by visualizing his or her most effective imagery, whether auditory (verbal), visual (mental pictures), emotional, or kinesthetic (body sensation). Because feedback is instantaneous, the trainee is able to determine immediately the success or lack of success of the mental strategies being used. Eventually an individual is able to replace the machine's information with direct psycho-physiological self-awareness and is able to use in everyday life the regulatory skills he or she has gained.

Green and Green (1986) stress that biofeedback machines themselves do not produce something, or do something to people. Therefore, biofeedback is not a conditioning tool and has in fact been unsuccessful when used in this fashion: "Biofeedback used as a conditioning tool, rather than as an aid in developing consciousness and self-regulation, has had consistently negative clinical results" (p. 562). Biofeedback training is training not of the body but of *awareness* of the body. As Green and Green put it, "Again, the point is that the training of the body with biofeedback machines really is the training of the CNS. And that means the training of the mind. We are not aware of our CNS; we are aware only of our states and contents of consciousness. Therefore, the conscious and willful training of what we call the involuntary nervous system involves becoming conscious of, and training, the so-called unconscious. . . . Self-regulation, by definition, means *conscious* self-regulation. If it is not conscious, it is not self-regulation" (p. 560).

Biofeedback training has been most widely used by health professionals as treatment for such ailments as anorexia, cancer, colitis, diabetes, epilepsy, esophageal spasm, glaucoma, fibrillation, hypertension, insomnia, migraine, multiple sclerosis, pain of various types, tension headache, tinnitus, and more. Educators have been slower to realize and take advantage of its implications for learning (Roberts, 1985). Two dissertation studies (Hanson, 1988; Schindler, 1987), however, review research reports of some applications in elementary and secondary schools, in colleges and universities, and in training programs in business and industry. Biofeedback training has been used with positive results to reduce test anxiety in college freshmen, to improve reading achievement among hyperactive adolescent learning disabled students, to overcome learning blocks, to improve attention, to enhance creativity, and to improve self-image with elementary-age children. Schindler (1987) lists more than 500 companies and business organizations, "ranging from the federal government to small business," that have used biofeedback and other consciousness-regulating techniques (meditation, hypnosis, guided imagery, autogenic training, and cognitive self-control). These techniques have been used with managers and workers to promote greater productivity, increase job satisfaction, improve performance, explore more effective methods of communication, and decrease absenteeism.

Biofeedback provides objective visible evidence of a link between conscious and unconscious body-mind processes and also provides an effective way to learn to self-regulate these processes for a more holistic functioning, including learning and creativity. When used properly, biofeedback is particularly potent as visualization training, "and skill in visualization is the essence of psychophysiological self-regulation" (Green and Green, 1986, p. 562).

Self-Regulated Imagery. Thinking in images—visualizing, fantasizing—is a cognitive process with which we are all familiar. For many, fantasizing is a spontaneous event that occurs throughout the day with little conscious awareness or direction given to the process. It is a universal experience, not unique to any particular age, gender, or culture. As common as it is, however, some measurable individual differences have been reported (Starker, 1985). For example, when asked to recall a simple incident (their morning breakfast), some individuals reported little or no mental imagery. In her study (cited in Starker, 1985), Roe (1951) observed some basic differences in image consciousness among social scientists (psychologists, anthropologists, sociologists), who leaned more in the direction of verbal thought, and physical scientists (physicists, biologists, chemists), who relied more on imagery. Examples of "pure" verbalizers or visualizers were found to be rare, however.

The adept use of imagery has been associated with the creative process (Houston, 1982; Starker, 1985). Einstein, exploring the source of his own creativity, stated, "When I examine myself and my methods of thought I come to the conclusion that the gift of fantasy has meant more to me than my talent for absorbing knowledge" (cited in Starker, 1985, p. 12). It is known that the brain can handle multiple patterns and relationships characteristic of imagistic thinking in almost simultaneous fashion, while logical-linear verbal thought takes place in a slower, sequential fashion (Houston, 1982). Houston speculates, "The so-called 'creative breakthrough' might then be seen as the manipulation of larger patterns of information that are part of the imaginal, symbolic process" (p. 125).

Starker (1985) has analyzed the imagistic process and suggests the following four distinctions, which he identifies as F-states (F represents fantasy):

1. *Imagery.* Imagery is often in the nature of mental pictures that form in the imagination. However, imagery can also be auditory, emotional, or kinesthetic.
2. *Daydreams.* These images have movement and usually some sort of theme or direction. Contrary to common perception, studies have revealed that most daydreams are not mere "wish fulfillment" but deal most frequently with problem-solving or future plans or actions.
3. *Reveries.* These are the images that appear when one is in the state between waking and falling asleep. They tend to be particularly vivid, often intense, and have a dream-like, hypnagogic quality. Researchers have discovered that individual differences in mental activity at sleep onset seem to be associated with personality differences. Individuals who experience vivid, almost hallucinatory images tend to be more self-accepting, less rigid about conforming to social standards, and more adept at producing waking fantasy stories than those whose reveries remain on the level of abstract thinking.

4. *Nocturnal dreams.* Sleep and dream research of twenty-five years has confirmed that dreaming is a nightly affair even when we do not recall having dreamt. When we do recall our dreams, they often make little sense. Imagistic thinking in general, and dreams in particular, have their own language. "Image-consciousness is a functionally normal alternative mode of being in the world, having its own 'laws' and its own language based on the exhibition of information through form" (Tolaas, 1986, p. 38). Understanding the images and metaphors of dreams takes effort, but many have found nontherapeutic dreamwork a fruitful method for linking unconscious and conscious processes and meanings in ways that have brought increased self-understanding, better problem solving, and enriched creativity (Ullman and Limmer, 1987; Ullman and Zimmerman, 1979).

Through imagery, conscious and unconscious mind processes can communicate. Spontaneous hypnagogic imagery can provide valuable information from the unconscious, while self-regulated visualization (for example, guided imagery) is a powerful method for programming the unconscious (Green and Green, 1986).

Guided imagery is consciously created visualization, guided by information. One can practice guided imagery alone, using a cassette tape of one's own voice or of another's or in a group. To take part in guided imagery, the person should be comfortable, relaxed, and in a place where distractions are minimized. Sometimes relaxing background music is also included. Attention is passively focused on the words or prompts of the leader. The most significant factor in using guided imagery is the attitude. A negative attitude that devalues imagery and fantasy as illogical and unreal will prevent its effective use. Some individuals have found it helpful to inform the critical, rational mind that the exercise is only a pretense and therefore does not need to be analyzed and evaluated, only experienced. Analysis and evaluation can come after the activity, if desired.

The significance of learning to use imagistic thinking in a self-regulated way is noted by Green and Green (1986). An individual's capacity to bring about physiological change through visualization was understood when it was noticed by those working in the field of self-regulation "that yoga, biofeedback training, hypnosis, self-suggestion, placebos, certain forms of meditation, all had something important in common— namely, visualization. Not necessarily mental pictures, but imagery of all kinds, verbal, pictorial, emotional, kinesthetic, depending on the nature and preferences of the visualizer" (p. 566). It is not surprising, then, that guided imagery has had widespread applications, a few of which are discussed briefly.

In sports training, guided imagery is called mental rehearsal and has been used by Olympic teams in many countries, by competitive athletes in professional sports, by college and high school athletic teams, and by individual sports competitors to improve their performances (Ostrander and Schroeder, 1979; Schindler, 1987). These athletes may practice mentally erasing past mistakes, eliminating the fear of failure, visualizing error-free skill practice, and imagining success in competition. The more completely one is able to enter into the experience, the greater the potential for its effectiveness. To participate more fully, the individual is encouraged to experience the fantasy with all the senses. Sports scientists have discovered that "when mental rehearsal is practiced by conditioned athletes, it is as effective and beneficial as the actual physical training they do for their sports" (Schindler, 1987, p. 45). Alleviated fears, increased self-confidence, and improved performance have commonly been experienced with persistent mental rehearsal.

Facilitators of adult learners have also made use of visualization and guided imagery as a way to help adults to gain better understanding and direction over themselves in their own learning processes (Griffin, 1987; Melamed, 1987; Smith, 1982). David Hunt (1987) helps teachers and counselors to identify and better understand their own learning/teaching/counseling styles through the use of guided imagery exercises, during which they are encouraged to create a personal metaphor that can give them direction in improving their professional practice.

Teachers have used guided imagery successfully with children in the classroom as a creative way to introduce a new topic, to help children improve their concentration and memory, to increase self-confidence, to accelerate learning, and to improve self-image (Ostrander and Schroeder, 1979; Schindler, 1987). Learning to use guided imagery is easy and direct (Roberts, 1983) and does not take special professional training. Several authors have detailed examples of exercises that have been used with children and/or adults (Hendricks and Roberts, 1977; Hendricks and Wills, 1975; Houston, 1982; Murdock, 1982).

Meditation. Meditation is a very old procedure that seeks a shift in awareness from an externally oriented, active mode of awareness to a receptive, internal focus. Forms of meditation are many and varied. Some emphasize isolation and sensory deprivation; some focus intently on a meditational object, word, or sound; some use ritual movement to unite body and mind; and some seek to expand awareness of the senses. Ornstein (1986) divides the many forms of meditation practice into two general varieties: "those exercises that involve restriction of awareness, focusing of attention on the object of meditation or on the repetition of a word (*concentrative meditation*); and those that involve a deliberate attempt to 'open up' awareness of the external environment" (p. 191). Carrington (1986) also notes a general distinction between meditational activities that teach strict concentration on a meditational object and those that are more permissive toward intruding thoughts.

Just as there are many forms of meditation, there are also a variety of goals. Traditionally, meditation training has been a part of religious and spiritual practice; the goals sought by these techniques have included enlightenment, direct knowledge of an absolute or of a Divine Being, spiritual growth, self-acceptance, and a mystical communion or oneness with all things. Contemporary Western societies, however, have developed techniques they call meditation or centering (these two words are used interchangeably), which emphasize more practical goals. These include using meditation/centering practices to reduce stress, improve skills performance, increase intellectual functioning, achieve personal development, gain deep levels of physical and psychological relaxation, increase creativity, and enhance one's general ability to operate more effectively in life (Carrington, 1986; Hanson, 1988; Schindler, 1987). Carrington notes that though the West considers meditation and centering to be synonymous, in the great traditions of meditation they are not. Rather, centering applies to those techniques (for example, repetition of a mantra, breathing exercises, concentration on a meditational object) used to prepare the meditator for the deep nonactive state of passive awareness that characterizes true meditation. However, in keeping with the accepted Western practice, Carrington, in her exploration of the subject, refers to centering techniques as meditation; this discussion follows her example.

A well-publicized contemporary form of meditation, Transcendental Meditation (TM), served as the basis for a technique developed by Herbert Benson, M.D. (1975). Known as the Relaxation Response, this technique has been applied by health professionals, in educational settings, and in training programs in business and industry. The Relaxation Response includes the following basic steps:

1. Find a quiet place free from distractions.
2. Choose a word or phrase on which to focus (for example, one, peace, love, relax); the word is not as important as the individual's response to it.
3. Sit or lie in a comfortable position.
4. Close the eyes and take a few moments to relax the body and quiet the mind. Taking a few deep breaths in a natural rhythm will help prepare one for meditation.
5. Breathing normally, become aware of each breath. With the slow natural rhythm of your breathing, repeat the word or phrase silently on each exhalation.
6. Disregard distractions. Don't fight intrusive thoughts; let them gently drift in and out of the awareness.
7. Continue the exercise for ten to twenty minutes daily. When it is finished, remain quiet and allow the mind to readjust to normal awareness slowly.

The Relaxation Response is representative of modern forms of meditation that stress practical application. These methods are easy to learn, do not involve the use of special postures or particular forms of breathing, and are not tied to any particular belief system. Carrington (1986) notes that research shows these new approaches, in spite of their simplicity, can be very effective in reducing stress (some evidence suggests meditators may even develop some immunity to stress); increasing alertness (meditators have been shown to react faster on visual tasks and have freer flow of ideas; improving manual dexterity (test scores have improved following meditation); and dissolving blocks to creativity. Improvement in stress-related illnesses, control of substance abuse, sleep, greater self-acceptance, and greater internal focus have also been reported as effects of meditation practice (Schindler, 1987). A more detailed description of the use of meditation in combination with other mind–body techniques is included in discussions of accelerated learning methods (Lozanov, 1976; Ostrander and Schroeder, 1979). Suggestopedia, developed by Lozanov, is a learning program that includes meditative exercises in a systematic way. Students in this program were taught Raja Yoga breathing exercises for improved concentration and in preparation for "supermemory" sessions for learning a foreign language. Meditation, special music, relaxation techniques, visualization, and oral presentation of material according to a specific rhythmic tonal pattern are all basic components that are combined to achieve extraordinary results in accelerated learning (Hanson, 1988; Ostrander and Schroeder, 1979).

Hypnosis. For many, hypnosis is a "trance" state in which unusual effects can be achieved. Among those experienced with the technique, however, there is little agreement that this is an accurate definition of hypnosis. In fact, a hypnotized subject is not always distinguishable from a waking one. Research has yet to identify physiological indicators associated with hypnosis, such as in the way brain wave patterns, blood pressure, pulse rate, skin temperature, and so on have been correlated through biofeedback with meditation and relaxation states. Among researchers and practitioners there is agreement, however, that one of the most prominent features associated with hypnosis is suggestion (Hanson, 1988).

Suggestions are ideas proposed to the subject, either by one's self or another, that the person reacts to as though the phenomenon the ideas represent were actually present. Suggestions can be received in a relaxed, waking state, but they seem to elicit special results under hypnosis when suggestibility, a condition of "unusual obligation" to follow directives, is increased (Hanson, 1988).

Hypnosis can be induced by a variety of techniques, which usually include some of the following: comfort and relaxation, concentration restricted to the words of the hypnotist (which can be self), and suggestions of drowsiness or sleep. There are, of course, degrees of receptivity and suggestibility, ranging from the light states a person can drift into when daydreaming, reading a book, watching a movie, television, or drama, or listening to music to deeper states such as one in which subjects can undergo surgery without anesthesia.

Another characteristic critical to hypnosis involves one's sense of reality. Through hypnotic induction a person's ground of reality shifts from the external environment to imaginal fantasy. Hypnotic suggestions usually contain two components. "First, subjects are asked to change their cognitive frame of reference from natural to fantasizing. Second, they are asked to construct an imaginary situation which would lead to the same results as the test suggestion. For example, if the hypnotist wanted the subject's hands to become hot, he might suggest that he imagine a hot coal burning in the palm of his hand" (Hanson, 1988, p. 143). Several researchers have noted that processes used in hypnosis, for example, redundancy, rhythm, counting, silences, intonation, gestures, and vivid imagery, are mind–body processes used every day when individuals become engrossed in an activity such as reading a book, watching television, listening to music, or daydreaming. They speculate that suggestion is as critical a means of communication in these everyday forms as it is in hypnosis (Hanson, 1988).

Self-hypnosis is the most practical technique for educa-

114   Learning to Learn Across the Life Span

tional applications. Individuals have been taught methods for self-hypnosis that have been used to improve athletic performance, to accelerate learning, to increase self-image, to improve concentration, and to overcome test anxiety (Schindler, 1987). Dale (1972) has identified nine educational uses for hypnosis: "(1) reinforcing positive habits and relinquishing negative ones; (2) expanding consciousness by increasing sensory and sensual responses; (3) improving concentration; (4) aiding memory; (5) building motivation; (6) releasing 'mental blocks'; (7) reducing anxiety; (8) increasing original and divergent thinking; and (9) developing self-confidence and self power" (cited in Hanson, 1988, p. 229).

Relaxation Training. Two processes seem to be basic components of all other approaches to self-regulation: visualization, or imagery, and relaxation. The relaxation required, however, is of a special kind—the body is relaxed while the mind is passively alert. This state of relaxation is rarely an automatic response, so to bring it under conscious control takes training and practice. Two techniques have been especially effective: progressive muscle relaxation (using the body to relax the mind) and autogenic training (using the mind to relax the body).

Both of these methods require a relaxation-producing breathing pattern. Fast, shallow breathing from the chest is associated with tension, while slow, deep breathing that uses the abdominal muscles promotes relaxation and alertness (Borysenko, 1987). One simple method for abdominal breathing is to slowly inhale, expanding the abdomen as well as the chest, hold the breath a few moments, then exhale in one long breath with a sigh of relief. One should maintain a normal, relaxed rhythm and not force an unnatural breathing pattern. Often in relaxation training one is given the suggestion to "let the air breathe for you."

Progressive relaxation was developed in the 1920s by Edmund Jacobsen, a psychiatrist (Padus, Gottlieb, and Bricklin, 1986). Under mental stress, the body becomes tense, which, in turn, puts more stress on the mind so that a tense mind–tense body cycle is set up. Progressive relaxation breaks this cycle by forcing the consciousness to recognize the actual feeling of physical tension and relaxation. Starting with one hand, the trainee clenches the fist, holds this for seven seconds, then slowly relaxes the hand. By doing this the person learns to identify the difference between the two states. Gradually, starting with the systematic tensing and relaxing of the feet, then the buttocks, legs, pelvic area, and so on, one learns to relax the body's muscle groups. Normal rhythmic breathing is maintained. The trainee inhales when muscles are tensed, exhales while slowly relaxing, and silently repeats "I am calm" with each exhalation. To conclude the exercise, one counts slowly from one to five, all the time giving self-suggestions to slowly leave the feeling of deeper relaxation and gradually become more alert and ready to go about one's daily activities.

Autogenic training was developed in the 1930s by Johannes Schultz from research on sleep and hypnosis that was first conducted in Germany in 1903 (Schindler, 1987). The early research discovered that intelligent hypnosis subjects were able to use mental techniques to achieve a state that greatly reduced their fatigue and tension. Two sensations were present, a feeling of heaviness in the extremities and a feeling of warmth, two feelings that are central to autogenic training.

Autogenic training enables one to control various physiological processes consciously through mental suggestions (Green and Green, 1986). There are three basic components to autogenic training: (1) restriction of sensory signaling, both internal and external; (2) mental rehearsal of specific verbal formulas; and (3) passive concentration, a casual, relaxed attitude contrasted to an intense, goal-directed focus. Beginning conditions are the same as those for progressive relaxation: wear comfortable, loose clothing, choose a room free from interference and distractions, sit or lie comfortably, and close the eyes.

The exercises begin with a feeling of heaviness in the limbs. The mental suggestion might be, "my arm is heavy." Next the focus is on the sensation of warmth, and suggestions are given to the areas of the body where warmth is being experienced. Physiological measures have correlated feelings of heaviness with muscle relaxation and sensations of warmth with emotional quiet (Green and Green, 1986). The entire body is systematically relaxed and warmed, and the final exercise suggests, "my forehead is cool." Visualization and rhythmic breathing are included and combined throughout the exercise. Once the relaxed state is entered, then other techniques, such as meditation, guided imagery, and hypnotic suggestion, may begin.

Summary. The various strategies and techniques developed for conscious-unconscious mind communication, including many not explored in this chapter, share the common viewpoint of the individual as a whole. Although each of the strategies and techniques has been considered here in separate fashion, to view them in such a manner does disservice to understanding the integrated, holistic nature of the mind–body processes involved. Two of these processes, deep relaxation and imagistic thinking, seem to be key elements included in all other strategies for consciously accessing nonconsciously stored material. Results obtained when using these techniques indicate that in many instances the problem may not be so much that learners forget information as that they are unable to retrieve from storage that which they already possess. When rational, logical learning modes are combined with intuitive, metaphoric modes in an integrated, systematic manner, as in the various superlearning approaches, results indicate exceptional learning capacities that normally remain untapped (Ostrander and Schroeder, 1979). When used in a purposeful manner, these processes seem especially effective in improving and/or increasing generalized learning capacities, such as attentional focus, concentration, motivation, memory, self-regulation, self-esteem, self-image, and self-understanding as a learner.

Dimensions of Learning to Learn in Whole-Mind Learning

As Gibbons notes in Chapter Three, any learning can include specific content as well as generalized process. Candy (Chapter Two) states that learning to learn "occurs both prior to and coincidental with learning endeavors." Joyce and Weil (1986) also emphasize that these same dimensions exist in the way material is taught and learned: "The process of the method itself is also learned by the student as he or she practices learning in a particular way. Models based on ways of inquiring teach methods of thinking as well as the content that is mastered" (p. 403). In facilitating or training for learning to learn with the whole mind, one must consider, then, these two dimensions: mind–body techniques as learning-to-learn strategies and learning to learn with the whole mind. A third dimension is the consideration of the learning-to-learn concept itself as a holistic paradigm for learning.

Mind–Body Techniques as Learning-to-Learn Strategies. It has already been noted that research findings implicate mind–body techniques as effective learning-to-learn strategies (Ferguson, 1980; Houston, 1982; Schindler, 1987). These nonrational processes are not context-specific and have been used effectively with a variety of subject matter in a wide range of learning situations.

Holistic learning approaches encourage open-mindedness and flexibility and can thus expand a learner's understanding about the nature of knowledge — its creation and validation. Rational thinking processes interpret and organize ideas; intuitive processes generate and create ideas (Samples, 1987). Old categories, mind-sets, and the single perspective are bypassed. Old information is looked at in new ways, as in the use of fantasy, and "new" information already stored in the mind is retrieved, as with hypnosis, meditation, and biofeedback techniques.

Intuitive mind–body processes emphasize patterns, connections, and relationships, and their use in learning enhances creativity, whether in problem solving, artistic expression, or other endeavors. Through consciously experiencing a variety of the conscious-unconscious mind communication processes and learning to self-regulate these, the individual's understanding of what it means to learn is enhanced and the learner is empowered to take greater control over his or her own learning processes and contexts (Langer, 1989). Continued evolution in awareness and understanding of learning processes, as well as increased self-control over those processes, are considered basic to learning to learn.

Facilitating Ability to Learn with the Whole Mind. Smith (1982) and Hammond in Chapter Six advise trainers and educators seeking to facilitate learning-to-learn capacities to expect to encounter resistance — especially when they require change and unlearning. Overcoming resistance to learning in a holistic mode requires persuading people to set aside beliefs that learning always means acquiring content, that in learning one must focus on a predetermined goal, that the learning process must be logical and sequential, and that the only valid knowledge is that which is validated externally.

In using intuitive, metaphoric approaches with adults in higher education, Griffin (1986) stresses that understanding and attitudes concerning the processes involved are critical. Learning to learn in this mode requires that the individual learn to suspend rational, logical mind processes temporarily, to remain open to the unexpected, and to believe that learning will occur. Griffin has found that individuals are often helped to enter more fully into the experience of mind–body techniques when they recognize that the processes are not unknown and mysterious but, rather, are the states of awareness in which they already operate and learn regularly in their daily lives. She also points out to learners that "letting go" and entering into the flow of the process does not mean becoming controlled by it.

An experimental, playful attitude can also facilitate learning to learn holistically. Both Samples (1976) and Bruner (1985) describe the importance of play as a metacognitive approach to problem solving among young children. Bruner suggests that play may, in fact, be "*the* form of early metacognition" (p. 603). Erik Erikson (cited in Bruner, 1985) discovered in his studies "that the most creative people were the ones with the least separation in daily life between work and play" (p. 605).

Imagistic thinking is a basic component of intuitive mind–body processes. Much of the information retrieved through conscious-unconscious mind communication, however, is presented in images that make little sense logically. Dreams are a prime example. Learning to think in metaphors facilitates imagistic thinking and meaning making. For example, one participant in a theory-building conference on learning to learn (Smith, 1988) likened learning in higher education institutions to trying to drink from an open fire hydrant. No rational, logical explanation could convey the same meanings and feelings that this simple metaphor does. Practice in metaphoric thinking can be incorporated into other learning-to-learn exercises. Smith (1982) uses the "Thinking About Learning Exercise" to encourage people to explore their own learning processes by searching for themes that characterize their personal learning experiences, both pleasant and unpleasant. Stating these themes in metaphors also facilitates imagistic thinking. Synectics (Joyce and Weil, 1986) is another method that stimulates thinking in images and metaphors and encourages breaking set and forming new categories. "Creative thinking becomes a conscious process . . . by connecting the familiar with the unfamiliar or creating a new idea from familiar ideas" (p. 166).

Learning to Learn as a Holistic Paradigm. Learning to learn, as described in this volume and in others (Ferguson, 1980; Griffin, 1986; Smith, 1982, 1988), focuses on learning in terms of process, higher-order thinking skills, increased self-understanding and self-control by the learner, transformation and empowerment of learners, appropriate and effective use of learning skills, an increased repertoire of learning approaches by the individual, the evolution of understanding concerning the nature and creation of knowledge, and the transcendence of self-imposed limitations in learning. The emphasis is on the learner's perspective: on the individual as a whole person and on learning as a whole experience. Among other things, learning to learn includes learning to make connections, understand relationships, and perceive patterns concerning one's own learning and to be able to act on these awarenesses in effective ways.

In these terms it can be argued that learning to learn is itself a holistic paradigm. In practice, research, and the literature, however, learning to learn with the intuitive, metaphoric mind–body processes has not received the same investigative attention and development as learning to learn in rational, logical, analytical modes. In fact, it has received little attention. It would seem, therefore, that, although learning to learn is a whole-learning–whole-person paradigm, it is one waiting to be wholly developed.

References

Benson, H. *The Relaxation Response.* New York: Morrow, 1975.

Borysenko, J. *Minding the Body, Mending the Mind.* Reading, Mass.: Addison-Wesley, 1987.

Bruner, J. "On Teaching Thinking: An Afterthought." In S. F. Chipman, J. W. Segal, and R. Glaser (eds.), *Thinking and Learning Skills.* Vol. 2. Hillsdale, N.J.: Erlbaum, 1985.

Carrington, P. "Meditation as an Access to Altered States of Consciousness." In B. B. Wolman and M. Ullman (eds.), *Handbook of States of Consciousness.* New York: Van Nostrand, 1986.

Colorado, P. "Bridging Native and Western Science." *Convergence,* 1988, *21* (2/3), 49–72.

Ferguson, M. *The Aquarian Conspiracy.* Los Angeles: Tarcher, 1980.

Gardner, H. *Frames of Mind.* New York: Basic Books, 1983.

Gardner, H. *The Mind's New Science.* New York: Basic Books, 1987.

Green, E. E., and Green, A. M. "Biofeedback and States of Consciousness." In B. B. Wolman and M. Ullman (eds.), *Handbook of States of Consciousness.* New York: Van Nostrand, 1986.

Griffin, V. "Holistic Learning/Teaching in Adult Education: Would You Play a One-String Guitar?" In J. Draper and T. Stein (eds.), *The Art of Teaching Adults.* Toronto, Canada: Culture Concepts, 1986.

Griffin, V. "Naming the Processes." In D. J. Boud and V. Griffin (eds.), *Appreciating Adults Learning: From the Learners' Perspective.* London: Kogan Page, 1987.

Hanson, C. "State-of-Consciousness Psychotechnology and Instructional Technology: An Investigation of the Theories and Practices of Systems for a Deliberate Change in Consciousness." Unpublished doctoral dissertation, Department of Leadership and Educational Policy Studies, Northern Illinois University, 1988.

Hendricks, G., and Roberts, T. *The Second Centering Book.* Englewood Cliffs, N.J.: Prentice-Hall, 1977.

Hendricks, G., and Wills, R. *The Centering Book.* Englewood Cliffs, N.J.: Prentice-Hall, 1975.

Highwater, J. *The Primal Mind.* New York: Harper & Row, 1981.

Houston, J. *The Possible Human.* New York: Tarcher, 1982.

Hulmes, E. *Education and Cultural Diversity.* New York: Longman, 1989.

Hunt, D. E. *Beginning with Ourselves.* Cambridge, Mass.: Brookline Books, 1987.

Joyce, B., and Weil, M. *Models of Teaching.* (3rd ed.) Englewood Cliffs, N.J.: Prentice-Hall, 1986.

Langer, E. J. *Mindfulness.* Reading, Mass.: Addison-Wesley, 1989.

Lewicki, P., Hill, T., and Bizot, E. "Acquisition of Procedural Knowledge About a Pattern of Stimuli That Cannot Be Articulated." *Cognitive Psychology,* 1988, *20,* 24–37.

Lozanov, G. *Suggestology and Outlines of Suggestopedy.* New York: Gordon and Breach, 1976.

Melamed, L. "The Role of Play in Adult Learning." In D. J. Boud and V. Griffin (eds.), *Appreciating Adults Learning: From the Learners' Perspective.* London: Kogan Page, 1987.

Murdock, M. *Spinning Inward: Using Guided Imagery with Children.* Culver City, Calif.: Peace Press, 1982.

Ornstein, R. *The Psychology of Consciousness.* (2nd rev. ed.) New York: Penguin Books, 1986.

Ostrander, S. and Schroeder, L. *Superlearning.* New York: Dell, 1979.

Padus, E., Gottlieb, W., and Bricklin, M. (eds.). *Your Emotions and Your Health.* Emmaus, Pa.: Rodale, 1986.

Pribram, K. *Languages of the Brain.* Englewood Cliffs, N.J.: Prentice-Hall, 1971.

Roberts, T. "State-of-Consciousness Psychology and Learning Capacity." In R. M. Smith (ed.), *Helping Adults Learn How to Learn.* New Directions for Continuing Education, no. 19. San Francisco: Jossey-Bass, 1983.

Roberts, T. "States of Consciousness: A New Intellectual Direction, a New Teacher Education Direction." *Journal of Teacher Education,* 1985, *36* (3), 55–59.

Samples, B. *The Metaphoric Mind.* Reading, Mass.: Addison-Wesley, 1983.

Samples, B. *Openmind/Wholemind.* Rolling Hills Estates, Calif.: Jalmar Press, 1987.

Schindler, D. "An Examination of Alpha Learning as a Viable Instructional Approach to Teach People to Learn." Doctoral dissertation, University of Akron, 1987.

Smith, R. M. *Learning How to Learn: Applied Theory for Adults.* New York: Cambridge Book Company, 1982.

Smith, R. M. (ed.). *Theory Building for Learning How to Learn.* DeKalb, Ill.: Educational Studies Press, 1988.

Sperry, S. P. "Educating the Two Sides of the Brain." *American Educator,* 1989, *13* (1), 32–37, 52.

Starker, S. *F-States: The Power of Fantasy in Human Creativity.* North Hollywood, Calif.: Newcastle, 1985.

Sternberg, R. J. *Beyond IQ: A Triarchic Theory of Human Intelligence.* New York: Cambridge University Press, 1985.

Sternberg, R. J. (ed.). *The Nature of Creativity.* New York: Cambridge University Press, 1988a.

Sternberg, R. J. *The Triarchic Mind.* New York: Penguin Books, 1988b.

Tolaas, J. "Transformatory Framework: Pictorial to Verbal." In B. B. Wolman and M. Ullman (eds.), *Handbook of States of Consciousness.* New York: Van Nostrand, 1986.

Ullman, M., and Limmer, C. (eds.). *The Variety of Dream Experience.* New York: Continuum, 1987.

Ullman, M., and Zimmerman, N. *Working with Dreams.* Los Angeles: Tarcher, 1979.

Vitale, B. *Unicorns Are Real: A Right-Brained Approach to Learning.* New York: Warner Books, 1982.

Chapter 5

Fostering Competence
in Self-Directed Learning

Malcolm S. Knowles

This chapter is premised on the research findings that adults are fairly competent when they undertake to learn something on their own in day-to-day life situations (Tough, 1979), but that when they enter into a formal instructional situation they fall back on their previous conditioning and adopt the attitude that their proper role is a relatively passive one in which they are dependent on others to instruct them (Knowles and Associates, 1984). Experience has shown that when adults are exposed to a situation in which they are expected to take responsibility for their learning they typically react with confusion, resentment, and resistance. Hence, it is important to provide them with preparatory experiences that will free them from their conditioned dependency and provide them with the attitudes, intellectual understanding, and skills necessary to enter into self-directed learning projects with confidence and pleasure.

Although people seem instinctively to engage in self-directed learning in certain situations, relatively few have developed the competencies required to be consistently successful. Among these competencies are the following:

- An understanding of the difference between teacher-directed and self-directed learning and the circumstances under which each is appropriate

123

- The desire and ability to maintain a sense of curiosity
- The ability to perceive one's self objectively and to accept feedback about one's performance nondefensively
- The ability to diagnose one's own learning needs realistically and to seek the help of peers and experts in this process
- The ability to translate learning needs into learning objectives in a way that makes it possible for the degree of accomplishment of the objectives to be assessed
- The ability to identify resources—human, material, and experimental—for accomplishing various kinds of learning objectives
- The ability to design a plan of strategies for making use of appropriate learning resources effectively
- The ability to carry out a learning plan systematically and proactively
- The ability to collect and validate evidence of the accomplishment of objectives
- The ability to relate to peers collaboratively as resources for helping one's own learning and to make one's resources available to them
- The ability to relate to teachers and other experts as facilitators and resource persons and to take the initiative in making use of these resources

The purpose of this chapter is to describe some ways that facilitators foster these competencies.

I have used or observed three distinct approaches or formats for helping adults to take more responsibility for their own learning: (1) orientation sessions and workshops; (2) self-paced modules, handbooks, and guidelines; and (3) individual instruction, mentoring, or tutoring.

Orientation Sessions and Workshops

Many institutions, particularly those catering to adult learners in external degree programs, independent study programs, and weekend colleges, provide a learning-to-learn experience as part of the orientation program for entering students. In fact, there is growing evidence from research on adult students that they typically enter an academic setting, especially if they have been away from one for a while, in a state of anxiety, with a nagging fear of failure and a set of unrealistic expectations regarding their role as students (Apps, 1981). They need to be helped to make a transition from their prior conditioning as dependent learners to their new role as self-responsible learners. This reorientation process may be launched by a short exposure or it may be a fairly lengthy sequence of experiences.

For example, I conducted a three-hour workshop for entering students in my graduate programs at Boston University and North Carolina State University. Mercy College in Dobbs Ferry, New York, has a one-semester orientation course, Career and Life Planning: College Orientation for Adults. The University Without Walls at the University of Minnesota provides a Seminar in Process Education that meets for twelve two-hour weekly meetings. Alverno College in Milwaukee has a sequential series of learning-to-learn experiences that continue progressively throughout the undergraduate program. The Fielding Institute in Santa Barbara, California, requires all entering students to participate in a five-day Admissions and Contract workshop that includes skill training in self-directed learning. Somewhat similar orientation experiences are found in many inservice education programs in hospitals, government agencies, and business and industry. All of these programs include in their design adaptations of the components I include in workshops on self-directed learning: climate-setting activity, presentation of a cognitive map of self-directed learning, and skill-practice exercises, which include learning plan construction.

Establishing a Climate for Learning. In a climate-setting exercise, I ask the participants to form groups of from four to six persons each and to share the following information about themselves in each group: *What* they are (in Martin Buber's terms, their "Its"), relating their present work roles and past experience; *who* they are (in Buber's terms, establishing an I-Thou as well as an It-It relationship), sharing one thing about themselves that will enable others to see them as unique human beings, different from everyone else in the room; any *special resources* they bring with them that are relevant to this course or workshop, gained through previous experience or study, that would be useful for others to know about; and any *questions, problems,* or *concerns* they have about the unique characteristics of adults as learners and about taking responsibility for their own learning.

I seek to model what I mean by sharing by giving this information about myself. I then ask one member of each group to volunteer to serve as a reporter for the group. When I sense that the groups have completed their sharing (usually in about twenty minutes), I invite the volunteer reporter from each group to summarize what he or she has learned about the other members of the group. I list the reported questions, problems, and concerns on a newsprint easel or blackboard.

At the conclusion of the exercise, I give my rationale for "wasting" this first half-hour or so with words something like this: I believe that a prerequisite for effective learning to take place is the establishment of a climate that is conducive to learning. Early in my experience, under the pressure of time constraints, I occasionally skipped this step, which usually takes about an hour, but I soon learned that the quality and efficiency of learning was considerably sacrificed. I have learned never to skip this step, although I have at times condensed it to thirty minutes.

There are two aspects to a climate for learning: physical climate and psychological climate. Regarding physical climate, the typical classroom setup, with chairs in rows facing a podium in front, is probably the least conducive to learning that the fertile human brain could have invented. It announces to anyone entering the room that the name of the game here is one-way transmission, that what is important is what takes place at the front of the room, that the proper role of the learner is to sit and listen (and, presumably, to take notes). I make a point of getting to my assigned room well before the participants are scheduled to arrive and if I find it set up this way (and most custodians know no other way) I place the chairs in one large circle, or, if this is not possible, in small circles or semicircles. My preference is for participants to be seated at tables (round or rectangular) in groups of five or six, with the tables arranged in a fan shape with one end facing the front. This setup announces loudly and clearly that the name of the game is interaction — within groups and between groups and the resource person — and that the role of the learners is to participate.

Important as physical climate is, psychological climate is even more so. The first characteristic of psychological climate that I try to bring into being is one of mutual respect. People are more open to learning when they feel respected. If they feel that they are being talked down to, ignored, or treated as objects, their energy is devoted to dealing with this feeling rather than with learning. I do several things to promote a climate of respect. (1) I make it easy for people to begin associating names with faces by providing large cards that can be folded into tents, with each participant's name printed on it with a felt-tipped pen. (2) I have the participants identify the special resources they are bringing with them that others might tap into for learning — thus conveying that I value what they have to contribute. (3) I listen carefully when a participant says something, and if I am not clear about what he or she is trying to communicate, I repeat it in my own words and ask if that is what he or she means.

A climate of collaborativeness needs attention. Because of their earlier school conditioning in which competition for grades and teachers' favor is the norm, adults tend to enter into any educational activity with an attitude of rivalry toward fellow participants. Although for many kinds of educational situations peers are the richest resources for learning, competitiveness can make these resources unavailable. To counter this situation, the climate-setting exercise with which I open all my workshops and courses puts the participants into a sharing relationship from the outset.

People learn more from those they trust than from those they mistrust, so it is important to establish a climate of mutual trust. And here we who are put in the position of teacher or trainer have a couple of strikes against us, for children learn at an early age that on the whole teachers are not among the most trustworthy subspecies of homo sapiens. They observe early on that teachers tend to have "pets." But more important, teachers have power over students; they give the grades, determine who passes or fails, and issue other punishments and rewards. In addition, the institutions in which teachers work present them in their catalogues and program announcements as authority figures; and it is built into the bloodstream of those of us who grew up in the democratic tradition that authority figures are to be mistrusted, at least until they are tested and their degree of trustworthiness is determined. I do several things to try to overcome this tendency to mistrust. (1) In presenting myself in the opening session I emphasize who I am as a human being— my family background, special interests, and hobbies—rather than my credentials as an expert. (2) I urge people to call me by my first name as soon as they feel comfortable doing so, explaining that when they call me "Dr. Knowles" or "Professor Knowles" I feel a cold, distant relationship between us, whereas when they call me "Malcolm" I feel a much warmer, closer relationship. (3) I emphasize that I perceive my role to be that of a facilitator in their achieving their goals rather than imposing my goals on them and controlling their behavior so as to achieve them.

People learn better when they feel supported rather than judged or threatened. Maslow (1970) has pointed out that human beings are most likely to change in an environment in which they feel safe. I convey my desire to be supportive by accepting learners with an unqualified positive regard, matching any diagnosis of a weakness with the valuing of a strength, empathizing with their problems or worries, and defining my role as a helper. But I also organize them into peer-support groups and coach them on how to support one another.

A climate of openness and authenticity is also essential. When people feel free to be open and natural, to say what they really think and feel, they are more likely to be willing to examine new ideas and risk new behaviors than when they feel a need to be defensive. In school we often have to pretend to know things that we don't or to feel things that we don't in order to live up to the system's expectations, and this interferes with learning. I try to model openness and authenticity in my own behavior on the faith that this is a model the learners will adopt. For example, I make it clear that there are some aspects of a content area in which I am not an expert, but that I know or can find experts with whom I can link the learners.

Then there is the matter of a pleasurable climate. Learning should be one of the most pleasurable and gratifying experiences we have; for, after all, it is one way people can become what they are capable of being — can achieve their potential. Learning should be an adventure, spiced with the excitement of discovery. In other words, whenever feasible, it should be fun. I think it is tragic that our educational system was established in the early nineteenth century, at the peak of the Calvinistic era, when anything pleasurable was automatically considered sinful. I make use of humor in my own practice to try to overcome this tradition — not canned jokes, but highlighting of things that happen when people start interacting with one another, things that we can laugh with (not at).

Perhaps what has been said about climate can be summed up with the adjective "human." Learning is a very human activity. The more people feel they are being treated as human beings — that their human needs are being taken into account — the more they are likely to learn and learn to learn. This means, among other things, providing for human comfort — good lighting and ventilation, soft seats on the chairs, availability of refreshments, designation of nonsmoking areas, frequent breaks, and the like. It also means providing a caring, accepting, respecting, helping, social atmosphere.

Presenting a Cognitive Map of Self-Directed Learning. Important findings from recent research about the characteristics of adults as learners include the following: (1) They have a deep need to be self-directing, but they have to be helped to overcome their conditioning from previous experience, that students are dependent on teachers. (2) They usually bring into any learning situation previous experience and training that provide a rich resource for helping each other learn. (3) They tend to be task-centered, problem-centered, and life-centered (rather than subject-centered) in their orientation to learning. (4) They are primarily intrinsically (rather than extrinsically) motivated to learn, given the right conditions and support. I emphasize that what people learn through their own initiative they usually learn more effectively and retain longer than what is imposed on them by others.

Conducting Skill-Practice Exercises. After explaining that a different set of skills is required for self-directed learning than in learning from an authority, I engage the participants in one or more exercises designed to develop such skills as realistic diagnosis of their own needs (using a self-rating instrument), translating needs into objectives, identifying appropriate learning responses, successful interviewing of resource people, reading a book "proactively," and giving and receiving help (Knowles, 1975).

I explain how to go about constructing a learning plan (often called a learning contract). This specifies (1) the learning objectives, (2) the resources, material and human, that will be used for achieving each objective, (3) the evidence of accomplishment of each objective that will be collected, and (4) how that evidence will be judged or validated. I then invite each participant to draft a practice contract for some simple learning goal, such as the ability to make a public speech (Knowles, 1986). I ask participants to identify any problems they experienced with this whole process, and I discuss with them the reasons for and solutions to these problems.

Several problems seem to be almost universal. The first is how to state objectives so that their accomplishment can be measured. I suggest that there are some learning operations that lend themselves to objectively measurable terminal behaviors, such as "To develop the ability to type sixty words a minute with a maximum of five errors per page." Most objectives having to do with the acquisition of psychomotor skills fit into this category. Other learning operations, however, are too complex for measurement. Those objectives that have to do with the acquisition of knowledge and understanding, interests, and values fit into this category and are more appropriately stated in terms of direction of growth or improvement, such as "To develop a knowledge and understanding of the theory of relativity to the point that I feel confident in discussing it with researchers at RCA." I point out that since the utility of objectives in self-directed learning is to give guidance to the learner rather than control to the teacher, I authorize learners to use terminal behavior objectives or directional objectives according to which is most meaningful for the learner. I go a step further and suggest that even exploratory objectives, such as "To explore the literature of group dynamics to determine if this is a field of inquiry that I wish to study in depth," are appropriate in some situations.

When participants ask about finding the best resources for learning about a particular topic or problem, I can often suggest particular books or articles; but if I cannot I suggest that they talk to the reference librarian in their local library. I also urge them to think of people in their environment—fellow learners, experts in their workplace, specialists in government agencies, or teachers in nearby educational institutions—who may know what they want to know.

A final major problem concerns collecting and validating evidence of learning. The kind of evidence that is appropriate depends upon the nature of the objective. If the objective is concerned primarily with knowledge acquisition, then the evidence must provide some indication of the knowledge acquired—such as a carefully annotated bibliography, a cognitive recall test, or an essay highlighting the information gained. Preferably there should also be some indication of the learner's understanding of the knowledge by some application exercise. The simplest way to get this kind of evidence validated is to submit it to someone (such as a more advanced peer or a teacher) who is in a position to evaluate such criteria as clarity, comprehensiveness, and accuracy. If the objective is concerned with skill acquisition, then the evidence must be some sort of performance—real or simulated—that qualified observers can observe and rate according to such criteria as precision, speed, and style. Finally, if the objective is concerned with affective outcomes—attitudes or values—then the best source of evidence is usually the learner's own introspection, although there are some instruments available, such as attitude and value scales, that can provide clues.

Self-Paced Modules, Handbooks, and Guidelines

Several institutions have developed student handbooks or guidelines, videotape programs, film-strip programs, or combinations thereof to help learners develop competence in self-directed learning. For example, the McMaster University School of Nursing in Hamilton, Ontario, has a combination film-strip and workbook that all entering students complete before starting on their regular curricular learning packages. Learners' (and sometimes facilitators') handbooks or guidelines are provided by Lloyd's Bank of California; the customer-training program at DuPont Company in Wilmington, Delaware; Mercy College at Dobbs Ferry, New York; and the Cardiovascular Nursing Program at Doctors Hospital, Little Rock, Arkansas (Knowles and Associates, 1984). Similar handbooks or guidelines for use especially with contract learning are provided by Nova University Center for Higher Education; the Cornell University Internship Program; the Fielding Institute; the Self-Directed Learning Project for Physicians, University of Southern California; Whatcom Community College in Bellingham, Washington; and the College of Liberal Studies, University of Oklahoma (Knowles, 1986). A growing number of institutions are finding that my little paperback book, *Self-Directed Learning: A Guide for Learners and Teachers* (1975) can serve as a ready-made resource for either individual or group orientation.

An increasing number of institutions are converting entire degree programs to self-paced, competency-based, modular curriculums. This movement is especially strong in Canada with the development of the DACUM (*Developing A Curriculum*) approach. For example, Holland College in Prince Edward Island offers a wide variety of credit courses through learning packages. Each package contains a model of the competencies a given course is designed to help learners develop, a diagnostic rating scale to enable each person to determine which competencies he or she needs to strengthen, a set of resources (human, printed, and audio-visual) relevant to each competency, and postevaluation procedures to determine the level at which each competency has been achieved. There are no lecture halls, but faculty members are available in each resource area (which contains audio-visual equipment and the learning packages for a given set of courses) to assist individuals and facilitate small group discussions. Upon completion of the learning packages for each course, the participants receive a "Record of Achievement" indicating the level at which each competency has been achieved. Employers of Holland College graduates have told me that the Records of Achievement provide them with much more useful information about applicants than do the traditional grade transcripts, and that these graduates are much more responsible and capable than graduates of traditional colleges.

Individual Instruction, Mentoring, and Tutoring

Primary responsibility for providing orientation to self-directed learning sometimes comes from mentors, tutors, counselors, or "information brokers," with or without the assistance of printed guidelines. Examples of this approach are found in the independent study or contract learning programs in several of the institutions listed above. And the institutionalization of mentoring as a principal approach to human resource development is spreading rapidly in a number of corporations, including the Department of Aviation in Australia and the Motorola Government Electronics Group, both of which have published excellent manuals for mentors. Daloz (1986) provides a state-of-the-art overview of this phenomenon.

The Role of Facilitator. As I see it, the role of a facilitator of learning involves taking responsibility for fulfilling two tasks. The first and primary task is to design and manage a *process* or set of procedures for enabling the learners to acquire the content required by the situation and their own self-diagnosed learning needs. This process is described in the last section of this chapter. The second task is to provide the *content* resources necessary for the learners to accomplish their objectives — either directly, out of the facilitator's own store of knowledge, experience, and skills, or (usually more important), indirectly, by linking the learners with other printed, electronic, or human resources. In this way he or she serves as an "educational broker." A critical aspect of performing both dimensions of this role is providing the learners with constant psychic support — conveying the facilitator's unqualified positive regard for their worth as persons, empathizing deeply with their ideas and feelings, and encouraging them to risk trying out new ideas and behaviors, and doing all these things as an absolutely authentic person rather than as a player of a role ("I think. . ." or "I feel. . ." instead of "You should. . .").

This is in sharp contrast to the traditional role of teacher, which is defined as having total responsibility for deciding what should be learned, how it should be learned, when it should be learned, and if it has been learned. The teacher then proceeds to deliver the content more or less didactically and tests the students' ability to recall the content, usually assigning norm-referenced grades to the result. When I made the transformation from a didactic teacher to a facilitator of learning, I discovered that several changes were taking place in me. (1) I had to reconceptualize (or redefine) my role along the lines described above. (2) I had to develop a quite different set of skills from those I had been trained to use as a didactic teacher, which were skills having to do primarily with transmitting and testing content material; the new skills were much more like those of the client-centered counselor described by Carl Rogers. (3) I had to change my value system from one in which I derived my psychic rewards from success in controlling learners and learning to one of success in releasing energy and control to the learners, together with taking pride in their learning achievements and their growing ability to accept responsibility for the overall process.

The Role of Learner. In essence, the shift in the role of the learner on which much of this book is premised is away from that of one who is dependent on another to direct and control his or her acquisition of content to that of a self-directed learner. In its broadest sense, "self-directed learning" describes a *process* in which individuals take the initiative, with or without the help of others, in (1) diagnosing their own needs for learning, (2) formulating their own learning objectives, (3) identifying effective human and material resources for accomplishing their objectives, (4) choosing and implementing effective strategies for using these resources, and (5) evaluating the extent to which they have accomplished their objectives. Of course, self-direction in learning does *not* mean learning alone or in isolation; it usually takes place in association with various kinds of helpers, such as teachers, tutors, mentors, resource people, and peers.

Conclusion

A number of responsible thinkers who are concerned about the future of our civilization (Botkin, Elmandjra, and Malitza, 1979; Faure and others, 1972; Naisbitt, 1982; Schön, 1983; and Toffler, 1971) have emphasized that in the world of accelerating change (the knowledge explosion, the technological revolution, the information society) that we are entering, learning must be a lifelong process if we are to avoid the catastrophe of human obsolescence. The single most important competence that people must possess to survive is the ability to learn—with or, more important, without a teacher. Although this ability should begin its development through the schooling of children and youth, all institutions in our society have a responsibility to foster it over a lifetime. And, fortunately, we now know that this is a competence that *can* be fostered. The present chapter seeks to describe the state of this art, but I predict that our body of knowledge about the art of fostering self-direction in learning will at least double in the next decade.

References

Apps, J. W. *The Adult Learner on Campus.* New York: Cambridge Book Company, 1981.
Botkin, J. W., Elmandjra, M., and Malitza, M. *No Limits to Learning: Bridging the Human Gap.* Elmsford, N.Y.: Pergamon, 1979.

Brookfield, S. D. *Self-Directed Learning: From Theory to Practice.* New Directions for Continuing Education, no. 25. San Francisco: Jossey-Bass, 1985.

Brookfield, S. D. *Understanding and Facilitating Adult Learning: A Comprehensive Analysis of Principles and Effective Practices.* San Francisco: Jossey-Bass, 1986.

Cross, K. P. *Adults as Learners: Increasing Participation and Facilitating Learning.* San Francisco: Jossey-Bass, 1981.

Daloz, L. A. *Effective Teaching and Mentoring: Realizing the Transformational Power of Adult Learning Experiences.* San Francisco: Jossey-Bass, 1986.

Faure, E., and others. *Learning to Be.* Paris: UNESCO, 1972.

Knowles, M. S. *Self-Directed Learning: A Guide for Learners and Teachers.* New York: Association, 1975.

Knowles, M. S. *Using Learning Contracts: Practical Approaches to Individualizing and Structuring Learning.* San Francisco: Jossey-Bass, 1986.

Knowles, M. S., and Associates. *Andragogy in Action: Applying Modern Principles of Adult Learning.* San Francisco: Jossey-Bass, 1984.

Knox, A. B. *Helping Adults Learn: A Guide to Planning, Implementing, and Conducting Programs.* San Francisco: Jossey-Bass, 1986.

Long, H. B., and Associates. *Self-Directed Learning: Application and Theory.* Athens: Adult Education Department, University of Georgia, 1988.

McGlagan, P. A. *Helping Others Learn.* Reading, Mass.: Addison-Wesley, 1977.

Maslow, A. N. *Motivation and Personality.* (2nd ed.) New York: Harper & Row, 1970.

Naisbitt, J. *Megatrends.* New York: Warner, 1982.

Schön, D. A. *The Reflective Practitioner.* New York: Basic Books, 1983.

Smith, R. M. *Learning How to Learn: Applied Theory for Adults.* New York: Cambridge Book Company, 1982.

Smith, R. M. (ed.). *Theory Building for Learning How to Learn.* DeKalb, Ill.: Educational Studies Press, 1987.

Toffler, A. M. *Future Shock.* New York: Bantam, 1971.

Tough, A. M. *The Adult's Learning Projects.* Toronto, Canada: Ontario Institute for Studies in Education, 1979.

![decorative ornament] Chapter 6 ![decorative ornament]

Designing and Facilitating Learning-to-Learn Activities

David Hammond

The chapter begins with an overview of five comprehensive approaches for enhancing people's effectiveness in learning. Then it presents some guidelines for design and facilitation of the process. Finally, it makes suggestions for the application of electronic media to learning-to-learn activities.

Some Comprehensive Approaches

This section briefly reviews some well-developed models or approaches to implementing the learning-to-learn concept: (1) High/Scope, (2) Walkabout, (3) concept mapping and Vee diagramming, (4) repertory grid-based technology, and (5) participation training. The first two approaches are oriented to children and youth, the third and fourth to people of all ages, and the fifth to adults. The models vary in the extent to which they make available a blueprint for implementation. Some require more highly skilled facilitation than others.

High/Scope. This is a preschool program to develop the child's capacity to plan and carry out his or her own learning experiences. Children learn to solve problems and make decisions as they work with real-world materials and objects. Learning to learn is regarded as an integral part of the program. High/Scope is described as an open framework model derived from Piagetian developmental theory, the result of over two decades of research and field testing and nationally recognized as a bona fide curriculum. Originating from the Ypsilanti (Michigan) Perry Preschool Project, one of the first early childhood programs of the 1960s, the curriculum emphasizes the process of learning. Key experiences for children, teaching and parenting strategies, and observation of children form the base for this developmental approach. The curriculum encourages the initiation of learning experiences by both children and adults. The idea is that through daily planning and evaluation sessions, teachers provide activities and generate strategies to challenge children and encourage them to develop and pursue their own interests, talents, and goals. Many learning experiences are readily available when children are best able to master them and relate them to their past, present, and future experiences. The curriculum enables teachers to implement developmental principles and build on children's existing strengths and accomplishments (Hohmann, Banet, and Weikart, 1979).

Preschool teachers plan and initiate developmentally appropriate activities around key experiences that reflect the basic, long-range goals teachers have established for each child: (1) to develop the ability to make planning decisions about what to do and how to do it; (2) to develop self-discipline and the ability to identify personal goals and complete self-chosen tasks; (3) to develop the ability to work with other children in various collaborative efforts; (4) to develop the ability for self-expression; (5) to develop the ability to apply the reasoning capability in a range of naturally occurring situations; and (6) to develop a spirit of inquiry and openness to knowledge and various points of view.

The High/Scope Classroom Program seeks to encourage active learning. The daily routine is centered in a sequence: the children plan an activity to carry out, implement the plan, and recall and evaluate what was done. Parental involvement is extremely important to the success of this kind of effort, so the parent program is designed to establish contact between teachers and parents before school begins and to provide parents with appropriate teaching strategies for the home environment (Hohmann, Banet, and Weikart, 1979). Given today's time constraints on most working parents, sustained parental reinforcement of the process becomes a challenging task. Another limitation of the approach is the lack of trained professionals. High/Scope attempts to address this shortage with a teacher trainer program that sends a High/Scope-trained teacher to any participating state to train other teachers in implementing the curriculum; those trained then return to their schools to train others. Workshops and seminars are also conducted at the High/Scope Educational Research Foundation in Ypsilanti, Michigan.

High/Scope has a comprehensive and self-contained program that provides a complete range of materials and resources in the form of books, manuals, and videotapes to assist the beginning facilitator. A main resource for the program is the *Young Children in Action and Study Guide,* which describes the curriculum and the key experiences used as guidelines in working with children.

Walkabout. Originally titled "Walkabout: Searching for the Right Passage from Childhood and School," this unique program has been introduced successfully in several schools. It was designed by Maurice Gibbons of Simon Fraser University (British Columbia) and described in several articles in the prestigious *Phi Delta Kappan;* reader response was unusually vigorous and positive (Gibbons, 1984).

Gibbons's idea was triggered by the film "Walkabout" and the observation that many cultures mark the transition from youth to adulthood with an appropriate but demanding test of adult skills. He posed the question, "What would be an appropriate test for transition to adulthood in our more complex and sophisticated society?" His answer was to challenge the students in their senior year. For the young person who has just finished twelfth grade, a graduation ceremony in the Walkabout mode might include demonstrations of competence in five basic challenge categories: adventure, creativity, service, practical skill, and logical inquiry (Gibbons, 1974, p. 598). The purpose is to create a pattern of competence and success for all students, one that will affect everything else they do. As with High/Scope, at the center of this model is a process that enables students to design and manage their own learning. The approach should be practical, adaptable to all grade levels, and appropriate for use throughout life: "By teaching students to carry out this process and to master the many skills that are involved, we lay a foundation that will ultimately enable them to develop their own learning activities" (Gibbons, 1984, p. 594).

The process Gibbons proposes involves:

(1) *Goal-setting:* reviewing the choices for learning, making decisions about what is important to learn, and setting clear goals to pursue

(2) *Strategic planning:* outlining exactly what has to be learned and accomplished, selecting those methods of learning that are appropriate for the task and for one's learning style, and organizing a plan of action for achieving the goal

(3) *Self-management:* learning to organize and manage time and effort by recognizing and solving such personal problems as disorder and lack of self-discipline when they arise, and by securing resources necessary for implementing the learning plan

(4) *Self-evaluation:* determining in advance what would constitute a high-quality learning outcome, seeking and using information about one's progress, and making a final judgment about one's success

(5) *Review:* reviewing what was learned and achieved, considering what worked well and what didn't (in order to focus on key improvements in the next cycle), and only then making decisions about the next goal and endeavor.

Gibbons states that this process can be introduced in a simple form with an easy task at any level of schooling. As students progress, they can apply the process to tasks of increasing complexity and duration, until eventually they are designing and carrying out major portions of their own learning programs. In the years following school, "The process will still be appropriate for learning and doing for personal and professional development. . . . We will also note a radical change in our teaching role, which will shift from presenter of content to coach of our students' performance. In the new paradigm we have to somehow inform, train, guide, counsel, and inspire students in ways that help them become excellent at what they decide to learn and do. . . . In teaching the process of self-direction we will also be struck by the uniqueness of individual students expressed in the activities they choose and in their struggles and progress. . . . To set personally important goals, for example, students must have inner clarity, not confusion, about who they are, what they do well, what they value and what they wish to become" (Gibbons, 1974, p. 595).

Walkabout depends on a balance between reflection and action. Reflection can be developed through the working journal or a similar device, in which students record what they are learning and explore their interests and talents. They "examine the struggles they are facing, describe their emerging visions of what they want to accomplish and in what ways they wish to be different, tell the stories of their experiences, and outline the ideas they are beginning to shape" (Gibbons, 1984, p. 597). From this record goals and plans emerge. In order to transform reflections into action strategies, students can learn how to write formal proposals, contracts, or plans that specify what they intend to do and how they intend to do it. Having a plan of action in hand enables the student to negotiate his or her proposal with the teacher, other adults, and parents.

Walkabout calls for all program components to be directed at increasing students' abilities to direct their own lives and learning. The program should be cumulative in order to prepare students fully to carry out their tasks and meet their goals in the final, challenge year. A supportive management system should be provided. The three major management practices presented are the contracts, timetables, and baseline evaluations for teaching; the three-block, four-mode program structure; and provision of a larger context of support. A picture of a complete and integrated program to teach students to direct their own learning emerges, one that prepares students to manage their own education during and after their graduating year.

This approach offers the potential for an in-depth program for enhancing learner motivation and control of the learning process. Its strength lies in the vision, optimism, and quality of its goals. Extremely dedicated and persistent leadership by school administrators is almost certainly required for successful implementation. A drawback might be student complacency and lack of willingness to rise to the challenges inherent in the approach. It seems that Walkabout's best chances to flower lie in the private school environment where all or parts of the program can be incorporated into the school curriculum without undue resistance.

Concept Mapping and Vee Diagramming. Joseph Novak and D. Bob Gowin have developed an approach designed to enhance education by helping people to learn about human learning, about the nature of knowledge, and about the construction of new knowledge. The approach involves strategies for better curriculum design and is based on a theory of how children learn and how teachers and others can help children learn to think more objectively. Novak and Gowin (1984) believe that when students learn about the learning process, they understand how they learn, and that helps them to facilitate and direct their own learning. The authors offer evidence that their propositions work, that children and youth can learn how to learn.

The approach is centered in two of the constructs described and discussed at length in the book — concept mapping and Vee diagramming — constructs seen as critical to learning how to learn. Concept mapping is a tool to help students and educators see the meanings of learning materials. Novak and Gowin describe it as a schematic device for representing meanings embedded in a framework of propositions. Propositions are concepts linked into semantic units. Maps illuminate the key ideas students and teachers need to focus on for a specific learning task. Since people think conceptually, concept maps serve to externalize concepts and improve thinking. Novak and Gowin demonstrate that Vee diagramming based on epistemological study of an event is a simple and flexible way to help students and teachers grasp the structure and meaning of the knowledge they seek. Students need to be helped to recognize (1) the events or objects they are observing, (2) the concepts they already know that relate to these events or objects, and (3) the records that are worth making.

The learning theory proposed by David Ausubel seems to be the main underpinning of the Novak-Gowin approach, from the point of view of theoretical orientation: "The most important single factor influencing learning is what the learner already knows. Ascertain this and teach him accordingly" (Ausubel, 1968, epigraph). Concept maps appear to be an effective tool for pinpointing the misconceptions and nuances of meaning that a learner holds, suggesting linkages between new knowledge and what the learner already knows. *Learning How to Learn* describes carefully how to introduce and employ concept mapping. There are directions for grades one to three, three to seven, and seven through college.

The Novak-Gowin approach emphasizes learning meaningfully, and "the best way to help students learn meaningfully is to help them explicitly to see the nature and role of concepts and the relationship between concepts as they exist in their minds and they exist out there in the world or in printed or spoken instruction" (p. 24). The approach employs procedures that help students to extract specific concepts (words) from printed and verbal material and identify interconceptual relationships. Mapping aids recall, and maps become increasingly more useful as students become more proficient in their development and interpretation.

The knowledge Vee is used as a heuristic—a problem-solving aid and an aid in understanding a procedure. It helps students to see the interplay between what they already know and knowledge they are producing or attempting to understand. The Vee emerged from twenty years of research and represents a tool for helping students understand the structure of knowledge and the ways in which people produce it. It has been shown to facilitate metalearning and metaknowledge acquisition by linking in a complementary manner the nature of knowledge and the nature of learning: "The Vee points to the events or objects that are at the root of all knowledge production, and it is crucial that learners become acutely aware of the events or objects they are experiencing, about which knowledge is to be constructed" (p. 54). Detailed directions for introducing and presenting the Vee are found in *Learning How to Learn.* Mapping should be introduced before the Vee so that students are already familiar with two elements of the Vee concepts and the objectives and/or events pertaining to them. Scoring keys for evaluating both maps and Vee diagrams are included. Finally, Novak and Gowin maintain that the Vee diagram and concept map can help educators with curriculum design "by structuring educational experience in a way that requires that teacher and learner pay explicit attention to metaknowledge issues, whatever the specific context of the learning" (p. 59).

This approach appears to enjoy a solid theoretical base and it is backed up by considerable empirical research. The main purpose is to provide workable strategies to help students learn to learn. The two constructs are purposefully designed to foster metacognitive understanding of knowledge acquisition. Both deal with reflectivity and epistemology, which should facilitate the acquisition of new knowledge. The collaborative aspect of learning is also not overlooked: "Students need practice in reflective thinking just as teams need time to practice a sport. The making and remaking of concept maps and sharing them with others can be seen as a team effort in the sport of thinking" (p. 19).

Another advantage of the approach is that it is readily adaptable for use with out-of-school adults. For example, community-based and "liberatory" adult educators frequently seek to help minorities and disenfranchised people to understand knowledge as power and the implications of lacking their own interpretations of their culture and history. Concept mapping and (especially) the Vee heuristic show real promise as tools for effecting these purposes. An added advantage is that concept mapping and Vee diagramming are available on computer software.

Two potential limitations suggest themselves: math and

science receive greater emphasis (in sample maps and diagrams, for example) than other subject areas; and the model's rather comprehensive philosophy, teaching-learning theory, and curriculum-building stance rest on research and experience centered in two heuristic devices.

Repertory Grid-Based Technology. The architects of this approach, Laurie Thomas and Sheila Harri-Augstein, describe it in *Self-Organised Learning: Foundations of a Conversational Science for Psychology* (1985). Elsewhere they defined self-organization as the ability to "converse with oneself about one's own learning process and to observe, search, analyze, formulate, review, judge, decide and act on the basis of such creative encounters" (Harri-Augstein and Thomas, 1983, p. 39). They assume that most people are almost entirely unaware of how they assign personal meaning to the events, activities, and objects they experience. Their research has focused on developing technologies to "represent personal meaning in ways which enable reflection, review, and effective transformation of the quality of human experience and performance" (Thomas and Harri-Augstein, 1985, p. xxvii). Underlying the approach are these principles: (1) Real personal learning depends upon an ability to use oneself as a test-bed for personal validity and viability. (2) The dynamics of self-organized learning depend upon an ability to monitor the construction and reconstruction of personal meaning over time. (3) Shared meaning, as opposed to public knowledge, must be truly negotiated.

The reflective learning technology used in the approach has evolved from George Kelly's repertory grid technique (1955), central to personal construct psychology. Conversational grids become a tool for exploration of personal meaning and the learning process itself. The grid enables the conversation to have structure, meaning, and depth. A major purpose is to eliminate emotional barriers that block the learner from achieving his or her learning goals. The process by which the facilitator elicits the grid from the learner was described in Chapter Two.

Thomas and Harri-Augstein (1985) discuss the methodology as follows: "The process of reflection upon experience is the nub of the methodology advocated. . . . The grid is designed to help people explore such items of experience as concepts, books, learning, studying or deeply personal thoughts and feelings about any issue that creates a major barrier or resource of learning" (p. 6). The grid also enables the individual to explore his or her thoughts and feelings about a topic in his or her own terms, which helps to make the topic personally interesting and relevant: "The learner who has challenged his or her own personal myths and who has acquired the knack of making all learning personal is ready to increase his or her capacity for learning" (p. 39). As a reflective technology, the approach links directly to the kind of reflection on learning processes that is central to learning to learn. It is clear that previously hidden feelings and attitudes can be brought to the learner's awareness. Incorporated into the description of the Thomas–Harri-Augstein approach in *Self-Organised Learning* are computer programs used to raise people's awareness of the learning process, ten of which are based on the repertory grid and can be used with individuals, pairs, and groups.

Thomas and Harri-Augstein describe another technology for helping people to read and study more effectively, the Brunel Reading Recorder. This machine produces a "read record" that reveals how time is spent as an individual reads a text. The learner and the instructor then examine, discuss, and interpret the implications for more effective practice. An organized talk-back to oral review "enables the learner to identify key habits and allows him or her to challenge these so that new strategies are explored, in a quest for effective understanding of a given text within the context of personally relevant purposes" (Harri-Augstein and Thomas, 1983, p. 45). Thomas and Harri-Augstein provide training in the use of these technologies in a variety of workshops offered through the Center for Human Learning at Brunel University (United Kingdom). Topics include self-organized learning of languages and the improvement of skills for reading, listening, and discussion.

The conversational science paradigm is based on the idea that people cannot know themselves unaided and must therefore exploit their potential through facilitation by a nondirective practitioner. Only the learner has direct access to his or her experience, but an observer is required to describe the learner's behavior with accuracy and precision. The repertory grid is a technique with which changes in one's perceiving, thinking, and feeling about learning-related events can be systematically examined. It therefore seems to be an excellent tool for discovering and ridding oneself of personal obstructions to learning, as well as for the examination of one's assumptions about learning. Although *Self-Organised Learning* does demonstrate with detailed diagrams how one can develop a program without the use of a computer, it is clear that the computer programs greatly enhance the workshops the authors recommend. (See Appendix B of the book.)

The major strengths of the approach include its learner-centeredness, the provision for externalizing normally internalized learning-related processes, the conceptualizing of learning enhancement as a long-term process involving far more than study tips and suggestions, and the adapting of technologies developed for therapy and other purposes to the purpose of learning to learn. A major limitation is the need for a well-trained facilitator to assist the learner in interpreting the grid, identifying its implications, and supporting appropriate attempts at improving learning-related behavior. At times the approach seems to be on the verge of requiring the facilitator to possess skills most likely to be found in consulting psychologists and therapists. And the approach, as described in *Self-Organised Learning*, can seem formidable as a result of the amount of technical and numerical manipulations involved in its application.

Participation Training. This approach to helping adults become effective in collaborative learning and group problem solving was developed at Indiana University by Paul Bergevin and several associates and has been used in a wide range of settings for a variety of purposes for over three decades. Among the settings are health agencies, business and industry, religious organizations, and correctional institutions. Among the purposes are team building, problem posing, and problem solving, providing a system for a long-term education or development program within the organization.

Major goals of participation training include the following: (1) to understand the conditions under which adults learn most effectively in face-to-face groups, the uses and potential benefits of collaborative learning, and the roles and responsibilities of group members; (2) to become a "learning team" that can identify common needs, interests, problems, and goals; and (3) to employ appropriate tools, strategies, and behaviors for meeting group needs and problems while maximizing opportunity for individual expression, responsibility, and growth. More specific objectives would be more effective listening; increased sensitivity to the needs, opinions, and value frameworks of self; and improved ability to give, request, and receive feedback from peers and facilitators.

Participation training reflects a philosophical position that has its roots in the earlier writings of John Dewey and Eduard Lindeman and is later reflected in the writings of Malcolm Knowles (*The Modern Practice of Adult Education,* Association Press, 1980) and Bergevin himself (*A Philosophy for Adult Education,* Seabury, 1967). This position emphasizes the active involvement of the learner in the educational process. It assumes that, for adults at least, the learner can and should take considerable responsibility for what is learned as well as how it is learned and evaluated. In this process of self-direction, the learner represents a primary resource for learning, and educators create the conditions for learners to assume as much control as possible of learning-related activity. Participation training represents a framework for enabling people to function in education undergirded with this philosophy.

Collaboration is also stressed. The literature of group dynamics and the experience of laboratory learning contributed to the development of participation training, providing concepts (for example, group norms) and methods (for example, the T-group) that were adapted into the training design and its implementation.

Participation training involves theory sessions about collaborative learning and the training design itself together with guided practice sessions in face-to-face groups. The tightly structured practice sessions require group members to plan and carry out a series of discussions and similar activities; the participants choose the topic and set the objectives for each practice exercise. By such means as trainer interventions, postdiscussion critiques, and various handouts, the facilitator guides group members in becoming effective in communication, consensus decision making, supportive behavior, and the like. This requires the participants to become sensitive to intra- and interpersonal processes. Emphasis is on the *process* of the discussion—not because the content or substance is devalued but rather because the approach teaches that when adults have learned to collaborate effectively, the quality and utility of their problem solving or exploration of an issue will be ensured.

A residential five-and-one-half-day experience, an institute, is considered an ideal format for participation training; some four hundred institutes have been conducted at Indiana University by the Bureau of Studies in Adult Education. To carry on the work, persons trained there conduct many other institutes. A variety of other formats are employed also—for example, two weekends or twelve weekly sessions of three hours each.

The role of the facilitator in this approach is a relatively complex one, involving modeling, instruction, sensitivity to process, active listening, climate setting, supportive behavior, and staying within a well-structured framework. However, in contrast to such methods as T-group and sensitivity training, the facilitator need not possess a background in therapy. The approach is centered in education—for example, making better learning-related decisions, identifying educational needs, bringing resources to bear, and evaluating learning. In the early sessions, the facilitator assists the group in learning certain procedures and focusing on processes while modeling some of the behaviors the participants will acquire or sharpen. Various responsibilities are gradually transferred to the training group members so that, in the institute, the trainer usually withdraws completely in a key and symbolic session near the end.

The person experiencing participation training must be

willing to enter it with something of a suspension of precon-
ceived attitudes and beliefs regarding groups. He or she may
well have a history of participation in groups that were inefficient, frustrating, or threatening. The experience may er-
roneously be perceived as therapy, or as superficial because it
can appear to be "all process and no content." The trainee's role
requires using unfamiliar terms and procedures in the presence
of others. It entails some self-examination and acceptance of
responsibility for voluntarily performing certain tasks (for example, leading a discussion or a planning session or serving as
observer).

Participation training was developed and tested through
action research in about fifty local organizations (hospitals,
churches, and libraries). As applications of the approach began
to proliferate, it was refined by experimental and quasi-experi-
mental research and by meetings and networks of those using
the approach. The result is a practical program with a wide
variety of manuals and other tools for both the facilitator and
the group member. Despite the relatively high amount of structure involved in teaching the system, the design and select
portions of it have proved to be adaptable to various types of
clientele, organizations, and purposes; applications have been
made with the undereducated, the blue-collar worker, the incar-
cerated, and the professional. The design has proved safe to use
despite the fact that self-examination is involved and some
interpersonal confrontations may arise.

Those who developed participation training were careful
to make provision for application, transfer, and dissemination.
The complete system has three parts: (1) team building (or
"discussion team work"), (2) applying group skills, and (3) post-
training application ("back home application," as it is termed in
the one-week residential institute). An example of a relevant
activity in phase two is one subgroup's being required to plan
and conduct an educational activity for another — an immediate
opportunity to apply skills acquired in phase one. In phase
three participants plan and conduct activities relating to post-
training applications. In addition to the institutes, consultation,
networking, and diverse publications, dissemination has taken

the form of a systematic trainer development effort tied to the conducting of institutes at Indiana University and throughout the country. There are, of course, also limitations. A persistent problem has been interpreting participation training to potential sponsors and participants (which has also often been a problem for providers of laboratory, sensitivity, and other forms of human relations training). One cause of this problem can be descriptions that include excessive jargon or unfamiliar terms (Bergevin and McKinley, 1965; McKenzie, 1975; McKinley, 1980). The result is that many who might benefit may avoid the experience or enroll with unrealistic expectations.

The kind of comprehensive learning-to-learn programs just described are likely to be effective and gain acceptance to the extent that they (1) include a credible theoretical base; (2) undergo field testing and evaluation; (3) provide the learner with relevant experience, practice, application, and reinforcement in the use of new behavior; (4) make available useful materials for both the learner and the facilitator; (5) make provision for facilitator training (if required); and (6) implement a systematic approach to dissemination.

Guidelines for Designers and Facilitators

The expanding knowledge base concerning learning to learn contains considerable information that is potentially relevant to designing and facilitating activities to help people to learn more effectively and make better educational decisions. However, implementing the learning-to-learn concept often requires adapting existing materials and inventing formats, strategies, and materials. This endeavor, which often proves in the long run to be more rewarding than merely adopting what is available, can be aided by understanding and implementing some guidelines for design and facilitation.

One area in which some useful guidelines are available involves systematic activity to help individuals take increased responsibility for their own learning activities and learning projects (often called "becoming self-directed learners"). Facilitators (counselors, teachers, supervisors, or consultants) can provide specific training events or try to build process awareness and learning skills acquisition into routine encounters with those they serve; or they can combine the two approaches. The individual needs to be helped to acquire a mental map of areas over which learner control can be exercised (for example, assessing educational interests, goal setting, resource selection, and evaluation). He or she needs to understand that exercising total control over all aspects of a learning project is seldom practical or desirable—learning how to make better use of peer and expert support is usually in order. The facilitator provides transition structures to assist the individual in gradually assuming greater control in managing the overall process. Structure comes from direct supporting behavior and from the provision of process theory, as well as from such tools as checklists and self-evaluation forms. The facilitator often collaborates with the individual in negotiating the amount of control to be undertaken by the learner and in diagnosing the process skills that need improvement. Training is especially likely to succeed when it occurs in a larger, personally relevant and meaningful context, such as career planning or entry into an educational program that emphasizes self-direction (Cheren, 1983; Hiemstra, 1988; Knowles, 1975).

Donald Maudsley developed five principles that underlie the facilitation of learning-to-learn activity, which he termed *metalearning*. For Maudsley, metalearning refers to the ways in which learners become aware of and take increased control over previously internalized processes of perception, inquiry, learning, and growth. Maudsley derived his principles from a critical analysis of the theories of Argyris and Schön, Bandler and Grinder, Bateson, Grof, and Piaget, as well as an examination of theory emanating from T-group and laboratory learning and the ideas of Lewin and others concerning planned change. He states that metalearning comes about when people examine the assumptions and rules by which they make sense of things and habitually interact with the world around them. Examples of assumptions might be that one can't learn X or Y, is too old to learn Z, or finds learning in groups a waste of time. Effective facilitation requires the following:

- Providing the learner with a framework for searching for new meanings and alternate ways of proceeding
- Ensuring that learners' current assumptions and rules are manifested (discovered) by them
- Challenging learners by revealing where rules, assumptions, and perceptions may be inaccurate and dysfunctional
- Creating new opportunities for learners to "re-organize themselves by means of new rules or the reduction of reliance on rules" (Maudsley, 1979, p. 43)

A few other writers have suggested guidelines for the design and facilitation of learning-to-learn programs. For children, Ann Brown makes the following recommendations: (1) training in general thinking skills of self-criticism as well as in task-specific skills, (2) interactive learning situations where the teacher acts as a coach, and (3) instruction aimed at increasing self-confidence. She advises teachers to aim at the child's existing level of knowledge, to proceed from the "concrete specific experience" to the general principle, all at the child's own rate (Brown, 1986). She describes this as the "training approach advocated today by psychologists and educators for all children" (p. 329).

Derry and Murphy (1986) suggest that the nature and shape of design are determined by "who is to be trained" (the characteristics and learning-to-learn needs of those to be trained), the kind of learning material the learner will be involved with (for example, the subject to be learned or the learning-related task to be carried out more effectively), and the amount of time available for training. For basic skills learning by both children and adults, they recommend concentrating on four learning strategy domains: (1) memory strategies—for remembering items, lists, vocabulary, and the like; (2) reading/study strategies for specific types of text (for example, teaching people to generate questions and to summarize as they read); (3) problem-solving skills applicable to arithmetic (for example, learning to employ a four-step problem-solving model); and (4) affective support strategies—goal setting and scheduling, self-support, and "mood-management" techniques (p. 32).

Graham Gibbs's views on design pertain primarily to learning-to-learn activities for students in higher education. He points out the need to generate or "bring up" content. By *content* is meant such matters as the experience of undergoing an examination, reading a chapter of text, and taking notes during a lecture. Students' notes from lectures and reading experiences as well as their answers to exam questions, therefore, become content to be analyzed by the student with the instructor's guidance. Effective training requires that the student become aware of the characteristics of the subject matter to be learned, the instructor's expectations, and the key learning tasks involved. The student is encouraged to examine present assumptions and practices and, as needed, to experiment with alternatives. Training works best when the instructor minimizes his or her role as the authority in subject matter. Appropriate activity should be built in throughout a subject matter course and tied to situations likely to motivate interest in strategy improvement. For example, an ideal time to introduce training for improving performance on examinations is shortly before a scheduled examination (Gibbs, 1981).

With regard to the design of learning-to-learn activities for adults, Smith (1982) cites a tendency for adults to resist learning process training, stating that "people do not necessarily like to have [for example] their inability to listen actively or dysfunctional study practices brought to the fore, [nor do they] usually change habits or basic orientations to learning without some conflict or frustration" (p. 43). Proposed learning-to-learn activities often need to be carefully justified to potential participants. The creation of a climate of security and trust during training helps to minimize resistance, conflict, and apprehension. Smith stresses the importance of clear and modest objectives to successful design, as well as provision for application of newly acquired understandings and strategies. He suggests minimizing theory while maximizing hands-on experience through such activities as projects, skills practice exercises, simulation and role play, analysis of case studies, and the like (Smith, 1982, Chapters Nine and Ten).

Some Principles of Design and Facilitation

The following generalizations describe some major design and facilitation principles based on information found in the learning-to-learn literature and elsewhere in this book. They are directed to the educator, but it is well to keep in mind that people do enhance their own learning skills and capacities without benefit of intervention. The principles are meant to be so generic as to apply to a wide variety of purposes, client groups, and age levels.

Maintain a Learner-Centered Orientation. The individual and how he or she experiences education and learning become the starting point for efforts on behalf of learning to learn. Novak and Gowin introduce *Learning How to Learn* with a question they have sought to answer in their long-term research: "How can we help individuals to reflect upon their experience and to construct new, more powerful meanings?" Gibbs subtitles *Teaching Students to Learn* with the phrase "A Student-Centered Approach," stating, "I have been trying for a student-centered approach . . . ever since the first didactic [learning] skills courses I ran were a disaster" (p. 88). Maintaining a learner-centered orientation is aided by active listening, engaging in dialogue with the learner, and the employment of tools and exercises that elicit learners' perceptions of their purposes for employing learning strategies, their personal blocks to learning, the results of dysfunctional strategies, and areas of needed improvement.

Strengthen the Foundations of Learning to Learn. Three foundations of learning to learn are (1) awareness and understanding of self-as-learner, (2) the ability to monitor one's learning processes and to reflect on them, and (3) the ability to access and utilize a wide variety of modes, resources, and strategies for learning. Becoming more aware of self-as-learner enables the individual to gain valuable insights into personal blocks to learning, strengths and limitations as learner, and personal preferences for methods of learning and learning environments. Awareness of one's own learning processes and procedures represents a starting point for improvement. Monitoring and reflection foster that awareness and are also critical to learning material of depth and complexity. The requirements of contemporary living call for alternately learning on one's own, in the informal group, and in the classroom—for employing and being subjected to an array of methods, techniques, and strategies. Experience and training that directly support and strengthen these capacities and competencies stand to be especially important; training for more limited or specific purposes can usually be conducted in such a way as to support them also.

Make the Idea of Learning to Learn Understandable and Palatable. Expect resistance as a result of such factors as apathy, apprehension, the complexities of some of the relevant concepts and processes, and people's natural tendency to be subject matter-oriented. It is often necessary to sell the idea of training and to label it appropriately. Cheren (1987) has found "learning management" a useful term in the no-nonsense environment of the for-profit organization. Smith (1982) states that people tend to find this kind of activity most acceptable when it (1) has the possibility of a larger payoff (for example, acquiring skills that can be used in comparable situations) and (2) when it clearly relates to previously encountered learning problems (for example, apathetic groups, aborted personal learning projects, or exam anxiety).

Establish and Maintain a Climate Conducive to Change. Installing a comprehensive learning-to-learn program may entail considerable change within an organization—change in such matters as curriculum, staffing assignments, and the reward system. Less ambitiously, for a teacher to adopt and act on a learning-to-learn orientation usually requires changes in his or her ingrained assumptions, attitudes, and behavior. Such changes can be threatening, and they are unlikely to be made unless he or she receives encouragement and support from the supervisor (Bowes and Smith, 1986). Peer support is often helpful; two or three persons experimenting together with learning-to-learn activities can go far toward creating their own climate of mutual support. Becoming a more effective learner usually calls for the individual to examine existing beliefs and behaviors and to modify them—a potentially unsettling experience. Designers and facilitators pay close attention to the psychological, social, and physical environment in which learning-to-learn activity transpires and seek ways to establish or take advantage of an optimum environment.

Adopt, Adapt, and Improvise. Sometimes the training activities, exercises, and resources of others can be used for one's purposes with little or no modification, but more often they require careful adaptation (for example, modifying an exercise or re-writing an instrument). Not infrequently, a resource or activity will need to be invented. Examples of collections of models, activities, and resources that can be used or adapted for a variety of training purposes are found in Gibbs (1981), Joyce and Weil (1986), Knowles (1975), Nisbet and Shucksmith (1986), Novak and Gowin (1984), Pfeiffer and Jones (1972–1989), and Smith (1982, 1983).

Applications of Electronic Media

Existing and potential applications of electronic technology to learning to learn are broad and diverse. A learning-style instrument, a concept map, or a conversational grid can be converted to videotape or computer software. Study skills enhancement advice is available on videotape. People can be taught to access data base information systems. In Great Britain, a computer-based simulation game has been developed to assist students to make the transition from secondary to higher education (Entwistle, Odor, and Anderson, 1988). In a program originally developed in the armed forces, the JSEP Basic Learning Skills Curriculum features twenty hours of computer-assisted video, audio, and workbook instruction on learning strategies and tactics; it helps the student to reduce anxiety and negative attitudes toward learning, use a four-step problem-solving procedure, and employ several strategies for reading with comprehension (Wilson, 1989). Rapidly evolving electronic technologies thus offer promise of sophisticated multimedia approaches that make sound learning-to-learn information available in home, school, and workplace.

A first step in making an electronic application of the learning-to-learn idea is to consider the installed base (the number of devices available to run the application). The video cassette recorder (VCR) represents an ideal starting point because it probably has the largest installed base. Surveys suggest that 60 percent of American homes have a VCR, making videotapes viewable in most homes and classrooms. A good example of a videotape application is Malcolm Knowles's cassette course entitled *The Adult Learner Video Workshop* (Gulf Publishing Company), which allows the facilitator to interact with the group during pauses planned so that tasks can be executed, as outlined in the facilitator's guide. It is also feasible for most facilitators to rent a video recorder (for example, Camcorder by Sony) and, with a well-designed presentation, offer a similar, if not quite as professional, program to a proposed audience.

Computers have the next largest installed base, but they are a long way away from having the market penetration enjoyed by VCRs. Computers, however, are much more flexible and have greater potential for group instruction and home study. In a classroom setting where there is only a single computer available, an opportunity for each member to use the computer to access major data bases relevant to individual learning projects could be included in course design. This would be helpful on two levels: developing the skills of students or clients to locate, access, or organize information for use in their learning projects, and developing a general awareness of a resource that will become more and more important to them if they are to learn efficiently.

As computers proliferate or where there is already a computer available to every member of a group, one can consider the fuller potential of the computer with such programs as those offered by Novak and Gowin (1984 and 1989) and Thomas and Harri-Augstein (1985). For the instructor or facilitator with no background in computers or computer programming, Hypercard (a software program now available) makes it possible to develop a software program of a course to assist in classroom instruction. Many instructors have already done so and have found it to be very effective, and the graphic nature of Hypercard makes it relatively easy to use. The approach facilitates the access of data bases, which often seems threatening to the neophyte. Since using resources is such an integral part of the learning-to-learn process and since more and more of the information people will be seeking will be available on data bases, it is important for the development of data retrieval skills to be included in training. Becoming comfortable with these electronic tools increases confidence and willingness to employ them when learning. Witness the popularity of the pocket size electronic dictionary; it is clear that people are more willing to look up a word when the task is made easy.

In addition to existing platforms for launching learning-to-learn programs in the classroom and home, it is useful to consider some technologies about to come on the scene and how they will probably affect applications. The focus here will be on those with the most immediate and potentially meaningful impact, with the best prospects for incorporating interactivity and for maximizing dissemination of information related to learning-to-learn.

The concept of interactivity is not new; it has been around for a number of years in the form of computer-assisted instruction (CAI) and interactive videodisc. For a number of reasons, neither of these two vehicles has been able to fulfill its educational potential. There exist, however, two remarkable new technologies that when combined should be able to fulfill that potential: Compact Disc-Interactive (CD-I) and Intelligent Tutorial Systems (ITS). Compact Disc-Interactive has information digitally encoded on an optical disc with which a learner can interact. An Intelligent Tutorial System is a software program composed of three expert system programs and an interface. In their present form these technologies apparently cannot help becoming a boon to education and efforts on behalf of learning to learn. It is not unreasonable to speculate that when they are combined in the very near future, the end result could be a tool of unprecedented power.

Interactive videodisc (sometimes referred to as optical disc or laser disc), long recognized in education and training for its multimedia capabilities, has been praised by many writers, including Kenworthy. "When properly designed and executed, interactive videodisc offers individualized, flexible, simulation based training at a reasonable price per trainee hour. And, because the medium teaches through practice, it is especially successful at addressing skills topics. Because interactive videodisc combines the realism of video with the individualized interaction of computer based instruction, trainees enjoy learning, and they learn more. In fact, studies comparing interactive videodisc to other teaching methods repeatedly have shown that those trained with disc reduced their learning time while increasing their retention" (1988, p. 6). To be sure, problems exist. The biggest has been lack of format standardization (the ability to play the same disc on different machines). The size and the cost of the units are substantial, and there is the deterrent to moving beyond the classroom: the need for three separate units (a videodisc player, a computer, and a monitor).

The compact disc has now eliminated these problems, however. Most people are familiar with the very popular compact disc players (commonly referred to as CD players) used for listening to music, usually seen attached to a stereo system or as a portable device carried on one's hip. The compact disc stores music as digital data on rotation five-inch platters that are "read" by beams of laser light. Compact disc-text players are available primarily as a computer peripheral in most computer stores; the player reads the text stored in digital form on the discs. The newest players have been reduced in size and can now be built into the computer. Functioning much like a hard drive, the player's hallmark is extraordinary storage capacity; for example, a single disc may contain an entire encyclopedia. The problems of portability and standardization have thus been solved. With the forthcoming introduction of the CD-I player, the cost and size will also have been reduced. This new technology augers a revolution in the learning industry.

CD-I: Compact Disc-Interactive System. This system, currently a prototype, is being developed by both the Sony and N. A. Philips companies, in two basic forms. The first is a TV attach-ment that will offer powerful, simple-to-use, home computing and graphics functions at a price projected at less than $300. These information appliances will be able to store and simul-taneously play back on a television set graphics, information, voices, stereo music, and TV images, and run software as well. The new CD-I systems that hook to televisions already installed in the home will include a pointing device, such as a mouse or light pen, for control. Portable versions with their own flat-panel displays will also be produced. This product is intended for home use and will be able to read ordinary audio compact discs as well as CD-I discs. The user will be able to listen, view, read, or any combination thereof, depending on personal selection or the design of the software.

A recent advance, Digital Video Interactive (DVI), allows the CD to have full motion video. This player unit, whether it is CD-I or DVI, will make it possible to view a multimedia ex-pression of any subject one chooses. Finally, Philips, Sony, and Microsoft have recently collaborated in the development of the CD ROM Extended Architecture (CD ROM XA). This format will infuse standard CD ROM players already attached to computers with the same capabilities as the stand-alone Compact Disc-Interactive (CD-I) systems.

Multimedia Software. Technically remarkable, the CD-I player and its high-capacity storage disc are, nonetheless, only half of the story. The other half is the technology that allows one to *interact* with the data on the compact disc, the software. Software enables the learner to use the material interactively in exciting ways. This mixed-media format can make an encyclopedia come alive in a way that neither print products nor text-only can. For example, one could not only *look up* Glenn Miller in the en-cyclopedia but *see* and *hear* him play over the text along with film clips of the band performing. "Real multimedia software sug-gests that the audio, graphics, motion video, and data are built into the production rather than added on as an after-thought, and . . . so integrated [as to] deliver a new experience to the learner" (Lambert and Ropiequet, 1986, p. 309). The CD-I or DVI portable player has the potential to become the ultimate educational tool, but to do so it will need to incorporate expert systems to handle the complete needs of a sophisticated program for learning to learn.

An expert system is a software program that imitates the thinking capabilities of an expert in a specific field. It enables programmers to capture some of the knowledge, methods, and rules of thumb a human expert uses to solve problems. Expert systems can be used in nearly any field, from financial investment analysis to geometry, but they work best in a narrow domain of knowledge. Expert systems are similar to human experts in that they can describe and explain their reasoning and conclusions, but, unlike human experts, they have no general or commonsense knowledge. Instead, these systems contain highly detailed knowledge about a specific area. The detail of this knowledge is such that the system does not have to think; it knows.

There are many types of expert systems. Some do all the problem solving with minimum interaction with the user, as in the Oil Discovery System or Auto Mechanic System, where all the user does is input the data and receive the expert's answer to the problem. Other types have the user input the data but also teach the user how the expert would deal with the situation; thus the user can compare his or her approach with that of the expert, as in the case of a medical model for student doctors. And there are other systems designed to teach a subject as if taught by an expert in that subject who is also an expert teacher.

The development of a learning-to-learn expert system is described by Entwistle, Odor, and Anderson (1988). The purpose is to encourage higher-education students to reflect on and improve their study strategies. The expert system is incorporated into a computer-based adventure game. The computer simulation makes use of research-based concepts, stemming from students' experiences, that describe the processes of studying: "In essence the design of the game . . . envisaged a database of information about studying, derived from research studies, together with advice tailored to the decision strategies and inferred characteristics of the individual student. In other words, it would be a simple expert system providing a form of 'intelligent' tutoring" (p. 237). The game takes the student through a series of events and decisions encountered in higher education. The student experiences and makes decisions regarding such problems as how to find accurate information about a course or instructor, how to cope with fear of failure and with frustration resulting from the unavailability of materials in the library, and how to balance study with other priorities. A "mentor" component allows the student to request comment on the experiences and provides advice concerning choices of strategy. Other interactive mechanisms are built in to allow the player to discover the rules governing the consequences of actions taken. The authors provide their model of the teaching-learning process in higher education, a diagram of the architecture of the computer simulation, and examples of actual frames of information the user encounters.

Intelligent Tutorial Systems. The most sophisticated way that expert systems are being put to use in learning or training is by combining three expert systems and an interface into a single system called an Intelligent Tutorial System (ITS). This is a computer-based learning environment in which system and student share control; the system has expanded ability to analyze student responses, tailor curriculum, and generally interact, much as a good teacher would. Currently there are a number of ITS systems functioning in the educational arena, the best known and most successful of which are the Anderson Lisp Tutor (for teaching Lisp computer language) and the Geometry Tutor. The strength of an ITS is that it functions very much like a private tutor, offering the learner a one-on-one experience, which in most cases has proven to be the most effective way of teaching. The system contains four modules: student, expert, tutoring, and environment.

The expertise of the student module is in understanding the student's knowledge so tutoring can be tailored to the user and the progress ascertained and updated over time, a continuous process until the subject is mastered. In the case of learning to learn, it is able to assess what the individual already knows about an aspect of the subject and what his or her capability and potentiality are. The expert module represents all the knowledge of the particular domain. It could, for example, reflect the combined knowledge of the experts in the field with regard to the concept and processes of learning to learn. The tutoring module is based on the student module and on the curriculum. It decides what information should be presented and how and what instruction to give next, based on the user's responses. A tutoring module needs to act like an expert teacher/facilitator or coach, knowing when to ask questions, generate problems, offer advice, and allow the preset curriculum to proceed. The environment module is the interface between the student and the program: student interaction with the program, keyboard, "mouse," touch screen, and so forth. For a learning-to-learn tutorial, a simple interface that does not distract from the tutoring process should be all that is required.

Since intelligent tutorial systems and compact interactive discs exist, and their combination would create a powerful educational tool, it is not unreasonable to speculate as to what form their merger might take and how they would operate. A first application might be played on a portable CD-I player about the size of a notebook with a voice or touch screen interface. (Apple computer has a prototype in design called the Knowledge Navigator.) If a larger screen were desired, the players could be attached to a television set or a monitor. The program, for example, could contain all the information the designer wished to include in an introductory course on learning to learn. Through its interactive capacities, the ITS would be able to diagnose the user's state of knowledge (student model), assess his or her learning style, bring to awareness any emotional barriers to learning (through conversational grids, for example), and evaluate the user's potentialities and capabilities. The result would be a customized program for introducing the individual to learning-to-learn concepts and for involving him or her directly in activities known to foster more active, meaningful, and effective learning. An existing electronic presentation, such as

Knowles's workshop for the adult learner, could be redesigned so that the user could have a sense of interacting personally with the expert, as if the latter were actually present, answering questions and giving suggestions.

Professionals interested in disseminating information and training activities related to learning to learn now have available the means to replicate their expertise accurately and render it accessible to a much broader audience than ever before thought possible. In the near future we can expect them to have available even more sophisticated means of presentation for dissemination. As professionals begin working with these new media, new kinds of design will emerge and commercial producers of materials stand to become much more active in producing and marketing appropriate electronic software.

Finally, merely converting information about learning to learn to electronic media does not ensure effective training. More often than not, current state of the art limits learning-to-learn software to the role of a useful tool for a curriculum builder, facilitator, or individual user. Applications that take full advantage of the potential of the media and minimize the inherent limitations will abstract the learning and study processes of the individual so they can be made manifest and compared with the performance of others. The individual's learning style will be taken into account, interactivity will be maximized, and care will be taken to avoid fostering "user-dependence" and "learning-to-be-taught." The individual will not be told how to do better but rather led through a process that reveals present assumptions and practices, offers alternatives, and motivates and supports behavior change — considerations that are equally essential when training with or without electronic media.

References

Ausubel, D. P. *Educational Psychology: A Cognitive View.* New York: Holt, Rinehart & Winston, 1968.

Bergevin, P. E., and McKinley, J. *Participation Training for Adult Education.* St. Louis, Mo.: Bethany Press, 1965.

Bowes, S. G., and Smith, R. M. "Directing Your Own Continuing

Education." *Lifelong Learning: An Omnibus of Practice and Research,* 1986, *9* (8), 8–10.

Brown, A. "Mental Orthopedics, The Training of Cognitive Skills: An Interview with Alfred Binet." In M. Segal and others (eds.), *Thinking and Learning Skills.* Vol. 12. Hillsdale, N.J.: Erlbaum, 1986.

Cheren, M. E. "Helping Learners Achieve Greater Self-Direction." In R. M. Smith (ed.), *Helping Adults Learn How to Learn.* New Directions for Continuing Education, no. 19. San Francisco: Jossey-Bass, 1983.

Cheren, M. E. (ed.). *Learning Management: Emerging Directions for Learning to Learn in the Workplace.* Information Series no. 320. Columbus: National Center for Research in Vocational Education, Ohio State University, 1987.

Derry, S. J., and Murphy, D. A. "Designing Systems That Train Learning Ability: From Theory to Practice." *Review of Educational Research,* 1986, *56* (1), 1–39.

Entwistle, N., Odor, P., and Anderson, C. "Encouraging Reflection on Study Strategies: The Design of a Computer-Based Adventure Game." In P. Ramsden (ed.), *Improving Learning: New Perspectives.* London: Kogan Page, 1988.

Gibbons, M. "Walkabout: Searching for the Right Passage from Childhood and School." *Phi Delta Kappan,* 1974, *55* (9), 592–602.

Gibbons, M. "Walkabout Ten Years Later: Searching for a Renewed Vision of Education." *Phi Delta Kappan,* 1984, *65* (9), 591–607.

Gibbs, G. *Teaching Students to Learn.* Milton Keynes, England: Open University Press, 1981.

Harri-Augstein, E. S., and Thomas, L. F. "Developing Self-Organized Learners: A Reflective Technology." In R. M. Smith (ed.), *Helping Adults Learn How to Learn.* New Directions for Continuing Education, no. 19. San Francisco: Jossey-Bass, 1983.

Hiemstra, R. "Self-Directed Learning: Individualizing Instruction." In H. B. Long and Associates (eds.), *Self-Directed Learning: Application and Theory.* Athens: Adult Education Department, University of Georgia, 1988.

Hohmann, M., Banet, B., and Weikart, D. *Young Children in Action.* Ypsilanti, Mich.: The High/Scope Press, 1979.

Joyce, B., and Weil, M. *Models of Teaching.* (3rd ed.) Englewood Cliffs, N.J.: Prentice-Hall, 1986.

Kelly, G. A. *The Psychology of Personal Constructs.* 2 vols. New York: Norton, 1955.

Kenworthy, N. W. *Instruction Delivery Systems.* Vol. 6. Warrenton, Va.: Communicative Technology Corporations, 1988.

Knowles, M. *The Adult Learner Video Workshop.* Houston, Tex.: Gulf.

Knowles, M. *Self-Directed Learning: A Guide for Learners and Teachers.* New York: Association Press, 1975.

Lambert, S., and Ropiequet, S. *CD ROM: The New Papyrus.* Washington, D.C.: Microsoft Press, 1986.

McKenzie, L. (ed.). "Participation Training." *Viewpoints,* 1975, *51* (entire issue). College of Education, Indiana University.

McKinley, J. *Group Development Through Participation Training: A Trainer's Resource.* New York: Paulist Press, 1980.

Maudsley, D. B. "A Theory of Metalearning and Principles of Facilitation." Unpublished doctoral dissertation, University of Toronto, 1979.

Nisbet, J., and Shucksmith, J. *Learning Strategies.* New York: Routledge, 1986.

Novak, J., and Gowin, D. *Learning How to Learn.* New York: Cambridge University Press, 1984.

Novak, J., and Gowin, D. *Maps and VEE Diagrams.* New York: Exceller Software Corporation, 1989.

Pfeiffer, J. W., and Jones, J. E. *A Handbook of Structured Experiences for Human Relations Training.* San Diego, Calif.: University Associates, 1972–1989.

Segal, J. W., Chipman, S. F., and Glaser, R. (eds.). *Thinking and Learning Skills.* 2 vols. Hillsdale, N.J.: Erlbaum, 1986.

Smith, R. M. *Learning How to Learn: Applied Theory for Adults.* New York: Cambridge Book Company, 1982.

Smith, R. M. (ed.). *Helping Adults Learn How to Learn.* New Directions for Continuing Education, no. 19. San Francisco: Jossey-Bass, 1983.

Thomas, L., and Harri-Augstein, E. *Self-Organised Learning: Foun-*

dations of a Conversational Science for Psychology. London: Routledge and Kegan Paul, 1985.

Wilson, L. "One Answer for Workplace Literacy Efforts." *Online,*
1989, *6* (7), 4–5.

Woolf, B. "Artificial Intelligence in Education." Paper presented
at the Sixth National Conference on Artificial Intelligence,
Seattle, Washington, July 1987.

PART TWO

Empowering Learners
at All Levels

Chapter 7

Stimulating Thought and Learning in Preschool and Elementary Years

Mary E. Diez
C. Jean Moon

For many children, the passive, individually focused experiences of a typical school day militate against learning to learn. For the most part the early years of school involve learning to be taught, with an emphasis on content as facts learned primarily by rote. Furthermore, as the following vignette from a parental encounter with a seven-year-old indicates, school learning is often, by design, an isolated experience:

What did you learn at school today?
Nuthin.
Hm. Tell me what you did all day.
Well, it's kinda hard to explain.
What subjects did you have?
Spelling and math.
What did you *do*?
Well, we copied down words from the board. The teacher wrote them and we put them on our papers.

Did you help each other?
No, you're not supposed to. If some other kid had it wrong and
you copied it, then you'd have it wrong too.

As a result, as Resnick (1987a) observes, much of what one learns
in school is not seen as related to what one does outside school.
For example, she notes that the mode of learning in school is not
focused on groups of people thinking and working together,
which is the common mode in the working world.

   While we do not deny the importance of content in the
curriculum of early childhood and elementary education, it is
our premise that early learning would be better approached as
the beginning of a lifelong learning process if the connection
between content and process were made more explicit. Focusing
on learning to learn as the goal of preschool and elementary
education requires some fundamental rethinking of the assumptions that direct schools and, hence, the interaction of
parents and children about learning. Rethinking is necessary
because learning to learn is a different form of engagement for
both the teacher and the learner from merely teaching toward
content acquisition. From our perspective, this rethinking suggests a change in emphasis in the activity of the teacher and the
learner—to a focus on the individual's development *as a learner*
within the context of the various content areas. This reconcep-
tualization provides a structure for fostering abilities, in order
to allow the learner to link in-school and out-of-school learning.

   Learning to learn, as we will deal with it in this chapter, is
a process-oriented concept, centered in refining learning strategies or abilities that impact one's development as a learner.
These strategies or abilities are not a specified checklist of do's
or don'ts that can be readily graded. Rather, they are complex,
strategic patterns of action in which the learner constructs
meaning when he or she activates prior knowledge and links
information to be learned to existing knowledge structures. It is
our contention that the conscious use of these abilities enables a
person to make critical process choices that foster the development of learner independence, which will become increasingly
important with chronological age.

Do schools currently do enough to help children learn to learn? While there are some optimistic signs in recent literature—for example, the concept of learning as a process of active thinking appears to be gaining momentum among educators and researchers (Jones, Palincsar, Ogle, and Carr, 1987)—the answer, for the most part, must still be no. Much of what goes on for the majority of children in preschools and elementary schools remains somehow separate and apart from what is required in the life, personal and professional, of an adult.

It can be assumed that because most parents of preschool- and elementary-age children were educated within traditional educational frameworks, at-home learning situations generally reinforce what occurs in school settings. This assumption can be coupled with another: parents often feel a lack of confidence in their own skills and abilities as educators and defer to the "experts." However, traditional rote learning and repetitive worksheets, so much a part of formal educational experiences, do not readily transfer to the demands of everyday living.

As much as schools have tried to link development with learning, gaps in these efforts are being recognized. Mass education has been, from its inception, concerned with inculcating routine abilities: making simple calculations, reading predictable texts, reciting religious or civil codes (Resnick, 1987b). Resnick contends that "public education has never taken as goals for its students the ability to interpret unfamiliar texts, construct convincing arguments, or develop original solutions to technical or social problems" (p. 5). The National Research Council (1989) states that "today's schools labor under the legacy of a structure designed for the industrial age misapplied to educate children in the information age" (p. 11). Routinization of basic skills has thus exacted a certain price; employers today complain that they cannot count on schools to produce young adults who can move easily into more complex work. As a consequence, education as a whole is coming under increasing criticism.

Such verbal and written challenges come at a time, however, when new knowledge about the nature of learning and how one thinks about learning is available. This knowledge helps make explicit many of the abilities for which parents, teachers, and students may have had only some level of intuition. As abilities that bridge in-school and out-of-school learning, they provide a basis for understanding learning and learning to learn over a lifetime and, as such, should be cultivated and modeled early in childhood.

This chapter will explore some of the theoretical background of these abilities and provide examples of how to develop them during the elementary and preschool years.

Development of Abilities for Linking Learning Across Settings

Part of the problem is that school-based learning is seen by students as restricted to the school setting, separate from situation-specific learning outside of school. Appreciation for linking in-school learning with out-of-school learning has generally not developed. For this to change, at least in preschool and elementary years, teachers and parents need to become more knowledgeable about what it takes to be a learner in and out of school settings.

This chapter is organized around a major principle of learning to learn as herein defined: more emphasis should be placed on strategies that will enable the learner, regardless of age, to understand the meaning of the tasks at hand and, as a consequence, to monitor his or her own learning. This process implies that learners have potential for knowing what to do and when to do it, even if they do not know specifically what to do at every given learning moment. Our intention is to address three general abilities that people need to develop, regardless of age, to engage in learning effectively: reflecting on learning, connection making, and problem solving.

Each of the three abilities can be developed and demonstrated by the individual through the use of a number of strategies. If children incorporate these strategies into their learning, they will begin to assess what they know as learners and create links between new information and existing knowledge and between in-school and out-of-school learning.

Reflecting on Learning

The abilities we propose as characterizing the process of learning to learn are metacognitive in nature. Broadly described, metacognition is the individual's ability to monitor and evaluate his or her progress in a learning or problem-solving task (Gerhard, 1987; Jones, Palincsar, Ogle, and Carr, 1987). It is a degree of awareness of the skills, strategies, and resources needed to perform a task effectively. Implicit in this general definition of metacognition is the assumption that in being aware of one's thinking processes or in actively pursuing strategies that will make thinking explicit, one will be able to see how new information fits with existing information.

As a construct, metacognition has been criticized as being vague and hard to test (Reynolds and Wade, 1986). At the same time, metacognition as it particularly relates to its development in children can be described. Flavell and Wellman (1977) state that the origin of metacognition can be found in children's realization of awareness of the existence of a mental world. They describe a series of studies that suggest that even children as young as four appear to understand that a mental world exists. Wellman's main point (as cited in Reynolds and Wade, 1986) is that when children begin to reflect on these mental terms and concepts, they are demonstrating the beginnings of metacognition. As the concept of mental life grows, so too does reflection and, presumably, metacognitive ability. The research in metacognition establishes the potential for children to become consciously aware of their learning processes. But how do they gain that awareness of internal process? How do they learn to make tacit knowledge available for conscious use?

In many classrooms, student thinking takes place in isolation so internal, if not unconscious, that the student has no sense of its effectiveness until he or she receives a test grade. Whether the result is a success or failure, the student often lacks access to an explanation for the bases of the outcome. By contrast, the skill of reflecting on learning allows the student to move back from the outcome and address the process of thinking that produced it. The benefit to the student in so doing is to externalize what was internal and therefore better understand the reasons for his or her learning outcome.

One technique that promotes reflection is probing the learning-related activities that take place, regardless of their nature. Knowing what you are doing and being able to talk about it gives you the power over it that reproducing actions by rote does not. Like the other abilities discussed, reflection needs to be developed in the learner. Teacher and parent modeling and group interaction are all important means for making the process of thinking external. The following examples illustrate some of the possible strategies.

Strategic Teaching. Strategic teaching involves making mental processes visible. Teachers have long known that young children, having been socialized into the process of school, will usually do what they are directed to do, but that does not necessarily mean that they fully process and understand what they are doing. One lesson from the research in strategic, or explicit, teaching is that students who have a sense of *how* and *why* performing certain strategies or actions works can make conscious use of those strategies and actions in other situations. Learning, then, is strategic in the sense that learners are aware of and control their efforts to use particular skills and strategies (Jones, Palincsar, Ogle, and Carr, 1987).

When strategic teaching is employed (in the classroom and at home) the roles of teacher and student reflect a much more expanded view of learning than simply the retention of facts. This view reinforces the idea of learning as a process that involves organizing an experience so that two key elements are made explicit: (1) assistance to the learner in accessing prior knowledge and (2) provision for integrating or linking new knowledge to prior knowledge. Both elements require active modeling and use of specific teaching and learning strategies. Examples of such strategies are content organizers that identify categories of information, key elements, or questions; activities that compare and contrast new information or skills with prior knowledge or procedures; activities that promote written or oral reflection about the learning experience; and assessment activities that diagnose both the acquisition of content and strategy usage. Each strategy assists both teacher and learner to make explicit some specific aspects of the learning process. In turn, the strategies can be isolated for discussion and reflection in pairs (student and teacher or student and student), in small groups, and with the class as a whole. Bailey (1985) found that among the benefits of this kind of process sharing are improvements in rate and amount of and in attitudes toward learning, as well as greater proactiveness.

Thinking Aloud. A strategy called thinking aloud is a means of reflection on learning processes that is described by Whimbey and Loachhead (1981), among others. Learners are divided into dyads made up of thinker and listener and given such a problem as the following that might be used in an elementary school math class: What day follows the day before yesterday, if two days from now will be Sunday? The thinker says aloud what goes through her mind while attempting to answer the question or solve the problem. The other person listens with full attention, asking questions only to help clarify what the thinker has said. When each dyad has an answer, then the listener is responsible for explaining to the class as a whole what the thinker did and why.

In the debriefing by the teacher, the focus is less on whether the thinkers have obtained the correct answer (Thursday, in the example) than how they arrived at an answer. In the example, students will often be divided among those who start at the beginning and proceed to the end and those who restructure the problem to deal with the "if clause" first as "given" information. Some will have drawn a diagram or other visual representation to assist in their thinking. Some will have skipped information (for example, they look for "the day before yesterday" and so get Wednesday as the answer). Others will have brought in information from outside the problem in the effort to solve it.

The benefits of this exercise affect both teacher and learner. First, the experience gives the teacher access to the information processing approaches and skills of the students.

How does each student approach a problem? How does each see the links between parts? Second, thinking aloud gives the students access to a variety of models for approaching problems or situations. Hearing not only the teacher's problem-solving model but those of other students as well gives the participants a sense that a variety of strategies are open to them, that there are many ways to approach questions. They also come to understand that mistakes can be helpful in providing new information and tactics. Finally, attention is shifted away from "what is correct" to the process of obtaining an answer.

Reflective Journals. Providing students with specific times and places to think about their learning helps to build skill in reflection; asking them to write about it builds communication skills and provides information to the teacher about how learners react to what happens. For example, at St. Leo Elementary School in Milwaukee's inner city, the faculty asks students to make entries in journals twice a day. In the morning they write about something observed on the way to school. At the close of the day, they write down a specific example of something learned that day.

The following excerpts from an eighth grade student's journal show a growing awareness of the interaction of attitude and learning:

> *Tuesday, September 23, 1987*
> Today ended up a better day than I expected. I did have a bad attitude. But somehow it changed without my know-how.

> *Monday, September 29, 1987*
> Today my "experiment" worked really well. I went in with a positive attitude and I had a "capital" day (as Jo says in *Little Women*). I can just imagine what the results would have been if I had had a negative attitude.

Reflecting on Learning at Home. Parents can apply a number of techniques to encourage learning to learn through reflection and to build on the efforts of teachers. Most important is the quality of their questions and dialogue with children. The question "What did you learn at school today?" is often asked (in the same way as "How are you?") as a social ritual that clearly communicates no interest in a serious and complete answer. Even if the question is conveyed as a serious one, children often find it hard to explain *what* they have been doing in school, especially if their teachers do not use explicit explanations of the *how* and *why* of their school activities.

Parents may wish to try simulating a "person in the street" interview, like those that children have seen on television, to provide a context for talking about school activities. They may suggest playing roles: "You be the teacher and I'll be the first grader; show me what school is like." They may also be able to build more straightforward dialogue by using nonverbal cues that indicate genuine interest and openness. Parents can also model reflection by sharing what they themselves learned today, how they went about it, and what they learned about learning or self-as-learner. Attention to communication can be the beginning of a different kind of exchange between parent and child — an exchange that structures a context in which the child can probe her or his experience and thinking, finding links between experiences.

Connection Making

While reflection focuses on the inner processing of the learner and the learner's awareness, the ability of connection making pushes out to make links between and among elements of the experience of the learner. Connection making builds on reflection by expanding the breadth of information and experience the learner can process. As a strategy, it is a clear example of part of the conception of learning-to-learn put forth above: making links between existing knowledge and new information.

Connection making is a skill that has seldom been promoted effectively in the classroom. For the most part, what children learn in school are narrow, limited contexts that are not seen as relating to the real world and do not transfer readily to situations outside of school. Children's experience in school too often fails to set up the expectation that school learning is of value outside that setting. Consequently, by the time we reach adulthood there is often a serious lack of ability to relate formal knowledge with practical experience.

Resnick (1987b) gives an example that illustrates how learning math is more than learning numbers as abstractions, that students need to learn to negotiate transactions using the concrete materials of their world. In the illustration, fourth graders were asked to deal with a situation involving the buying of an ice cream cone. Students were given some coins: a quarter, a dime, and two pennies. The price of the cone was 60 cents. In answering the problem question of how much additional money was needed, most students quickly answered "a quarter." From a "real-world" standpoint, the answer of a quarter is correct: it is the simplest piece of change to round out the 60 cents. From a purely mathematical point of view, of course, the exact answer is 23 cents. Teachers need to bridge the gap between in-school and out-of-school contexts like this one to help students see that both answers are acceptable given clarity of context. The ability to estimate is, of course, critical in the out-of-school context (National Research Council, 1989).

The burden of Resnick's (1987a) argument is that we need to find links between in-school and out-of-school thinking and learning experiences. The following are examples of strategies for fostering connection-making skills.

Connecting Triangle. Many teachers in the Kamehameha (Hawaii) Elementary School use this device to promote critical thinking and encourage the making of connections. Teachers ask students to think of a triangle linking whatever they are learning to two other points: their own experiences and events in the larger, global world.

Class Focus

Larger   Personal
World   Experience

For example, a class in geography can focus on the cultural patterns of the people of a specific country. After reading about the culture of another country, the teacher can help make the idea of culture concrete by asking students to look at the customs in their own families—from the ways in which basic tasks are completed (for example, the preparation of foods) to beliefs made concrete in the celebration of holidays. Students can explore how such factors as climate, neighboring countries, and immigration patterns may affect differences. Extension to the larger world might involve a discussion of how and where people of different cultures have to work together. A relevant question might be: "How do the differences in beliefs and ways of viewing the world affect the prospects for world peace?"

Mapping. Another connection-making strategy that can take various forms also involves making certain content relationships visual: mapping or graphic outlining. This process allows learners to show what they see or to work from a preestablished structure to examine the information in a story or article. It provides support for the kind of reading and thinking skills that parents and teachers begin in preschool and that continue into college and beyond; these skills begin with the learner's ability to answer the question: "What is the main idea?" As many teachers who work with mapping have pointed out, the process requires careful, step-by-step preparation. However, once students have learned the process, they can begin to apply it across subject areas and in a variety of adaptations.

In primary grades, children, through the use of picture cards, can begin to develop the sense of how the parts of a sequence (for example, a story, a series of sizes, a series of numbered objects) fit together. Later, they can begin to design a graphic outline of a story or a series as a way to show its structure. As students begin to write their own stories and essays, mapping can also be used as a kind of design for the direction the writing will take. The following map illustrates the structure of an essay written by a fourth grader to compare and contrast butterflies and flowers.

		delicate
		small
		alive
	Similarities	colorful
While flowers and		live a short time
butterflies are alike		come at a certain time of the year
in many ways, they		are seen in gardens
have important		
differences		flowers stay in one place
		butterflies fly
	Differences	from place to place
		flowers are plants
		butterflies are insects

The map tells the teacher that the child knows a great deal—both about the qualities of flowers and butterflies and about the ways in which comparison and contrast operate. Comparison, for example, is displayed as a set of common qualities, arrayed in a pattern that suggests a fan, while contrast is displayed as "sets" of oppositions. A map that failed to display the difference in organization of similarities and differences would give the teacher/parent important information about the learner. Such a map aids in diagnosing the level of understanding of the processes of comparison and contrast—a building block for the development of higher-order thinking skills.

Very early, children can develop an ability to deal with simple maps as a means to take apart a communication (a story, a poem) in order to look at the separate pieces, to understand how they fit together into a whole and why it is constructed in the way that it is. They can also use prepared maps with pieces left for them to fill in as a way to examine a communication for information that they need.

The connection-making elements of mapping can be used to build more careful reading habits, as a result of guidance in identifying and representing ideas or objects and their relationships; to organize information as an aid in thinking, either from one source or several sources; to organize information for the learner's own writing or speaking preparation; and to enhance retention of knowledge through the processing of the relationships embedded in information. For more information about mapping across content areas, see Jones, Palincsar, Ogle, and Carr (1987).

Connections in Reading: PrEP. Langer and Purcell-Gates (1985) describe a problem-oriented prereading plan (PrEP) that assists students to examine what they already know about a topic to be assigned for reading. In the three stages of the plan, students are first asked to free associate about the topic, telling what comes to their minds when they hear a certain word or see a certain picture. The teacher records the associations on the chalkboard or overhead transparency. After all have had an opportunity to talk, the teacher asks students to reflect on their initial associations (for example, "What made you think of . . . ?"). This assists them to clarify connections they made and to see how theirs resemble or differ from those of their classmates. Finally, the teacher asks them to reflect on new ideas about the topics that emerged for them through the discussion.

Making how they use their prior knowledge explicit to learners assists them, first of all, to be aware that they have knowledge to build on and that it is connected to what they are about to learn. The role of the teacher in connection making is central. Once again, because the individual has "learned to be taught," the teacher can provide the stimulus to go beyond a concern for "correct" answers to a concern for the strategies employed.

Connection Making at Home. Connection-making ability is most appropriate to links between home and school. Parents need to know what is going on in school learning so that they can model ways of extending learning to other contexts, and to make this connection they can develop questions that will assist children to see links between school lessons and what is happening in the home. For example, geographical knowledge can be reinforced and expanded as parents watch the evening news and ask children to make comparisons between the countries being talked about and the children's experience of their own country and knowledge of other countries. Prices in media advertisements can serve as a basis for making impromptu math connections.

Parents can assist children to make contextual distinctions by understanding that children gradually develop an awareness of social knowledge. For example, parents may teach children to say "May I please be excused?" when they want to leave the table. The same child who masters that phrase will learn from experience not to transfer its use to the situation of leaving the sandbox. Parents can point out differences in language usage in different situations and raise children's growing tacit knowledge of context to the level of conscious awareness. As the child begins to recognize differences in social situations, he or she responds appropriately to peers, perhaps with "See you later."

It is thus the explicit awareness of contextual distinctions that relates such activity to learning to learn. Parents can role-play with children the different ways of talking and acting that are appropriate to different situations, thus building the child's awareness of a growing ability to read the environment and to choose language and actions appropriate to each setting.

Problem Solving

Many teaching situations assume the ability of the learner to use strategies for framing problems or action without providing assistance in acquisition of the skills required to use those strategies. Problem-solving ability has to go beyond the mere following of directions. Learners need to be able to draw upon different approaches to problems with some sense of why one approach is likely to be more effective than another.

Sternberg (1985) expresses the concern that, while problem solving is being emphasized more in schools, "we are preparing students to deal with problems that are in many respects unlike those they will face as adults" (p. 194). He goes on to characterize the difference in a number of ways, the most important of which, for our purposes, are that school problems are often decontextualized, well structured, and tidy, leading to one correct answer. In contrast, everyday problems depend on context, are ill formed and messy, and often have no single correct solution.

In the primary grades, problem solving can begin with real-life situations the students face. A teacher at Holy Angels School in Milwaukee's inner city uses problem solving to establish and maintain discipline agreements with first and second graders. Each year, she establishes a pattern with students of "calling time out" to discuss problems as they arise in everyday class activities: "Boys and girls, what is the problem here?" Responses vary, indicating the perceptions of the situation from the students' perspectives: "We can't all talk at once." "Some people can't get their work done because others are talking." "The people in the other rooms will think we're bad kids."

"What can we do about the problem?" the teacher continues. The students, in generating ideas, not only take some ownership in and responsibility for the environment of the classroom, but learn to look at a problem from various angles, generating several solutions before deciding on one to follow as a group. The teacher extends the problem-solving process to projects related to academic work, especially in the science area, where she wants children to first observe and then raise questions. The next step is to devise strategies to find answers to the questions.

Problem solving as an ability that can deal with everyday issues builds on both reflection on learning and connection making, extending these abilities as the learner faces new situations and bringing conscious use of specific strategies to the service of learning in a new situation. But there is an additional element that is essential in preparing learners for everyday problem solving: a sense of being responsible, as an active and aware agent, in addressing problems. The strategies in this section focus on ways that parents and teachers can begin to assist children to be responsible for their own learning and to be active in finding solutions to a range of problems.

Observation. Primary skills related to the ability to solve problems are those that relate to careful observation of the relevant data and to the questioning of the possible meaning of the data. The development of these skills needs to be explicitly addressed by the teacher, for example, to make clear to the learners what they are doing in a science or geography class as they identify all the things that can be described. Observational ability can be linked to the development of mapping skills in the early grades. Teachers can provide a partial graphic map or outline, which the students then use as a tool to record observations from reading or an experiment. Giving them a place to record observations underscores the importance of the activity.

   In both in-school and out-of-school settings, much can be done orally to build this skill. For example, in spaces between activities, children can be guided to focus on elements in the environment, such as the flowers and butterflies discussed earlier, identifying with careful attention the things that they see.

Creating Open-Ended Problems. Teachers can use questions to develop awareness of what the learners already know and to assist them in probing the meaning of what they know in new ways. The PrEP program previously described begins each new lesson with open-ended questions to get at the learners' prior knowledge, bringing it to the forefront. But questions can also push that knowledge out to make new applications.

   At Alverno Campus Elementary School in Milwaukee, one of the teachers asked third grade students after they had read *Jack and the Beanstalk,* "How would this story have been different if it had been told from the perspective of the giant?" She was seeking to enhance the learners' ability to take a situation and probe it from various angles, a skill that helps problem solvers to take new approaches to problems they encounter. She was also assisting the learners to see the effect of context on a situation—it's a different story if Jack is not the main character. Changing perspective assists learners to see the role of context in assessing the information they have available, and in the long run it is central to moral development.

Reciprocal Teaching. Palincsar and Brown have explored a technique that engages teacher and students in four strategies for creating meaning in reading. Called reciprocal teaching, it involves question generating, summarizing, clarifying concepts or vocabulary, and using information in the text to predict what will come next. In the process, teachers and students take turns in the role of leader. This allows the teacher to model the process of connecting old and new information and to assess the learners' ability to do so.

Reciprocal teaching is one method that can help to create the independence needed by the effective problem solver. When the teacher sees the learners using the strategies appropriately and effectively, she can pull back from modeling and directing, giving the learners the active and aware role of directing their own learning process (Jones, Palincsar, Ogle, and Carr, 1987; Palincsar and Brown, 1985).

Problem Solving at Home. Parents can draw upon many of these methods to develop or reinforce the child's use of strategies. Explicit discussions of context, for example, will assist the child to transfer awareness of the impact of perspective on real-life problems. Observation can be developed in games played while traveling in the car—looking for specific items on a "bingo" card (such games are available), reciting the alphabet as the letters are found in road signs or license plates, and so on. Parents can follow the reading of stories with open-ended questions about the characters: What are they likely to do after the story ends? The gathering of data can be modeled as parents involve children in solving day-to-day problems. For example, Sara is due at a birthday party at 4 P.M.; her mother is scheduled to attend a meeting at 3:30 P.M.; Sara is asked, "How can we solve this problem?"

When parents and children face real-life issues or problems, the same principles described for reciprocal teaching can be employed. For example, the child can be asked to lead a discussion about raising his or her weekly allowance, about whom to invite to a party when choices must be made, or about where to go on a family vacation. The same process of creating meaning in reading (reciprocal teaching) can be adapted to create a format for examining problems and making decisions within the family.

Conclusion

Implementing the concept of learning to learn as a top priority of preschool and elementary education requires some rethinking of the fundamental assumptions that direct schools, and, hence, direct the learning-related interactions of teachers, parents, and children. In its simplest form, this rethinking has to do with schools letting go of the responsibility for ensuring that students acquire a vast storehouse of knowledge that will last over a lifetime. Instead, children, at the youngest ages, need to acquire abilities to meet each situation as it presents itself and make judgments about what needs to be done within the structure of specified content.

This call for rethinking is not a denial of the importance of content but a call for making a legitimate place for fostering the acquisition of process-oriented skills along with the content, beginning at an early age. Focusing on knowledge acquisition almost exclusively as the goal of schooling has done little to improve the scholastic performance of students or to ensure their success in the workplace. A better approach would be through a blending of knowledge acquisition and practical strategies for learning to learn. Reflection, connection making, and problem solving are generalized abilities that show promise in assisting learners to move beyond low-level skills of recall and comprehension and to develop self-monitoring skills that transfer across contexts.

Note: We wish to extend our appreciation to schools that participated in Alverno College's 1985–1987 Fund for the Improvement of Post-Secondary Education (FIPSE) sponsored project,
"Partnerships in Teaching Critical Thinking" — St. Leo Elementary and Alverno Campus Elementary in Milwaukee and the
Kamehameha School in Hawaii — as well as to those instructors
who serve as cooperating teachers for Alverno College students
at Holy Angels School in Milwaukee.

References

Bailey, G. D. "Sharing Process with Students: Can It Make a
   Difference?" *Kappa Delta Pi Record,* Spring 1985, 81–85.

Flavell, J. H., and Wellman, H. M. "Metamemory." In R. V. Kail,
   Jr. and J. W. Hagen (eds.), *Perspectives on the Development of
   Memory and Cognition.* Hillsdale, N.J.: Erlbaum, 1977.

Fulwiler, T. "Writing and Learning in Grade 3." In T. Fulwiler
   (ed.), *The Journal Book.* Portsmouth, N.H.: Boynton/Cook,
   1987.

Gerhard, C. "What Every Educator Should Know About Reading
   Comprehension: Helping Students to Be Successful Beyond
   the Early Grades." *Research into Practice Digest #2,* 1987 (1),
   1–36.

Jones, B. F., Palincsar, A. S., Ogle, D. S., and Carr, E. G. *Strategic
   Teaching and Learning: Cognitive Instruction in the Content Areas.*
   Alexandria, Va.: Association for Curriculum Development,
   1987.

Langer, J. A., and Purcell-Gates, V. "Knowledge and Comprehension: Helping Students Use What They Know." In T. L. Harris
   and E. J. Cooper (eds.), *Reading, Thinking, and Concept Development: Strategies for the Classroom.* New York: College Entrance
   Examination Board, 1985.

National Research Council. *Everybody Counts: A Report to the
   Nation on the Future of Mathematics Education.* Washington, D.C.:
   National Academy Press, 1989.

Palincsar, A. S., and Brown, A. L. "Reciprocal Teaching: Activities to Promote 'Reading With Your Mind.'" In T. L. Harris
   and E. J. Cooper (eds.), *Reading, Thinking, and Concept Develop-*

ment: Strategies for the Classroom. New York: College Entrance Examination Board, 1985.

Resnick, L. B. "Learning in School and Out." *Educational Researchers,* 1987a, *16* (9), 13–20.

Resnick, L. B. *Education and Learning to Think.* Washington, D.C.: National Research Council, 1987b.

Resnick, L. B., and Klopfer, L. E. *Toward the Thinking Curriculum: Current Cognitive Research. Association for Supervision and Curriculum Development Yearbook.* Washington, D.C.: Association for Supervision and Curriculum Development, 1989.

Reynolds, R. E., and Wade, S. E. "Thinking About Thinking About Thinking: Reflections on Metacognition." *Harvard Educational Review,* 1986, *56* (3), 307–317.

Roehler, L. R., and Duffy, G. G. "Direct Explanation of Comprehension Processes." In G. G. Duffy, L. R. Roehler, and J. Mason (eds.), *Comprehension Instruction: Perspectives and Suggestions.* New York: Longman, 1984.

Sternberg, R. J. "Teaching Critical Thinking, Part I: Are We Making Critical Mistakes?" *Phi Delta Kappan,* 1985, *67,* 194–198.

Whimbey, A., and Loachhead, H. *Problem Solving and Comprehension.* Philadelphia: Franklin Institute Press, 1981.

Chapter 8

A "Thinking Curriculum"
for Secondary Schools

Frank P. Bazeli

Teachers in secondary schools work very hard at teaching their students the content and structure of their fields of knowledge. In the process, some students acquire or improve self-management capabilities that make them more effective lifelong learners, but for the most part these welcome successes are incidental outcomes of the curriculum. This chapter will describe some ways of intentionally improving the learning capabilities of secondary students, within the context of current public school reform movements.

One movement, the improvement of learning capabilities and thinking skills through a variety of training programs, apparently has had little impact on what goes on in public school classrooms, despite notably successful experimental results. A key reason is that the learning-to-learn movement has come in direct conflict with a much stronger and more general school reform movement. Galvanized by reductions in the competitive position of the United States in world economics, business groups and vocal supporters in the federal government have accused the schools of incompetence and the students of mediocrity. These accusations have been accompanied by public demands for accountability by the teaching force and for

demonstrated increases in measured student academic achievement (National Commission on Excellence in Education, 1983).

Responding to these demands, most state legislatures
have mandated wide-ranging public school curricular reforms
and new teacher certification requirements. Since 1983 the
states have generated more regulations on education than in the
previous twenty years (Timar and Kirp, 1989). In 1986, William
Chance reported that more than 275 task forces on education
had been formed by various groups in the 1980s, resulting in
increased high school graduation requirements in 43 states,
statewide student assessment programs in 37 states, teacher
competency tests in 29 states, and changes in teacher certification requirements in 28 states (Orlich, 1989). The central goal of
this reform movement is, as Buccino (1988) puts it, frankly
utilitarian: the United States must enhance the knowledge and
skills of its work force in order to win the international competition in high technology. The thinking goes that this pragmatic
goal can be attained by forcing the schools to achieve academic
excellence, which is defined in terms of increased scores on
standardized achievement tests (Corrigan, 1988; Shepard,
1989). Especially important are scores in science and math.
Unfortunately, the esthetic domain is less important in the
reform movement, according to Ducharme (1988). He contends
that such a narrow definition of excellence may lead to the loss
of the things that count most, for example, a sense of what is
beautiful. Aside from that line of protest, the point of conflict
between the movement to promote learning capabilities in
schools and what is being called the measured curriculum lies in
the nature of the consequences of this test-driven educational
system.

The Measured Curriculum

The ubiquitous measured curriculum has become all too familiar to American educators over the past generation. Seated for
the most part in behaviorist educational psychology, but also in
forms of cognitive psychology, curriculum and instructional
design have been based on tight definitions of performance

objectives and lock-step sequencing of content and skill acquisition. Principles of direct instruction, mastery learning, and behavior modification primarily with the utilization of extrinsic reinforcers to induce attainment of the performance objectives have been featured. In fact, these programs have often shown excellent results with some student populations in terms of observable and measurable achievements by individual students in content, skills, and attitude displays on criterion-referenced tests (Joyce and Weil, 1986, pp. 307–398). However, two concerns arise. First, rather than measuring individual student achievement on criterion-referenced tests, most schools have had to utilize standardized, norm-referenced, paper-and-pencil tests for reporting purposes. Second, Resnick (1989) and others contend that acquiring content and skills without the mental elaboration and self-regulation needed to make them generative—that is, usable for interpreting new situations and solving problems—is self-defeating.

Shepard (1989) makes the case against the way standardized achievement tests are used to evaluate the academic excellence of schools and students. She points out a number of problems. One problem is that large-scale testing programs are limited by political and practical problems in their ability to measure important learning outcomes. The content of the tests is negotiated by test makers to match that found in standard textbooks and the content choices of curriculum experts. This process of consensus building promotes market appeal but severely narrows the breadth of the subject matter covered on the tests. The effect is that the tests deal with only that fraction of the field of study covered by nearly all the teachers and schools. The vast amount of specialized material dealt with in the classrooms of innovative teachers is not tested. Test construction is also limited by focus on basic skills. Tests, especially those meant for minimum competency testing for promotion purposes, for the most part measure the lower levels of instructional objectives. Further, the multiple choice format of most tests limits the opportunity for students to demonstrate their ability to organize relevant information, present arguments, and explain their choices.

As limited as these tests are, their convenience as quick measures for public consumption (with all that entails in terms of political and professional consequences) forces many teaching faculties to "teach to the test." Curriculum becomes test driven rather than oriented to important educational goals. This phenomenon, which Madaus (cited in Brant, 1989) calls "high-stakes testing," corrupts both the curriculum and the test results. For example, Darling-Hammond and Wise (1985) found that untested parts of the curriculum were sacrificed so that teachers could teach the test content. They also found that teachers taught the precise content of the tests, not the controlling generalizations and principles. Rather than teaching practical application, teachers taught the content in multiple choice format (Shepard, 1989). This approach emphasizes rote study of content and drill and practice on decontextualized skills. Studied this way there is little chance for integrated learning to occur.

Effects on Teachers. For the teachers, the test-driven measured curriculum is particularly destructive. Caught up in a frantic race to cover the prescribed curriculum, often within spider webs of state or locally mandated performance objectives, with the threat of end-of-year high-stakes standardized tests looming, teachers are depowered and deprofessionalized. What McNeil (1988) calls "deskilling" occurs. Many teachers give up the exercise of their own expertise and professional judgment and sink into routine drills and expository instruction. Darling-Hammond (1988) cites an extreme case in which one large urban school district supplies teachers with a standardized curriculum plan that details precisely the content in each subject in each grade (from preschool through high school), with a pacing schedule, lesson plans for each day, prescribed grading standards, and prescribed assignments with weighted grading directions. Student promotion is determined by standardized tests. In this case there is little use for professional knowledge, collegial consulting, or planning and decision making. These curriculum policies operate at the same time the various states have been raising teacher certification requirements. Darling-

Hammond (1988) refers to this phenomenon as apparent schizophrenia.

Teacher Empowerment. These circumstances have given rise to a movement for teacher empowerment promoted especially by professional teacher associations (Glickman, 1989). The aim is to restructure the schools from the bottom up. Led by local districts and utilizing the expertise of teachers, the movement is meant to solve educational problems in ways that take local conditions into account. Standardized practices mandated by the state are viewed as too rigid and unworkable. In this plan, teachers are the primary decision makers and share responsibility for school operation with the administration. One such experiment, called the Home Base Guidance Program, is being carried out in Rochester, New York. The goal of the project is to empower teachers to create schools where students think. A new set of relationships was agreed to in negotiations for the Rochester teachers' contract in 1985. Details of the changes have been developed through collaborative efforts between the teachers and the administrative staff. Curriculum changes toward promoting critical thinking and collaborative learning are being supported by establishing a wide variety of magnet schools and programs. A career ladder system for teachers has been fashioned, which includes peer assistance and review for new teachers and "lead teachers" who mentor and carry out staff development programs. Increased salaries and a condensed salary schedule are incentives for working a longer school year and participating in much greater involvement with students by teachers.

Specifically, the Home Base Guidance Program assigns approximately twenty students to each middle school and high school teacher for personal attention and guidance. Teachers are case managers for their twenty students. They are responsible for home contacts, mentoring, affective guidance, and other forms of support. Through a process of shared governance, the stakeholders (teachers, administrators, parents, and students) are represented on planning teams that include a majority of teachers. Planning teams determine budgets, instructional goals, environmental conditions and culture, and often the processes for filling staff vacancies (Urbanski, 1988). Professional empowerment at the local levels would seem to offer the greatest hope for replacing the centralized test-driven, measured curriculum with something better.

The Thinking Curriculum

The 1989 *Yearbook of the Association for Supervision and Curriculum Development,* edited by Lauren Resnick and Leopold Klopfer, is entitled *Toward the Thinking Curriculum: Current Cognitive Research.* Resnick and Klopfer clearly have sought to promote a school curriculum based on theories of learning that focus on the internal management processes of the learner. The various authors explore ways that the traditional subject matter of the schools can be taught to help students develop mental elaborations and self-regulation strategies that increase their learning capabilities. In an overview of the yearbook, Resnick and Klopfer propose a number of organizing themes for such a curriculum.

1. *The centrality of knowledge.* The need for organizing schemas that can be used to interpret and elaborate new information; the importance of building up a scaffolding of the major concepts and generalizations in a field in order to increase capabilities for understanding conditions, situations, and problems encountered.
2. *Joining skills and content.* The use of standard school subject matter as the context for reasoning and problem solving rather than rote learning of content or separate study of generic thinking skills; active subject-specific reflection and practical problem solving.
3. *Joining cognition and motivation.* Promoting the willingness of learners to use what they have learned in problem situations; overcoming anxiety and accepting the challenge of solving a problem, which is part of learning to learn, especially for those who have been trained to be helpless.
4. *Shaping dispositions for thinking.* The role of social commu-

nities — the use of collaborative learning and problem solving in developing thinking capabilities. Group efforts to solve problems have long been known to promote solutions to problems not likely to have been achieved by any single member. Participation in group problem solving also promotes disposition toward critical thinking.

5. *Cognitive apprenticeship.* A new challenge — the process of learning to learn in a field of study by solving real problems of increasing complexity by novices within the context of ongoing participation in intellectual activity led by those who are more knowledgeable.

The authors of each chapter carry at least some of these themes into their treatment of how to teach learning strategies in reading, mathematics, writing, and science. (Other chapters deal with more theoretical and technical topics.) The work represents a major effort to loosen the hold of the measured curriculum on the public schools; it also demonstrates that two movements can be combined in order to achieve real academic excellence.

Learning How to Learn

Increasing learning capabilities means introducing new strategies and improving the efficiency of present strategies that students use when learning. Secondary teachers are (or ought to be) heavily involved in helping students to grow in the complexity of their schemas of knowledge, their social values, their emotional maturity, and their physical well-being. The goal is to help students become competent adults by developing their capabilities to continue to grow.

How can secondary school teachers contribute to this goal? From the myriad of possibilities for intervention I will focus on the following applications: the establishment of a classroom climate that promotes dispositions for learning; the use of a repertoire of teaching models that not only promotes effective learning but also encourages reflection on learning strategies; and the use of cooperative learning processes and activities that assist one in knowing when and how to use what has been learned, especially in out-of-school situations.

Classroom Climate

What motivates students to learn? Jere Brophy (1988) cites Feather's expectancy x value theory as a guide. According to this theory people will expend effort on a task to the degree (1) to which they expect to be able to perform the task successfully if they apply themselves and (2) to which they value participation in the task itself or the benefits or rewards that successful task completion will bring. If one or the other of these components is missing, they will expend little or no effort. None of us will waste time trying to learn something we believe we cannot learn, nor will we learn something that has no value to us in learning. Our motivation is raised or lowered as these factors are raised and lowered in our perception. With this theory in mind, teachers first need to establish a supportive classroom climate in which students are asked to learn content, skills, and attitudes that are clearly valuable and in which students see evidence that, with effort, they will be successful.

How do teachers establish such a classroom climate? A key component is to work on group cohesion — students need to feel included in the classroom group. The process involves first identifying each student, by recognition and territory, as a legitimate member of the group. Learning the names of students and something about them as quickly as possible fixes initial class membership. If this is followed up by activities that promote positive recognition among class members, such as self-introductions, interviews, and name recognition tests, membership will be firmed up. Territory is also important; within the classroom students need a place recognized as theirs or that of their work. Probably all of us have had the experience of attending class or meetings in the same room over a period of time. In the first session we stake out a favorite spot at the front of the room, or near the door, or in one corner with our back to the wall. By the second session that spot is ours; if we enter the room and find someone else occupying our territory we experience a definite emotional reaction to our loss. Establishing group ownership of a room is also important to a sense of mutual belonging. Following these initial procedures, occasional meetings concerning group maintenance, efficient predictable organizational procedures, and some distinctive rituals create a class culture that is cohesive and attractive.

Attribution research — the study of student perceptions of the causes of their successes and failures as learners — has focused on how students analyze the relationships among ability, effort, and achievement (Wittrock, 1986). The research suggests that success is not enough to increase learning and achievement if the students attribute success to easy tasks, luck, ability, or other factors (including excellent teaching) that are outside of their control. Wittrock suggests that this might be one explanation for the uneven results of behavior modification programs that provide only success experiences for "learned helplessness students" (in a 1975 study by Dweck). Persistence and motivation increase only when students perceive that success is brought about to a substantial degree by their own efforts in challenging learning tasks (Wang and Stiles, 1976). Teachers need to set learning tasks for individuals and groups that are challenging but within the abilities of the students to achieve. Goals are most likely to promote further disposition for learning if they are concrete and limited with helpful feedback from both teacher and peers concerning ways to improve.

Within the context of a supportive classroom climate, the content of the course needs to be perceived by students as being of value. There is nothing so defeating as being in a class where the purpose, nature, and practical usefulness of the content are vague at best. We have all gone through our personal purgatories in order to complete a long-term educational program. Often we suffer without knowing why — these experiences seem to be a rite of passage rather than the acquisition of valuable knowledge. To overcome this problem, instructional objectives should be related to the real world. Abstract principles need to be made personal, that is, constantly related to the students' own lives or their future goals. They also need to take on concrete forms. Students need to know where they might encounter and recognize these principles in their daily activities. For example, in a science class the study of Ohm's law can be dealt with in abstract form ($E = I \times R$) or students can talk about the last time the lights went out at home. The interaction of a supportive classroom group led by a teacher who encourages effort, experimentation, and some risk taking is essential for teaching secondary students how to learn.

One program with classroom characteristics similar to those proposed here is the Project for Enhancing Effective Learning (PEEL), begun in 1985 at Laverton High School, Victoria, Australia. It is discussed in Chapter Fifteen. In weekly meetings individual teachers in the project have worked out activities and teaching approaches that promote metacognition in their content areas. Hynes (1987), who teaches PEEL project history and geography at Laverton High School, describes an experiment. He wrote a series of nonsensical statements about rainfall and planting on the chalkboard and had the students copy them. When he asked if they had any questions, one student asked for the meaning of a term and a second questioned whether soil could evaporate as suggested in the paragraphs written on the board. This led to strategies requiring students to question and to interact with the instructor. In another session, Hynes presented a brief introduction to the settlement of New South Wales followed by a relevant videotaped presentation. Students were then asked to write whatever questions they could develop about the content of the videotape. Following discussion of fact and questions that start with "what if. . .?" students generated additional questions to the point where they began to see that the topic represented a complex set of interrelationships among the convict system, economic depression, and empire building. After being categorized, the questions generated served as a research agenda for individual and group investigation. This sort of activity contains the ingredients for successful learning and for learning to learn. The ownership by the students of the research questions they generate can be highly motivational. The group interaction in this approach develops cohesion and support for investigative learning.

Reflective Teaching Models

Bruce Joyce has taken the lead for over twenty years in the conceptualization of models of teaching. Rather than adhere to a single family of methods, derived from a favored psychology or philosophy of learning and instruction, Joyce points out that effective methods for teaching a variety of learning tasks can and do come from many sources. An effective teacher thus builds a wide repertoire of teaching models for use in improving students' learning capabilities. What turns some of these models into powerful aids are the nurturance activities of the teacher in promoting student reflection on the cognitive strategies they exercised as they participated in the instructional session (Joyce and Weil, 1986; Joyce, Showers, and Rolheiser-Bennett, 1987). In this section several examples of reflective teaching models will be presented.

Typologies and concepts (string instruments, culture, democracy, story plot, insects, inert gases) are the building blocks of structures of knowledge, forming the scaffolding that classifies the content in a field. Practitioners and experts acquire new learning in their fields, solve problems, and interpret situations through manipulations involving these hierarchies and matrices. The richer and more complex the elaborations the more rapid and creative the responses. Teachers tend to teach concepts through expository methods—that is, they define the concept, outline its attributes or characteristics, provide one or two examples, and possibly test for understanding with a quick oral question or two. While this approach has the advantage of speed, which is attractive to teachers who want to cover a large amount of content quickly, it has at least four problems. First, the chances are very good that a number of students will achieve only marginal, if any, understanding of the concept. Second, teachers will have no way of knowing the extent to which students have learned the concept until a later, more crucial, time. Third, this process generally results in the acquisition of inert knowledge that is difficult to use. Fourth, students have not learned anything about how to conceptualize on their own.

Concept Attainment Model. Joyce and Weil (1986) have developed a model of teaching based on the work of Bruner, Goodnow, and Austin. Called concept attainment, it can be used in most subject areas to promote active student learning of concepts. The model, with the nurturance of the teacher, also promotes student learning about how to conceptualize. Concept attainment has the following syntax:

Phase I   *Presentation of Data and Identification of Concept*

The teacher presents labeled examples of the concept to a group of students. These may be real or symbolic representations, such as objects, artifacts, pictures, descriptive phrases, designs, and so forth. Positive and negative examples may be presented alternately.

The students compare attributes in the examples, generating and testing hypotheses about the characteristics of the concept. Essential and non-essential attributes are differentiated by processes of elimination and group discussion.

When satisfied, the students present a consensus definition of the concept according to its essential attributes.

Phase II   *Testing Attainment of the Concept*

The students examine additional unlabeled items and decide whether or not each represents an example of the concept.

The teacher confirms their hypothesis, names the concept, and restates the definition.

Students may attempt to provide additional examples.

Phase III *Analysis of Thinking Strategies*

> The students describe their thinking strategies as they observe each new example.
>
> The teacher and students discuss the role of hypothesizing and testing.
>
> The teacher and students consider what can be learned about conceptualizing strategies in this area of content.

The following example of the concept attainment model illustrates its potential effectiveness. In a middle school English classroom the teacher, Jim Becker, introduces an activity by telling his class that he is going to show them a series of words. The students, grouped in triads, examine each word. Some will be "yes" examples of a concept he has in mind; others will be "no" examples. Each team tries to figure out why. As the activity goes on, Mr. Becker presents the following examples by showing the words written on cards and then rewriting them on the chalkboard. After he introduces each item, students discuss and venture guesses about the relationships among the meanings of the words.

Yes	No
sentiment	refuge
restless	commerce
irregular	

Following the presentation of the yes word *irregular* the students hypothesize that the yes words are emotional words. Following some discussion the next examples are presented.

Yes	No
consumer	standard
paraphrase	cliché
	tendon

As soon as the yes word *consumer* appears, several voices pipe up: "Oh! Oh! It's not emotions. Let's look for something else."

A class member suggests: "Rather than the meaning of the word, maybe we should be looking at the construction." "Yes," answers Mr. Becker. With a shift of focus the students quickly identify the prefixes and suffixes on the root words of the yes examples. Test words that follow include

interview   apostrophe

Following the review by the teacher, an intense general discussion ensues concerning the characteristics of prefixes and suffixes, their place in English composition, and the strategies that have paid off in identifying the concept.

Guided Inductive Model. Interactions within a body of knowledge tend to occur in patterns practitioners can identify and use to predict cause and effect and to solve problems. These generalizations are called relationships, equations, principles, or rules. They appear in every field of knowledge from the rules governing the writing of various forms of poetry to the principles for mixing colors in art. Often principles are quite abstract, making them difficult to learn by those who are new to a field or whose general intellectual development has not yet gone beyond the concrete operational level. To circumvent the problems often encountered in the deductive presentation of an abstract rule, generalization, or principle, the guided inductive model is often used. It has the additional benefit of lending its syntax to reflection and to the improvement of cognitive processes.

Orlich (1980) identifies the following characteristics of the model:

1. The thought processes require that the learners progress from specific observations to inferences or generalizations. The objective is to learn (or reinforce) appropriate processes for examining events or objects.
2. The teacher controls the elements—the events, data, materials, or objectives—and thus acts as the class leader.
3. The student reacts to the specifics of the lesson—the events, data, materials, or objects—and attempts to structure a

meaningful pattern based on his or her observations and on those of others in the class.

4. The classroom is considered a learning laboratory.
5. There is usually a fixed number of generalizations that will be elicited from the learners.
6. The teacher encourages each student to communicate his or her generalizations to the class so that the others may benefit from individual perceptions (p. 291).

The syntax of the model includes the following steps:

1. The teacher presents a collection of objects, events, or work products, such as entries in a bookkeeper's journal or video-tapes of people greeting each other at an airport.
2. The teacher directs the students to make a series of specified observations for each item presented.
3. The students and the teacher record observations onto tables or charts.
4. The students examine the data to discover a pattern.
5. The pattern is identified and restated in terms of a formula, principle, equation, or generalization.
6. The generalization is tested on more examples.
7. The students and the teacher discuss the nature of the generalization, its utility in understanding a culture, in explaining phenomena, in constructing an organization, or in planning a strategy.
8. The students and the teacher review the process, discussing ways to use inductive inquiry for discovering other patterns in the field as well as in everyday experiences.

The following illustration of the model should be especially helpful because of the instructional use made by the teacher of a student error. Denise Carlson is preparing a class session in geometry on relationships found in polyhedra (solids bounded by polygons). She lays out a number of polyhedra she has cut out of construction paper and fashioned into their three-dimensional forms. She also draws an empty table design, which will contain data collected by the students, on the chalkboard.

Following some preliminary classroom work, Ms. Carlson calls attention to the display of objects. She reminds the class of their introduction to polyhedra the previous day. She reminds them that polyhedra are solids with polygons for faces. The students review the concepts of various kinds of polyhedra, such as pyramids. After this review of prerequisite knowledge, Ms. Carlson tells the students that today they are going to study some relationships found in all polyhedra. After dividing the class into several groups, she then identifies and counts the faces, vertices, and edges of one of the polyhedra. Following this demonstration she distributes the polyhedra among the groups and asks them to count, as she has done, the number of faces, vertices, and edges found on each. She now has to review the process for Dennis, who asks to see her demonstrated observations again. As the groups report their observations, Ms. Carlson records the data on the table drawn on the chalkboard, hesitating briefly only to allow Dennis to report his observations for the "pup tent" his group has selected (the triangular prism). Upon completion of the data collection, Ms. Carlson asks the class to examine the table for any patterns that might occur in the data. As a cue she suggests that the groups let F stand for faces, V stand for vertices, and E stand for edges.

She puts a question to the students: If you were to take one set of data, could you write an equation setting off the relationship between the components? Wendy's group suggests that if you add the faces and vertices together you will have two less than the number of edges. Ms. Carlson makes another column for F and V and checks the table to see if the theory of Wendy's group holds. All but the "pup tent" (the triangular prism) data match the pattern of $F + V - 2 = E$. (See Table 8.1.) Dennis's group is coached to recheck the observation for the triangular prism, and they discover an error in the count of the number of edges, which should be nine rather than seven. With the pattern holding, Dennis asks how Wendy's group found the pattern, which triggers a discussion about the attempts made to look for some sort of regularity in sets of data by adding, subtracting, multiplying, and dividing numbers between and within the data sets. Ms. Carlson talks about the idea of playing with spatial

Table 8.1 Wendy's Theory: Faces + Vertices − 2 = Number of Edges in Polyhedra.

	Faces	Vertices	F + V − 2	Edges
Square pyramid	5	5	10	8
Pentagonal pyramid	6	6	12	10
Octahedron	8	6	14	12
Triangular prism	5	6	11 (X)	7 (9)
Tetrahedron	4	6	10	8
Pentagonal prism	7	10	17	15
Dodecahedron	12	20	32	30

relations in geometry. This leads to a discussion of learning strategies for making inductive observations and conducting searches for patterns that can be generalized to everyday life. The session closes with a discussion of the need for formal proof to verify the theory of Wendy's group.

Synectics. Throughout history, prophets, teachers, and orators have used metaphorical images and parables to capture the essence of a complex idea. Probably one of the most powerful learning strategies one can develop is the use of metaphors to gain new perspectives on old problems. American secondary schools offer relatively few opportunities to learn divergent thinking processes and to enhance creativity. One well-tested method is the synectics model developed by William Gordon, who has been working for well over thirty years on ways to help ordinary persons think divergently (Gordon, 1972).

There are two general approaches that fall under Gordon's model. The first approach has to do with learning about something that is complex and abstract. The key, according to Gordon, is to *make the strange familiar.* In many instances the organization and operation of a complex system is similar to that of some familiar, concrete, seen-every-day process that can be used as a metaphor for learning about the abstraction. For example, Gordon cites the work of William Harvey, who in the sixteenth century compared the action of the heart with that of a pump. Harvey's metaphor has served to teach blood circulation to countless numbers of medical students; however, Harvey himself had a difficult time overriding his previously held metaphor of sea tides to explain blood circulation. A current student of medicine, Gordon suggests, might think of the heart as a water pump for a swimming pool and then connect lungs and liver as filters to clean the blood. Another example of a concrete and intriguing way to present a lesson is seen in the study of the structure and function of the human eye, using a camera as the metaphor, breaking down its components, and comparing them to parts of the eye.

The second approach used by Gordon is intended to *make the familiar strange,* in order to develop new perspectives and promote divergent thinking. In this case the "familiar" are the stereotyped explanations and procedures that have outlasted usefulness. This is done by the sequenced use of analogies and compressed conflict that take participants farther and farther away from their original perspectives.

The syntax of the model follows these steps:

Phase I   *Description of Present Condition*

The teacher introduces a known topic, possibly a problem, issue, organization, work product, or relationship. The students are asked to give their current perspectives on the topic — how they see it now (for example, the state tax system or the role of elderly persons in our society).

Phase II   *Direct Analogy*

The teacher asks the students to suggest direct analogies from other contexts, for example, mechanical objects, plants, animals, other organizations that have similar characteristics. After a number of suggestions have been made, the most interesting one is selected for further study — for example, antique car for an elderly person.

Phase III *Personal Analogy*

> The teacher asks the students to "become" the direct analogy and to tell how they feel in their situation. The students suggest feelings and attitudes that may range from very positive to very negative. The teacher persists in encouraging these expressions until a good number are available.

Phase IV *Compressed Conflict*

> After discussion of the personal analogies, two that are in the most intriguing conflict are paired. Pasteur's "safe attack" and Shakespeare's "captive-victor" are well-known examples. For example, "cherished neglect" might be generated for the antique car analogy.

Phase V *Direct Analogy*

> The process of direct analogy, personal analogy, and compressed conflict is repeated, starting from the compressed conflict identified in the first cycle.

Phase VI *Reexamination of the Original Task*

> The teacher has the students return to the original topic to use the last set of analogies and compressed conflicts to bring new perspectives to the task. In the case of the elderly, for example, the task is to propose new roles for them as their numbers increase (Joyce and Weil, 1986).

Creative production and divergent thinking processes can be powerfully encouraged through these engrossing group efforts. In addition, as Joyce and Weil point out, the shared experience usually fosters good interpersonal relationships and a high level of participation and cohesion. Even the most timid are eventually caught up in a well-run process; however, the process can be threatening to insecure or rigid teachers since there is little they can do to predict outcomes. Sometimes the effort fails, but the potentially positive effects on learning to learn are worth the risk.

This illustration of a synectics lesson is a good example of the results that may be obtained through use of the model. Students in Alice Harris's literature class are reading Dickens's *Great Expectations.* In the past several days they have become acquainted with the main characters. As an exercise in character analysis, Ms. Harris asks the class to select one of the main characters for closer study. The class chooses Estella. When asked to choose words that describe Estella, class members list "beautiful," "man-hating," "elegant," "haughty," "adopted," and "only child."

Ms. Harris then asks: "What machines or mechanical things have similar characteristics?" As direct analogies the following list is volunteered: sports car (sleek, beautiful), missile (flashy, dangerous), ferris wheel (beautiful, haughty, standout, dangerous). The ferris wheel analogy is selected as the most interesting analogy, so Ms. Harris asks: "How would you feel if you were a ferris wheel?" As a personal analogy, the students mention the words bored, alone, powerful, disdainful, trapped, nauseous, impressive, and pampered.

Ms. Harris now says: "Look for opposites between these words" (compressed conflict). "Trapped-powerful" is selected. Ms. Harris asks: "What kind of animal might exemplify trapped power?" (second direct analogy). The students suggest watchdog, tiger in a cage, whale, Budweiser Clydesdales, King Kong, and circus elephant. When Ms. Harris questions: "Which has the most trapped-powerful feeling?" The class choice is "tiger in the cage." Ms. Harris says: "Visualize this tiger. What characteristics and states are there?" (second personal analogy). The responses are hate, pacing, restlessness, rage, tension, resentfulness, significance, fearfulness, embarrassment, and scheming.

As Ms. Harris begins the reexamination process, she offers these guidelines. "Think about Estella and the tiger in the cage. Compare their feelings and attitudes. Use the ideas you generate in writing a character analysis of Estella as she might be feeling in a given incident or situation you find in the book. For example, what is going on inside Estella at the party? How do you think she feels living in an old house with a woman who's been wearing a wedding gown for forty years and with all the clocks stopped at 9:20? We'll discuss your analyses on Friday."

Final suggestions from class members: "Ms. Haversham is in deep trouble." "That woman is living with a time bomb." "There's going to be a mess." "Maybe not—maybe she'll just leave or kill herself."

Generative Knowledge

All of us at one time or another have encountered problems that we could not solve only to have someone else solve them by using methods and information we also knew. Somehow it had not occurred to us to try those strategies or to tap that particular body of knowledge. This is an example of what researchers such as Anderson (1987) and Lesgold (1988) mean what they talk about the inability of learners to transfer declarative knowledge into procedural or use-oriented knowledge. Much of what we have learned remains inert and can be recalled only in the context in which it was learned. It is not enough to learn something—we also need to learn when to use it and for what purposes. This kind of outcome is called conditionalized learning (Simon, 1980) or generative knowledge (Wittrock, 1985).

How can teachers promote generative knowledge? What seems to work best are instructional designs that organize courses around the key generalizations and paradigms of a field of study and provide problem-centered and issue-centered engagement with content. In these designs students have many opportunities to elaborate their understanding of the content by building mental representations of the hierarchies and matrices of knowledge under study. There tend to be a wide variety of teaching methods involved in order to get at many types of instructional objectives, but active student learning is a key element, students as individuals and as members of cooperative learning groups. Active learning implies being engaged in activities that are exercises in self-regulated cognitive strategies. Some of these are relating information to oneself, interpreting, finding analogies and metaphors, observing and data collecting, inferring, predicting, imagining, and using such elaboration methods as laying successive overlays of new information over skeleton frameworks and other graphic representations.

As instruction proceeds students assimilate the structure of the field, using the paradigms as anchors and scaffolding. New content and skills are related to the mental representations being built up. The scaffolding is modified frequently as new information is encountered that requires modifications of the structure. In order to transfer these content structures into procedural schemata, students need to confront case studies and simulated or real problems that are complex enough to require the exercise of combinations of problem-solving strategies and a variety of content. Confronting complex problems tests and expands the students' procedural schemas and forces them to reflect on the strategies they are using to deal with the problem.

Bransford and Vye (1989) cite research that shows that solitary student practice on problems may not result in increases in generative knowledge, and they therefore recommend coached practice. Coaches can cue students to change approaches before they reach discouragement after encountering a series of dead ends. Coaches may help students reflect on their strategies by thinking out loud their attempts at solving novel problems. Coaches can assess and correct student misconceptions and inaccuracies about the precepts and content involved in the problem. As students struggle with problems, coaches can offer new strategies to apply or new ways to think about the problems or the various situations in which these problems are found. Finally, coaches can select problems and exercises that lead toward achievement of meaningful instructional goals.

Issue-centered and problem-centered courses became popular in the 1960s with the development of materials by scholars to teach students to think like scientists. In these courses students confront puzzling phenomena or real science problems; they must solve the problem or attempt to explain the phenomena by using the scientific method of inquiry. What is most important is not the solution to the problem but the learning of the inquiry method (Suchman, 1962). An approach developed by Schwab (1965) and called the Biological Sciences Curriculum Study (BSCS) focused on teaching high school biology students how to design studies and how to encounter the major ideas in the field. Since the 1970s, both curriculum projects have faded as major instructional designs in high schools despite research showing favorable results. For example, Joyce and Weil (1986, pp. 56–57) cite research by Schlenker in 1976 that found that inquiry training resulted in increased understanding of science, productivity in creative thinking, and skills for obtaining and analyzing information (although it was found to be no more effective than conventional recitation methods for the acquisition of information). It seems that the emergence of the measured curriculum has made this approach less attractive for teachers who are required to cover maximum amounts of information in the science curricula. A second reason might be that courses exclusively oriented to one format lose their appeal in time. However, while these programs have faded as formats for entire courses, the inquiry training models continue to be used frequently by innovative teachers, and not only in the sciences. The formats have been adapted for use in other teaching fields, and the problems format continues to be the focus for cooperative learning projects.

It is in cooperative learning approaches that the best conditions for promoting generative knowledge are found, and recently this format has become a popular topic for teacher inservice programs. Good and Brophy (1987) review the procedures used by several cooperative learning programs. In general, the approach involves small groups of students (four to six who work together on practice and application exercises after whole-class instruction is completed, receiving feedback from peers as well as the teacher and the curriculum materials. The methods differ as to task and incentive structures. Various assignments require students to help each other to learn or to produce a work product, or require individuals and teams to compete in order to complete the task. Tasks may be group-oriented with a team working toward a single work product requiring pooled resources and shared labor. An example might be to prepare a background report to the class on one recent example of political revolution, including the prediction of another in the making. Tasks may also be individually oriented. In this case group members assist one another by discussing how to respond to questions or assignments, in checking work, or in providing feedback or tutorial assistance. Individual students on the team are responsible for turning in assignments but they work on them with the support of the group.

The incentive structure may be individual, cooperative, or competitive. In the individual structure, each student is graded on his or her own assignment. In the cooperative structure, individuals are rewarded both for their own efforts and for those of the other group members; there is a group grade. In the competitive structure individuals and groups compete for grades or other incentives.

One such cooperative learning program is the Learning Together model developed by David and Roger Johnson, who suggest that four elements be present in the group effort:

1. Positive interdependence aimed at a mutual goal, division of labor, dividing materials and other resources among members, assigning each member to a specific role, or tasks. This ensures that each member is important to the group effort.
2. Face-to-face interaction among students to develop exchange of ideas.
3. Individual accountability for mastering assigned materials in order to promote contributions to the task by each group member.
4. Instruction of students in appropriate interpersonal and small-group skills, such as asking and answering questions, active participation in all decisions by all members, respectful treatment, and responsibility for carrying out assigned tasks (Good and Brophy, 1987, pp. 437–438).

Research results concerning cooperative learning reveal that of forty-one studies, twenty-six reported significantly greater learning in cooperative learning groups as against only one in a control group. Groups that ensure individual accountability by individuals to groupmates produce higher achievement than those that allow one or two outstanding students to carry the team. Finally, despite differences in entry-level achievement, student groups that required members to explain materials to other group members resulted in effective learning experiences for both the explainer and those receiving the explanation (Good and Brophy, 1987). It would seem that, used judiciously, the cooperative learning approach is a very useful tool for fostering the acquisition of generative knowledge when students are given practical problems complex enough to require a variety of cognitive strategies to solve and when teachers provide instruction pertaining to interpersonal and small-group skills.

Summary

The current reform movement that requires schools to be accountable for measured academic excellence is being challenged by a movement to promote the learning capabilities of students. In the public schools, the thinking curriculum movement, based on cognitive learning and instructional theories, can be linked to demands by teachers for empowerment to make professional decisions at the local school level without the constraints of oppressive and rigid state mandates. Within that context, teaching how to learn in the secondary schools can be accomplished by individual teachers through adjustments they can make in the instructional design of their courses and the interactions they establish in their classrooms. This chapter has reviewed some concrete suggestions within the framework of three key applications of the thinking curriculum: the establishment of a classroom climate that promotes dispositions for learning; the use of a repertoire of teaching models that encourages reflection on learning strategies; and the use of cooperative learning processes that activate what has been learned so that it can be used for interpreting situations and solving in- and out-of-class problems.

References

Anderson, J. R. "Skill Acquisition: Compilation of Weak Method Problem Solutions." *Psychological Review,* 1987, *94,* 192–210.

Bransford, J., and Vye, N. "A Perspective on Cognitive Research and Its Implication for Instruction." In L. Resnick and L. Klopfer (eds.), *Toward the Thinking Curriculum: Current Cognitive Research. Association for Supervision and Curriculum Development Yearbook.* Washington, D.C.: Association for Supervision and Curriculum Development, 1989.

Brant, R. "On Misuse of Testing: A Conversation with George Madaus." *Educational Leadership,* 1989, *46* (7), 26–29.

Brophy, J. "Synthesis of Research on Strategies for Motivating Students to Learn." *Educational Leadership,* 1988, *46* (3), 40–48.

Buccino, A. "Redefining Competitiveness and National Well-Being." In D. Corrigan (ed.), *The Purposes of American Education Today.* A publication of the Association of Colleges and Schools of Education in State Universities and Land Grant Colleges and Affiliated Private Universities. College Station: Texas A & M University, 1988.

Corrigan, D. "Creating the American School." In D. Corrigan (ed.), *The Purposes of American Education Today.* A publication of the Association of Colleges and Schools of Education in State Universities and Land Grant Colleges and Affiliated Private Universities. College Station: Texas A & M University, 1988.

Darling-Hammond, L. "The Futures of Teaching." *Educational Leadership,* 1988, *46* (3), 4–10.

Darling-Hammond, L., and Wise, A. "Beyond Standardization: State Standards and School Improvement." *The Elementary School Journal,* 1985, *85,* 315–336.

Ducharme, E. "The Purposes of American Education Today: Concerns and Assertions." In D. Corrigan (ed.), *The Purposes of American Education Today.* A publication of the Association of Colleges and Schools of Education in State Universities and

Land Grant Colleges and Affiliated Private Universities. College Station: Texas A & M University, 1988.

Gagne, R., Briggs, L., and Wager, W. *Principles of Instructional Design.* (3rd ed.) New York: Holt, Rinehart & Winston, 1988.

Glickman, C. "Has Sam and Samantha's Time Come at Last?" *Educational Leadership,* 1989, *46* (8), 4–7.

Good, T., and Brophy, J. *Looking in Classrooms.* (4th ed.) New York: Harper & Row, 1987.

Gordon, W. "On Being Explicit About Creative Process." *The Journal of Creative Behavior,* 1972, *6* (4), 295–300.

Hynes, D. "Chapter 4, Theory into Practice." In J. R. Baird and I. J. Mitchell (eds.). *Improving the Quality of Teaching and Learning: An Australian Case Study—the PEEL Project.* Melbourne, Australia: Monash University Printery, 1987.

Joyce, B., Showers, B., and Rolheiser-Bennett, C. "Staff Development and Student Learning: A Synthesis of Research on Models of Teaching." *Educational Leadership,* 1987, *45* (2), 11–23.

Joyce, B., and Weil, M. *Models of Teaching.* (3rd ed.) Englewood Cliffs, N.J.: Prentice-Hall, 1986.

Keefe, J. "Assessment of Learning Style Variables: The NASSP Task Force Model." *Theory into Practice,* 1985, *24* (2), 138–144.

Lesgold, A. "Problem Solving." In R. J. Sternberg and E. E. Smith (eds.), *The Psychology of Human Thought.* New York: Cambridge University Press, 1988.

McNeil, L. "Contradictions of Control. Part 3: Contradictions of Reform." *Phi Delta Kappan,* 1988, *69,* 478–485.

National Commission on Excellence in Education. "A Nation at Risk: The Imperative for Educational Reform." Washington, D.C.: U.S. Department of Education, 1983.

Orlich, D. "Education Reforms: Mistakes, Misconceptions, Miscues." *Phi Delta Kappan,* 1989, *70* (7), 512–517.

Resnick, L. B., and Klopfer, L. E. "Toward a Thinking Curriculum: An Overview." In L. Resnick and L. Klopfer (eds.), *Toward the Thinking Curriculum: Current Cognitive Research. Association for Supervision and Curriculum Development Yearbook.* Washington, D.C.: Association for Supervision and Curriculum Development, 1989.

Schwab, J. (ed.). *Biological Sciences Curriculum Study, Biology Teach-
ers' Handbook.* New York: Wiley, 1965.
Shepard, L. "Why We Need Better Assessments." *Educational
Leadership,* 1989, *46* (7), 4–9.
Simon, H. A. "Problem Solving and Education." In D. T. Tuma
and R. Reif (eds.), *Problem Solving and Education: Issues in Teach-
ing and Research.* Hillsdale, N.J.: Erlbaum, 1980.
Suchman, J. R. "The Elementary School Training Program in
Scientific Inquiry." Report to the U.S. Office of Education,
Project Title VII. Urbana: University of Illinois, 1962.
Timar, B., and Kirp, D. "Education Reform in the 1980's: Lessons
from the States." *Phi Delta Kappan,* 1989, *70* (7), 504–511.
Urbanski, A. "The Rochester Contract: A Status Report." *Educa-
tional Leadership,* 1988, *46* (3), 48–52.
Wang, M., and Stiles, R. "An Investigation of Children's Concept
of Self-Responsibility for Their School Learning." *American
Educational Research Journal,* 1976, *13,* 159–179.
Wittrock, M. "Teaching Learners Generative Strategies for En-
hancing Reading Comprehension." *Theory in Practice,* 1985,
24 (2), 123–126.
Wittrock, M. "Student's Thought Processes." In M. Wittrock (ed.),
The Handbook of Research on Teaching. (3rd ed.) New York: Mac-
millan, 1986.

Chapter 9

Helping College Students
Take Charge of Their Education

Ann Q. Lynch

When colleges and universities take seriously the implications of the learning-to-learn idea, substantial benefits can come to them, to their clients, and to society. There are many plausible reasons for implementing these programs: new audiences can be reached and assisted in making smooth transitions to higher education; students can learn more in less time; dropout rates can be reduced. Learning-to-learn programs give students the feeling that they "matter," that college is not merely the survival of the fittest. Students can be assisted to mature to higher levels of cognitive, ethical, and spiritual development by acquiring the skills of critical thinking, problem solving, and collaboration. By producing better educated graduates who have had positive college experiences, higher education institutions can expect to enjoy greater confidence and support from their various constituencies. Moreover, society benefits as a more effective workplace, a more responsible citizenry, and more generative leadership emerge (Schlossberg, Lynch, and Chickering, 1989). This chapter describes some of the many promising applications of learning to learn in higher education.

A small number of innovative institutions have made learning to learn an integral part of institutional or adult learner programs. For some colleges and universities, provision takes the form of special courses, seminars, or learning centers. In some cases the process of learning to learn has been infused into subject matter areas. A few professional and graduate schools have incorporated the process into their programs. The approaches described below are a sampling limited to some of the more creative practices in the United States, even though there are some very innovative programs abroad.

An Institution-Wide Response

The school that has taken the leadership in responding holistically to the need to address the important issues involved in learning to learn is Alverno College in Milwaukee, Wisconsin. Russell Edgerton, president of the American Association for Higher Education, wrote, "Ever since I first learned about Alverno's vision of liberal learning, I've regarded this college as a beacon—illuminating with rare clarity and intensity a path toward a more productive form of liberal learning" (Edgerton, 1984, p. 3). Alverno stands as a beacon because its faculty, staff, and administrators have taken a hard look at the question, "What is essential?" and they have made a commitment by designing curricula and assessment processes to prepare students for work, citizenship, and personal fulfillment in the postindustrial era. As Edgerton sees it, there is a desperate need for "take-charge" people, for people who have the versatility to change and who care enough and see the connections involved in community and public life. Individuals must develop intellectual and interpersonal skills and have opportunities to test them in real performance situations. Alverno faculty are deeply committed to developing abilities that last a lifetime, and they have created a culture that sustains this search for excellence.

A liberal arts college for women with about 1,400 degree-seeking students who attend in both weekday and weekend formats, Alverno prepares women for professional careers. The broad, complex abilities required of all Alverno students are as follows: communication, analysis, problem solving, valuing in decision making, social interaction, taking responsibility for the environment, involvement in the contemporary world, and esthetic response. Loacker and Doherty (1984) identified the core, consistent sequence through which their diverse learners progress toward self-direction in learning. "This seems to occur as the learner encounters three basic issues: (1) that learning is a change in the self; (2) that newly learned (or newly recognized) abilities can be adapted to varying situations, where they have the power to change the environment; and (3) that one can take charge of the learning process, integrating and to some extent directing the changes in one's self and one's world" (1984, p. 102f). These abilities are identified and taught by involving students in learning situations where simulations and other concrete experiences as well as reflection and conceptualization are evaluated. Besides the traditional academic and professional subjects, the experiential learning programs were expanded in such ways that all students are involved in sponsored, off-campus learning activities where they apply abilities in concrete situations.

Mentkowski and Doherty (1984) describe how Alverno's assessment process is central to the curriculum. The faculty have created criteria or descriptive statements that provide a picture of each ability to be assessed. Faculty, students, and external evaluators from the Milwaukee business and professional community use the criteria to evaluate the students' strengths and weaknesses. For example, videotapes of students making speeches and performing in group leadership situations are evaluated by outside assessors who offer constructive criticism for improvement. Since assessment focuses on the application of abilities, students learn to tie knowledge, theory, motivation, and self-perceptions to constructive action. From the faculty's perspective, the key to Alverno's impact is found in the consistency with which the core abilities are fostered throughout the curriculum. "It is the systematic, constantly evaluated use of abilities that characterizes our approach. For the faculty, the curriculum is a collaborative effort which transcends departments and divisional structures" (Mentkowski and Doherty, 1984, p. 6). As a method of teaching thinking across the curriculum, Ruggiero (1988) cites Alverno's assessment process as unique and ahead of its time.

An extensive research program evaluated the impact on 750 students in two different graduating classes and included 60 alumnae and 180 working professionals who were not Alverno students. The findings were as follows:

1. Students learned complex abilities that later functioned as organizing principles for role performance and career satisfaction.
2. Students became self-sustaining learners and identified curriculum elements most important to their learning.
3. Students came to value liberal learning.
4. Students experienced changes that included broad generic abilities, learning styles, ways of thinking, and personal growth.
5. Students developed moral sophistication.
6. Alumnae and other working professionals stressed the importance of intellectual and interpersonal abilities at work.
7. Alumnae achieved competence and continued as self-sustaining learners (Mentkowski and Doherty, 1984).

Several of these findings need elaboration in terms of learning to learn. In regard to becoming self-sustaining learners, three major components were identified: (1) taking responsibility for learning, (2) making relationships among abilities and their use, and (3) using different ways of learning. The curriculum is directly linked to changes in several frameworks of cognitive development (Kohlberg, 1981; Loevinger, 1976; Perry, 1970, 1981; Piaget, 1972; Rest, 1979); learning styles (Kolb, 1984); and generic abilities of critical thinking, achievement and leadership, motivation, self-definition, and personal maturity (Watson and Glaser, 1964; Winter, McClelland, and Stewart, 1981). The study of student perceptions indicated more sophistication in valuing, which was confirmed by faculty experience. Students used more principled reasoning in resolving moral dilemmas, with higher achievers in the curriculum showing more change than lower achievers. Although students appeared to change most during the first two years, the changes in the second half of college were more directly attributable to the student's successful participation in the college's curriculum.

Age does seem to confer some initial advantage, as reflected in cognitive development scores of entering students but not in the more specifically focused abilities. Both younger and older students' learning styles changed dramatically; that is, at entrance they showed marked preference for concrete over abstract thinking and for reflective observing over active experimenting. After exposure to Alverno's curriculum, learners moved toward a more balanced mode of thinking and came to rely equally on concrete and abstract thinking and to show flexibility in choosing reflective or active approaches. Older students had a consistent edge over younger students in decision making and career understanding at entrance and remained more sophisticated. Although starting at the same place in regard to classroom learning processes and roles, older students made more immediate progress than younger students in understanding concepts such as learning in multiple ways, learning from peers, and independent learning. Alumnae reported experiencing learning as a continuous process and regarded it as an intrinsically rewarding activity that motivates career development and job choice. In another key element in learning to learn, alumnae described combining knowledge, theory, and experience in new situations for action.

A Program-Wide Response

Several institutions have developed programs aimed at meeting the needs of adults. At DePaul University (Chicago), the School for New Learning (SNL) is an alternative degree program, offering the B.A. and M.A. degree, which serves about 1,000 students annually. SNL began with the assumption that adult learners come to college with significant college-level learning that may become certified through a self-assessment process. Justice and Marineau (1988) describe the integral part that self-assessment plays in the core curriculum at SNL. "By learning to systematically engage in self-assessment, adult learners can ascertain and clarify their needs and motivations for learning, identify learning goals, and measure the achievement of their learning. Self-assessment places the locus of control within the learner and draws on the best source of information about the characteristics of the learners. It directly enlists the student's motivation for learning and relates the outcomes of the learning enterprise to the initial reasons for beginning it" (p. 50).

SNL programs are structured around outcome criteria — explicit statements of the knowledge and ability expected of successful degree candidates. Focusing on the outcomes of learning allows maximum flexibility in designing individual programs, sets the framework for integrating and assessing knowledge and abilities gained outside the college, and, more important, fosters the habit of self-assessment. In a preadmission workshop, students reflect on themselves as learners and discuss inventories of skills, learning styles, and areas of knowledge and work experiences in a structured but open-ended manner. Through educational autobiographies, students describe the significant learning events in their professional and personal lives. This process reinforces the legitimacy of the self and helps create a coherent structure on which to build new learning.

In the second component of the core curriculum, students take a course to design a learning plan. They focus on what they know and how to document it, what they need to learn to achieve their goals, the requirements of the program, and how they will learn it. Students confront the development of standards by learning to generate their own criteria for assessment through examining categories of their own learning and preparing statements to describe the intended outcomes. Women's development and ways of knowing are examined using Gilligan's (1982) and Belenky, Clinchy, Goldberger, and Tarule's (1986) work.

In the third phase each student's learning plan is developed in dialogue with and supported by a committee, consisting of a faculty member, a professional from the student's chosen field, and often a peer. The committee provides a forum to examine and critically reflect upon the plan in relation to the requirements of the external world. A course on research and inquiry helps the learner use formal and informal methods to identify and clarify issues for investigation and problem solving. "Grounded in the work and life experiences of the learner, the inquiry course focuses on problem-framing techniques, the use of resources, and the role of research in decision making" (Justice and Marineau, 1988, p. 51). Acquiring the tools of inquiry helps put individuals in charge of their own learning.

Next students use assessment to examine what they have been learning in their programs. What knowledge, skills, and abilities have they used outside of school, what learning activities have worked for them, and why? Learners are then asked to design and execute an independent learning project, which is approved by the committee. In the independent project the adult learner draws on her work or life experience as well as academic knowledge gained and tests her ability to reflect in action. The seventh and final component is the culminating colloquium in which the learner brings together the experiences of her program at SNL and evaluates them in terms of her own goals, the goals of the school, and the standards of the work world. In the colloquium, learners exercise the skills of self-assessment by reflectively integrating what they have learned.

Self-assessment entails the analytical tools to take an idea apart and examine its components; the ability to marshal one's mind and one's commitment behind an idea, problem, issue, or cause; and the perspective from which to view each problem or issue in a larger context. Justice and Marineau (1988) contend that in the self-assessment process, as it is developed at SNL, "are contained the skills, motivation, and capacity for reflection associated with truly educated people, the capacity to see things clearly and in their own terms" (p. 61).

Learning-to-Learn Courses and Seminars

Many different courses and seminars have been implemented in various colleges and universities. In a recent American Council on Education survey of 2,600 institutions, 78 percent reported that they offered a credit or noncredit course on the topic

"Coping with College" (El-Khawas, 1985). Often these take the form of orientation and are intended to introduce the student to the institution and to higher education. Some are specifically designed to focus on the thinking, learning, and problem-solving aspects of learning to learn, and some are designed as developmental education for high-risk students. Several exemplary approaches will be presented.

Empire State University. Empire State (New York) University was the first major college designed for adults. Struggling with situational, personal, and institutional barriers (Cross, 1981), adult learners especially make considerable sacrifices to enter or return to college. To overcome returning adults' feelings of inadequacy and marginality, Steltenpohl and Shipton (1986) developed a comprehensive introductory learning experience that provides adults an opportunity for a realistic self-appraisal of their potential as learners, the achievement of a sense of belongingness, and a deeper understanding of higher education in general and the meaning of liberal education in particular. In groups of twelve to fifteen participants, students share their anxieties and sense of urgency and receive support from interaction with peers and faculty facilitators. "Our goal is to make the group a laboratory for learning how to learn" (Steltenpohl and Shipton, 1986, p. 641).

In applying self-assessment to the experience, the designers concurred with Malcolm Knowles's (1980) statement, "If one thing stands out about adult learning, it is that a self-diagnosed need for learning produces a much greater motivation to learn than an externally diagnosed need" (p. 284). The students complete a forty-seven-item self-assessment checklist to identify levels of competence and knowledge about topics related to persistence and success in college. They also write an essay on what it means to be an educated person, and they employ other standardized, self-interpreting instruments to help them gain control and responsibility for self-diagnosis. In assessing themselves on their competencies in self-directed learning, most students rate themselves low on their understanding of adult learning and their ability to diagnose their learning needs, to translate those needs into objectives, to identify strategies and resources for achieving objectives, and to evaluate outcomes.

The curriculum includes adult development theory, such as the study of life course, crises, transitions, and the dynamics of change, which provides a perspective on the adult students' discomfort and uncertainty as they begin college studies. Most adults return with a deep sense of urgency to complete their degrees and to increase their occupational skills. Recognizing that college is an "off-time" event (Neugarten, 1977) for them helps to explain some of the urgency they feel. As they study Whitehead's (1949) stages of romance, precision, and generalization in the learning process, they understand their own intellectual development more fully and come to recognize that their education is more than career oriented. By analyzing their own initial writing samples and studying the criteria that English faculty use to rate writing, the students assess their needs for improvement of academic skills.

Activities such as interviewing and listening to former students as well as reading and writing build confidence and capitalize on the strengths of these concrete learners. This self-knowledge highlights their need to develop abstract conceptual modes and to incorporate analytical skills. Writing assignments include an essay summarizing the outcomes of all their assessment activities; a learning autobiography describing learning situations and outcomes in their lives, including what it means to be an educated person; and a referenced paper drawing on course content to describe course outcomes in terms of impact on their educational goal setting.

Exploring the meaning of higher education and the relationship of career and liberal education is a significant component in achieving the goal of what it means to be an educated person. As Morris Keaton, president of the Council for Adult and Experiential Learning (CAEL) said, "Since learning how to learn is one result of a liberal education, the practical need of being employable is better fulfilled now more than ever before by an undergraduate education" (Watkins, 1989, p. A24f). Forty percent of the students have had no prior college and 18 percent more have had fewer than sixteen college credits. As shown in the current debate about the content of a college education, such as the National Institute of Education's report, *Involvement in Learning* (1984), exposing the students to faculty from various disciplines and exploring terms and issues helps them gain a knowledge base for future planning. Their individual purposes for education become connected with social issues and cultural heritage.

The success of the eight-week course can be measured in terms of the students' ability to translate the goals of identifying their educational needs and interests, of seeing themselves as adult learners, and of appreciating the various views of what it means to be an educated person into subsequent steps in their education. Often a short-term goal of an associate degree allows students to test their abilities and maintain a commitment to education while providing a strong sense of accomplishment on the road to a four-year degree. Opportunities for assessment of prior college-level learning contribute to the quality, ownership, and uniqueness of the educational programs as well as the confidence students gain in themselves as adult learners. A study of the difference between persisters and nonpersisters made it clear that adults with little or no prior college need to obtain as realistic an appreciation of the demands of college as possible at entry and to strengthen their academic skills.

Learning to Learn Seminar. A Learning to Learn (LTL) Seminar developed by Marcia Heiman and Joshua Slomianko (1987) can be the core course in the critical thinking curriculum, incorporated into an orientation course, used as an elective, taught in learning centers, or taught in content classrooms. At the University of Massachusetts, Boston, Robert Swartz, director of the Critical and Creative Thinking Program, described the LTL Seminar component: "Learning to Learn brings a breath of fresh air to the process of learning in higher education. It enables students who have relied on rote memorization and superficial understanding to discover questions asked by the fields they study. By engaging in a search for answers to their own questions, students begin to think critically about what they are learning—something we need more of in this society"

(Heiman and Slomianko, 1987, p. 30). The Learning to Learn Seminar helps students to become more aware learners. Susan Shapiro, director of the Methods of Inquiry Project at the State University of New York, Buffalo, reports that LTL students "learn that each discipline has its discrete vocabulary, set of issues and approach to problems. Furthermore, they learn that each course has instructional objectives based upon an investigation of fundamental questions in the field" (Heiman and Slomianko, 1987, p. 30).

The Learning to Learn Seminar is a system of reasoning strategies in which students become active participants in their own learning. LTL is a fully developed system of critical thinking skills that becomes a part of the students' natural thinking processes. Research on the thinking strategies of successful learners showed that four skills form the foundation of critical thinking:

1. Asking questions of new materials, testing hypotheses, and engaging in a covert "dialogue" with the author or lecturer
2. Learning course content by identifying key factual and conceptual component skills of complex principles and ideas
3. Devising feedback mechanisms to assess learning progress
4. Identifying professors' instructional objectives

Of these skills, Heiman and Slomianko (1987) assert, "the most important is the process of asking questions: without it very little learning occurs" (p. 4). The students' learning-to-learn strategies fall into three categories or stages of learning: input, organization, and output. During the input stage, students generate field-relative questions. They learn to view their lecture notes and reading assignments as a series of answers to implied questions, and then they learn to generate these questions. During this stage of instruction, emphasis is given to helping students shape their questions to fit the disciplines they are studying. Students learn to distinguish between definitional and problem-solving questions. They also learn to develop editing checklists to identify error patterns idiosyncratic to them and to edit systematically for those errors while doing math or prose writing. In the organization stage, students learn information mapping and flow charting. They learn to externalize their thinking processes by organizing information matrices for comparative analysis of interrelated concepts. This process helps students clarify complex relationships and identify areas where they lack information. They begin to see the relationships among the ideas and facts of a field and can begin to create a picture of what the field as a whole is asking. Rather than time management, they learn task management, which teaches them to break their assignments into smaller, more manageable tasks that incorporate LTL strategies. Included in these tasks are components that offer regular feedback on performance. In the output stage, students use systematic procedures for solving problems. They use step-by-step procedures, for example, to work through math problems by answering a series of questions about the presented problem. They also prepare for exams by predicting objective and essay questions from information matrices and mock exams, and they focus on central concepts in predicted essay answers. Finally, they learn to write papers as a series of answers to self-generated questions, rather than to follow a rigid outline format.

Research of LTL seminars shows that grade point averages of normally admitted freshmen at the University of Wisconsin enrolled in a four-week, noncredit LTL course were significantly different in favor of the experimental groups over control groups when they were equated on such variables as high school rank, college entrance test scores, and type and levels of college courses carried. The most impressive study targeted disadvantaged students at Boston College and Roxbury Community College and showed that LTL students achieved significantly higher grade point averages over disadvantaged non-LTL controls. They also completed more course credits, even though their SAT entering mean scores were significantly lower than for normally admitted students. Follow-up studies at both institutions indicated that a much higher percentage of LTL students continued or graduated as compared with disadvantaged non-LTL controls.

Learning Analysis. The University of Nebraska and five other Nebraska colleges and universities participated in a three-year project, originally conceived by K. Patricia Cross (1975) and supported in part by the Fund for the Improvement of Post-Secondary Education, entitled "Helping Students Become More Sophisticated Consumers of Their Own Education." The major component of the project was a course in learning analysis (LA), which was intended to help students become more knowledge-able and analytical about their own learning reactions. LA invites students to explore their own approaches to learning through a set of measures of cognitive style and through par-ticipating in exercises to develop skills for seeking information about teaching methods in use on campus. Besides participat-ing in a survey of the principles of learning and a discussion of various teaching models, students were helped to develop alter-native strategies to use in different learning situations.

The next part of the LA course was a series of content units taught by outstanding instructors from different disci-plines using different teaching techniques, such as self-paced instruction, experiential learning, gaming and simulation, lecture-demonstration, discovery, and open classroom. Students kept track of their learning reactions, analyzed their responses to different teaching methods, and learned the disciplinary content of each unit. The desired outcomes for students in-cluded knowledge of one's preferred learning style and the teaching-learning environments in which various strategies were optimally used, development of information-seeking skills for choosing courses, development of alternative learning strat-egies, experience with a variety of teaching methods, and intro-ductory knowledge about learning psychology and four other disciplines.

The results of the first two years of LA at the University of Nebraska, Omaha, were summarized by Trani, Cross, Sample, and Wiltse (1978). A majority of students reported that LA affected their planning in selecting future courses and seeking information about the instructional method in different courses. Results also showed that students' preferences for orga-nizational structure and for interactive group experiences were consistent with their generally field-dependent cognitive style. Field dependents have been described as preferring socially oriented subject matter to objective or scientific materials, as holistic rather than analytical thinkers, as tending to be guided by authority figures, and as preferring to work with others rather than independently. For example, in providing a self-analysis of preferred and nonpreferred learning situations, many University of Nebraska students were uncomfortable with the lack of structure and absence of articulated goals in the open-classroom environment. They preferred the structure provided by lecture-demonstration and the social experiences and mutually reinforced group learning occurring in the experiential learning format. This project provided a stimulus to other institutions to help students become more sophisticated consumers of education.

Learning to Learn Skills Course. At the University of Texas, Austin, Claire Weinstein has developed a Learning to Learn Skills course in educational psychology that has become so popular that all sixteen sections have been fully subscribed each semester for several years (Mangan, 1988). Weinstein supervises her graduate students as they teach this innovative course. Three types of students enroll: those who are in imminent academic danger, those whose advisers have recommended that they take the course, and those who are doing well but who want to be sure they have covered all the basics before they enter professional school. Students who read a chapter only to discover that they have no idea of what they have just read can learn to monitor their comprehension as they proceed: they learn to ask themselves questions and to paraphrase as they read. Students are taught to stop and take stock of what they have read, in order to be sure they have retained the material, and to apply the theory to something relevant to their own lives. Students analyze their study habits and discover their best time for studying. To overcome test anxiety, Weinstein teaches her students cognitive behavioral approaches, such as saying "Stop" when the anxiety becomes intolerable. This procedure results in the student's attention being refocused on the test rather than on the anxiety symptoms. She stresses the importance of active learning. Students set specific learning goals and develop a variety of learning strategies to assist them in reaching those goals. Alternative methods are applied when learners encounter difficulty. For example, when a student cannot understand an assigned reading, rather than reread the assignment, he or she is encouraged to talk it over with another student or to compare notes from lectures to find similar points.

Weinstein has found that the course can be especially helpful to academically disadvantaged students, usually those who did not grow up in an environment conducive to learning. She is quoted as saying, "I think you have an ethical obligation to help these students. If you let them in, but don't do anything to keep them in, you have a revolving door rather than an open door" (Mangan, 1988, p. A3).

University 101. At the University of South Carolina, Columbia, John Gardner directs the University 101 program, which he developed, and serves as director of USC's National Center for the Study of the Freshman Year Experience. Upcraft and Gardner coedited *The Freshman Year Experience: Helping Students Survive and Succeed in College* (1989). Drawing upon Chickering's (1969) seven vectors of student development, they define freshman success as making progress toward educational and personal goals in the following areas: (1) developing academic and intellectual competence, (2) establishing and maintaining interpersonal relationships, (3) developing identity, (4) deciding on a career and lifestyle, (5) maintaining personal health and wellness, and (6) developing an integrated philosophy of life. Jeweler (1989), codirector of USC's University 101 program, has described the underlying philosophy as focusing on the multidimensional *development* — as opposed to the *teaching* — of freshmen. He draws a parallel between the perplexities facing freshmen and the problems encountered by faculty at large universities. The question is how to involve students and faculty in the excitement of the learning experience. Because of experimenting with interactive teaching methods that foster the development of a community of learners, the benefits to students, faculty, and the institution have proven to be very real.

Building on Astin's (1985) involvement theory, University 101 begins with a series of collaborative learning exercises designed to unify the class as a group. The instructor must establish himself or herself as someone highly approachable. "If the student is convinced early in the course that a partnership for learning has been formed, the first goal of the course has been accomplished" (Jeweler, 1989, p. 202). Instructor and students together plan other elements of the course, which might include study skills, understanding professors, library research skills, and writing skills (academic); career planning and choice of an academic major (vocational); learning the value of contributing to the common welfare of the community (social); realizing the lifelong value of fitness, exercise, and nutrition and the risks of alcohol, drugs, and tobacco (physical); learning to cope with stress and anxiety and learning to express one's feelings (emotional); and feeling positive and enthusiastic about life, about one's aspirations, and about one's values, appreciating the value systems of others, having a sense of what is ethical, and achieving a general appreciation of "why I am here" (spiritual). Students are asked to write frequently, and they often keep journals of their reactions to different experiences. Variation in teaching methods among lecturers, small-group exercises, and large-group discussions emphasize that the *how* of teaching is as important as the content. USC's University 101 has become a model for many other freshman seminars and has been the impetus for national conferences focused on the freshman year experience.

Human Inquiry Program. At Slippery Rock (Pennsylvania) University, the core of the Human Inquiry Program was epistemology: learning how to learn in various academic disciplines and reflecting on some of the dominant modes of thought in Western civilization (Cobb, Combs, and Kemmerer, 1985). In addition to intellectual achievements of the human culture, the program emphasized the "how": how to create, how to define problems, how to appreciate, how to achieve, and how to learn from the past in order to create a desired future. The faculty generated commitments from students to study in three distinct ways: students discovered or created a setting for studying (library, lounge, empty classrooms, or friends' rooms) where they learned to be less distracted by interruptions; they kept journals describing their feelings about studying with other students; and they were encouraged to attend cultural events with classmates and model intellectual behavior on campus.

The faculty presented different models of thinking and introduced the students to Piaget, Kohlberg, and brain hemispheric dominance as heuristic metaphors for ways of knowing, experiencing, and creating the world. A "leap into learning" seemed to occur when students' became aware of their own patterns of thinking. Sometimes students with reflective, analytic, or esthetic modes tried to use that same mode for all subject matter areas. After becoming engaged in learning using their preferred mode, students were encouraged to risk learning through other modes. Students are said to have become aware of the mixture of intuition, observation, calculation, and organization needed to generate data, create patterns, and solve problems.

Professors had their preferred ways of perceiving and judging, and they discussed their preferences for learning and teaching with the students. Observing faculty members thinking aloud, investigating, making mistakes, and overcoming shyness was enlightening and encouraging to the students. "The results were a dimming of blind respect for expertise and an enhancement of students' sense of their own capacity to learn from productive mistakes" (Cobb, Combs, and Kemmerer, 1985, p. 52). Two years of program evaluation indicated that the Human Inquiry Program did not retain students significantly better than other programs but had positive effects on students' intellectual, interpersonal, political, and civic development. The program was also beneficial to disadvantaged students in the University Enrichment Program, who changed in the same directions as the regular students.

Career and Life Planning Course. At Rockland (New York) Community College, the staff has developed a Career and Life Planning course, which incorporates adult development theory, learning style assessment, decision-making strategies, career exploration, educational planning, and life skills development (Viniar, 1984). The credit-bearing course, taught by trained facilitators and offered in a variety of formats, time frames, and locations, is now a well-integrated part of Rockland's orientation and educational planning process (Cullinane and Williams, 1983). Several thousand adult students have developed life portraits, assessed their learning and decision-making styles, developed career profiles, and designed individualized learning plans. Some departments have created adaptations for their majors. Such a course introduces adult learners to the institution's programs and services in a holistic manner and provides a strong base for support groups and for developmental mentoring.

Sierra Project. Character development is a major focus of the Sierra Project at the University of California, Irvine, where John Whitely (1982) and his associates have researched the effects of a year-long academic and residential program to raise the character level in college freshmen, as well as studied the growth of character during the college years. Whitely (1989) asserts, "The challenge for college educators is to harness the hidden curriculum of moral experience and translate it into structured thinking about enduring values, moral choices, and long-term decision making" (p. 175). The curriculum for character development begins with assessing the developmental status of the students associated with ego development, moral maturity, principled thinking, and forms of ethical and intellectual development. The choice of curricula is influenced by constructs from developmental and counseling psychology, including the structural organization of thinking, developmental sequencing, interactionalism, equilibration, psychological sense of community, empathy, and social perspective taking and assertion training (Loxley and Whitely, 1986). From the beginning to the end of the freshman year, Sierra Project students grew significantly more in postconventional or principled reasoning than aggregated control groups. After thirty years of research and development, Whitely (1989) believes that the foundations are in place now for higher education to play a vital role in enhancing ethical sensitivity and moral maturity for those who will lead this nation into the twenty-first century.

Learning Centers

Many institutions offer learning centers or academic support programs that assist students to diagnose strengths and deficiencies and help them build needed skills to begin or continue college-level work. With encouragement and support, practically all students can overcome learning deficits. Having a professionally trained staff in the learning center provides essential consistency and continuity. Mature students, serving as peer helpers and tutors, can provide important role models for others. This kind of support can be crucial in helping students break through skill and anxiety barriers.

At Memphis State University, in addition to an Adult Student Center and an Adult Student Association, the Educational Support Program (ESP) developed by Donna Manske (1987) provides a comprehensive approach with the philosophy: "Everyone can learn how to learn." Students of all ages participate in the program to the degree that meets their needs. They can come to understand their learning preferences by taking the Myers-Briggs Type Indicator (MBTI). For example, adults who prefer extraversion and sensing may want classes that are practical and oriented toward group activities, while those who prefer introversion and intuition may want classes that allow them to work alone creatively and contemplatively (Kolb, 1984). The MBTI (Myers and McCaulley, 1985; McCaulley, 1987) shows students how their learning preferences as well as their reading, writing, listening, and problem-solving skills are reflected in their individual styles. When students are in classroom situations that differ from their learning preferences, the ESP staff, as learning specialists, introduces them to compensatory strategies. Students who fail entrance tests and are required to take state-mandated developmental courses to remedy learning deficiencies are helped in ESP where they receive inten-

sive tutoring and instruction in learning to learn. In these
courses, supplemented by computerized instruction, enthusiastic teachers help students overcome deficits in reading, writing, foreign language, and mathematics (Manske, 1987).

At Ball State University, high-risk students are helped
through a learning center to assess their learning styles using
the MBTI and other instruments. Nisbet, Ruble, and Schurr
(1982) studied 375 males and 283 females in the program. They
found that it could be predicted to a significant degree that
those freshmen whose preference was for judgment, meaning an
organized, planned, and orderly lifestyle, would receive higher
second-quarter grades than students whose preference was for
perception, meaning a spontaneous, flexible lifestyle. The students with a preference for judgment were also more likely to
complete the third quarter than those with a preference for
perception.

Learning to Learn in Professional Schools

Academic support services have begun in various professional
schools rather recently. Initiative for developing such support
services comes from a growing awareness of the needs of the
"new" student, who may be minority, female, older, or from a
lower socioeconomic class and, more important, inadequately
prepared to meet the strenuous demands of an advanced professional school education.

In the schools of medicine and pharmacy at the University of Missouri, Kansas City, Manzo and Casale (1980) developed a methodology called PASS—a Problem-Solving Approach to Study Skills. The approach grew from an awareness
that students learned standard study strategies but failed to
make even the slightest adaptations necessary to transfer strategies to varied course requirements. The developers hypoth-
esized that this inflexibility was fear based. They designed a
method to promote a more assertive posture, by creating an
impression of a manageable situation rather than an over-
whelming, amorphous problem. The PASS lesson begins with
the students making introspective judgments about their learn-

ing problems, stimulated by a list of common problems developed by the staff. The student is encouraged to take more responsibility for resolving the learning problem by conversing with the teacher, responding to appropriate diagnostic instruments, and using related resource materials. After defining the problem in specific terms, consideration is given to the way that the student intuitively dealt with the problem. More standardized techniques are discussed and the student is urged to develop a more enlightened approach to solving the problem. Casale and Kelly (1980) found an underlying dependency syndrome among their subjects and worked toward assisting the students to take a more assertive role in their learning. Also relevant here is problem-based learning, a simulation-based program with a learning-to-learn emphasis now in use in several medical schools and described in Chapter Eleven.

In a graduate course, Kasworm (1983), now at the University of Tennessee, Knoxville, examined self-directed contract learning as an instructional strategy. She examined the impact of a self-directed learning course upon participant self-directed learning behaviors and attitudes. Significant positive gains were noted on participant pre- and postgain scores on Guglielmino's (1977) Self-Directed Learning Readiness Scale (SDLRS). Observational diaries of selected students and the instructor were analyzed for major themes and transitions. Course evaluations showed a majority of positive participant responses regarding perceived changes in knowledge and skill in self-directed learning as well as reported value of the course experience.

In a related study at Virginia Commonwealth University, Richmond, Caffarella and Caffarella (1986) investigated whether using learning contracts in graduate education enhanced adults' readiness and competencies for self-directed learning (SDL). The study involved 163 students from six universities enrolled in graduate courses in adult education where learning contracts were employed. The findings suggest that the use of learning contracts had little impact on developing readiness for SDL because readiness was already high. However, the use of learning contracts did have a positive effect on developing competence in SDL, especially in translating learning needs into objectives, identifying human and material learning resources, and selecting effective strategies for using these resources.

The Future of Learning to Learn in Higher Education

In this last decade of the twentieth century, higher education can make giant strides by encouraging the process of learning to learn. Such exemplary programs as described above can benefit learners, the institution, and society. A more comprehensive model has been proposed by Schlossberg, Lynch, and Chickering (1989) in which the institution is restructured from the learner's perspective rather than for administrative convenience, as it is currently constructed. The following approach is a distillation of that model. It calls for the higher education environment to acknowledge the transitions through which students progress and, more important, to make each learner feel that he or she matters.

To implement this approach, student and academic affairs departments would work in an integrated manner with the welfare of the students being of primary importance. Essentially, programs and services would be structured to serve students from entry through departure—as they move in, as they move through, and as they move on. The educational purpose of all programs and services would be paramount. Student affairs staff would become student educational specialists and serve as faculty in development courses and as resources to other faculty about student and adult development theory and practices.

Entry programs and services would address the needs of potential students, serve admission and orientation functions, and help students adjust to the institution. An entry education center would coordinate the services and programs to help students build a solid relationship with the institution. Preadmission, recruitment, admissions, financial aid and planning, orientation courses, assessment of prior learning, and developmental assessment are areas to be included in the entry education center. Many of the outstanding seminars and courses described above speak to this phase. The emphasis is on the freshman year and all of the workshops and courses that focus on the needs of those new to college or returning to higher education. Much of the research conducted in the programs indicated that new learners have higher needs for concrete experiences and should be helped to become more reflective, conceptual, and capable of turning understanding into action. They must be taught to think critically and helped to develop intellectually, interpersonally, and ethically.

The second phase involves supporting students as they move through the institution. Learning center programs, academic advising, career development, personal counseling, cocurricular activities, residential life, family care, health, and other services form a cohesive support unit reaching all students with multiple purposes. An adult learner support center becomes the mainstay for those students who are older, part-time, or commuters and who need a place to study, meet friends and faculty, and receive messages. An adult learner association becomes the advocate with student government for the needs of this often disenfranchised group. The association can publish a newsletter, plan social and educational activities, and provide information at registration about programs and services, such as co-op babysitting, orientation, and the adult learner support center. Some adults may serve as peer tutors in the learning center and others may become adult peer counselors to help returning adults "get connected." Student educational specialists, faculty, and administrators may serve as developmental mentors, a new role to assist students in becoming more reflective about their college experience. They help students prepare developmental transcripts, based on student and adult development theory, and provide the needed challenge and support Nevitt Sanford (1966) advocated a quarter century ago.

The final phase, "moving on," is sorely neglected by most institutions. A culminating course similar to the orientation course would help students integrate their learning and take important steps toward the future. The developmental mentor can assist the student in reviewing her or his accomplishments both in the institution and outside in the workplace. At this or an earlier point, the mentor may make referrals to career planning and placement or to transition groups such as "Making the Plunge into the Professional World," "So You are Considering Graduate School," or "Coping with Graduation and After" to assist the student in taking the next steps. Besides the graduation ceremony, graduates need informal rituals to recognize the learning and development that has taken place and to acknowledge that learning is a lifelong process. Institutions can benefit at this point by keeping in touch as students graduate and become alumni.

Many of the concerns of traditional-age college students and adult learners can be addressed as institutions make a commitment to change. Professional development for faculty and educational services staff will be essential to facilitating that change. Alverno College and DePaul's School for New Learning light the way for other institutions and serve as models for helping students to feel that they matter. As learning to learn becomes an integral and comprehensive part of higher education, the purposes of learners, institutions, and society will be better served.

References

Astin, A. W. *Achieving Educational Excellence: A Critical Assessment of Priorities and Practices in Higher Education.* San Francisco: Jossey-Bass, 1985.

Belenky, M. F., Clinchy, B. M., Goldberger, N. R., and Tarule, J. R. *Women's Ways of Knowing: The Development of Self, Voice and Mind.* New York: Basic Books, 1986.

Caffarella, R. S., and Caffarella, E. P. "Self-Directedness and Learning Contracts in Adult Education." *Adult Education Quarterly,* 1986, *36* (4), 226–234.

Casale, U., and Kelly, B. W. "Problem-Solving Approach to Study Skills (PASS) for Students in Professional Schools." *Journal of Reading,* 1980, *24* (3), 232–238.

Chickering, A. W. *Education and Identity.* San Francisco: Jossey-Bass, 1969.

Clark, T. F. "Individualized Education." In A. W. Chickering and Associates, *The Modern American College: Responding to the New*

Realities of Diverse Students and a Changing Society. San Francisco: Jossey-Bass, 1981.

Cobb, L., Combs, C., and Kemmerer, A. "A Freshman Program: Learning How to Learn." In J. Katz (ed.), *Teaching as Though Students Mattered.* New Directions for Teaching and Learning, no. 21. San Francisco: Jossey-Bass, 1985.

Cross, K. P. "Grant Proposal: Helping Students Become Sophisticated Consumers of Education." Washington, D.C.: Fund for the Improvement of Post-Secondary Education, 1975.

Cross, K. P. *Adults as Learners: Increasing Participation and Facilitating Learning.* San Francisco: Jossey-Bass, 1981.

Cullinane, M., and Williams, D. *Life, Career, Educational Planning: A Facilitator's Manual.* Suffern, N.Y.: Rockland Community College, 1983.

Edgerton, R. "Abilities That Last a Lifetime: Alverno in Perspective." *American Association for Higher Education Bulletin,* 1984, *36* (6), 3–4.

El-Khawas, E. *Campus Trends, 1984.* Washington, D.C.: American Council on Education, 1985.

Gilligan, C. *In a Different Voice: Psychological Theory and Women's Development.* Cambridge, Mass.: Harvard University Press, 1982.

Guglielmino, L. M. "Development of a Self-Directed Learning Readiness Scale." Unpublished doctoral dissertation, Department of Adult Education, University of Georgia, 1977.

Heiman, M., and Slomianko, J. "Learning to Learn: Some Questions and Answers." Unpublished manuscript, Cambridge, Mass.: Learning to Learn, Inc., 1987.

Jeweler, J. A. "Elements of an Effective Seminar: The University 101 Program." In M. L. Upcraft, J. N. Gardner, and Associates, *The Freshman Year Experience: Helping Students Survive and Succeed in College.* San Francisco: Jossey-Bass, 1989.

Justice, D. O., and Marineau, C. "Self-Assessment: Essential Skills for Adult Learners." In P. Hutchings and A. Wutzdorff (eds.), *Knowing and Doing: Learning Through Experience.* New Directions for Teaching and Learning, no. 35. San Francisco: Jossey-Bass, 1988.

Kasworm, C. E. "An Examination of Self-Directed Contract

Learning as an Instructional Strategy." *Innovative Higher Education,* 1983, *8* (1), 45–54.

Knowles, M. S. *The Modern Practice of Adult Education: From Pedagogy to Andragogy.* (2nd ed.) Chicago: Follett, 1980.

Kohlberg, L. *The Meaning and Measurement of Moral Development.* Worcester, Mass.: Clark University Press, 1981.

Kolb, D. A. *Experiential Learning: Experience as the Source of Learning and Development.* Englewood Cliffs, N.J.: Prentice-Hall, 1984.

Loacker, G., and Doherty, A. "Self-Directed Undergraduate Study." In M. S. Knowles and Associates, *Andragogy in Action: Applying Modern Principles of Adult Learning.* San Francisco: Jossey-Bass, 1984.

Loevinger, J. *Ego Development: Conceptions and Theories.* San Francisco: Jossey-Bass, 1976.

Loxley, J. C., and Whitely, J. M. *Character Development in College Students.* Vol. 2: *The Curriculum and Longitudinal Results.* Schenectady, N.Y.: Character Research Press, 1986.

McCaulley, M. H. "The Myers-Briggs Type Indicator: A Jungian Model for Problem Solving." In J. E. Stice (ed.), *Developing Critical Thinking and Problem-Solving Abilities.* New Directions for Teaching and Learning, no. 30. San Francisco: Jossey-Bass, 1987.

Mangan, K. "A Pioneer in Teaching 'Learning to Learn' Skills." *Chronicle of Higher Education,* Sept. 14, 1988, p. A3.

Manske, D. H. "Report on Retention Strategies." Unpublished manuscript, Memphis State University, 1987.

Manzo, A. V., and Casale, U. "The 5 C's: A Problem-Solving Approach to Study Skills." *Reading Horizons,* 1980, *20* (4), 281–284.

Mentkowski, M., and Doherty, A. "Abilities That Last a Lifetime: Outcomes of the Alverno Experience." *American Association for Higher Education Bulletin,* 1984, *36* (6), 5–6 and 11–14.

Myers, I. B., and McCaulley, M. H. *Manual: A Guide to the Development and Use of the Myers-Briggs Type Indicator.* Palo Alto, Calif.: Consulting Psychologists Press, 1985.

National Institute of Education. *Involvement in Learning: Realizing the Potential of American Higher Education.* Report of Study

Group on the Conditions of Excellence in American Higher Education. Washington, D.C.: National Institute of Education, 1984.

Neugarten, B. L. "Adult Personality: Toward a Psychology of the Life Cycle." In L. Allman and D. Jaffee (eds.), *Readings in Adult Psychology: Contemporary Perspectives.* New York: Harper & Row, 1977.

Nisbet, J. A., Ruble, V. E., and Schurr, K. T. "Predictors of Academic Success with High-Risk College Students." *Journal of College Student Personnel,* 1982, *23* (3), 227–235.

Perry, W. G., Jr. *Forms of Intellectual and Ethical Development in the College Years: A Scheme.* New York: Holt, Rinehart & Winston, 1970.

Perry, W. G., Jr. "Cognitive and Ethical Growth: The Making of Meaning." In A. W. Chickering and Associates, *The Modern American College: Responding to the New Realities of Diverse Students and a Changing Society.* San Francisco: Jossey-Bass, 1981.

Piaget, J. "Intellectual Development from Adolescence to Adulthood." *Human Development,* 1972, *15,* 1–12.

Rest, J. R. *Development in Judging Moral Issues.* Minneapolis: University of Minnesota Press, 1979.

Ruggiero, V. R. *Teaching Thinking Across the Curriculum.* New York: Harper & Row, 1988.

Sanford, N. *Self and Society: Social Change and Individual Development.* Hawthorne, N.Y.: Aldine, 1966.

Schlossberg, N. K., Lynch, A. Q., and Chickering, A. W. *Improving Higher Education Environments for Adults: Responsive Programs and Services from Entry to Departure.* San Francisco: Jossey-Bass, 1989.

Steltenpohl, E., and Shipton, J. "Facilitating a Successful Transition to College for Adults." *Journal of Higher Education,* 1986, *57* (6), 637–658.

Trani, E. P., Cross, K. P., Sample, S. B., and Wiltse, J. C. "College Teaching and the Adult Consumer: Toward a More Sophisticated Student Body." *Proceedings of the IEEE,* 1978, *66* (8), 838–846.

Upcraft, M. L., Gardner, J. N., and Associates. *The Freshman Year*

Experience: Helping Students Survive and Succeed in College. San Francisco: Jossey-Bass, 1989.

Viniar, B. "Adult Development Theory: The Medium and the Message." *Insight — An Annual Collection of Articles on Teaching and Learning by Faculty of the Community Colleges and State Universities of New York, 1983*–1984. Albany: New York State Board of Regents, 1984.

Watkins, B. T. "With More Adult Students on Campuses, Some Colleges Are Adjusting Their Curricula and Teaching Methods." *Chronicle of Higher Education,* Jan. 18, 1989, p. A27f.

Watson, G., and Glaser, E. *Critical Thinking Appraisal.* New York: Harcourt Brace Jovanovich, 1964.

Whitehead, A. N. *The Aims of Education.* New York: New American Library, 1949.

Whitely, J. M., and Associates. *Character Development in College Students.* Vol. 1: *The Freshman Year.* Schenectady, N.Y.: Character Research Press, 1982.

Whitely, J. M. "Character Development." In L. M. Upcraft, J. N. Gardner, and Associates, *The Freshman Year Experience: Helping Students Survive and Succeed in College.* San Francisco: Jossey-Bass, 1989.

Winter, D., McClelland, D., and Stewart, A. *A New Case for the Liberal Arts: Assessing Institutional Goals and Student Development.* San Francisco: Jossey-Bass, 1981.

Chapter 10

Learning-to-Learn Needs
for Adult Basic Education

David J. Collett

The application of learning to learn in Adult Basic Education (ABE) programs offers considerable potential and challenge. The educational needs of ABE students differ considerably from those of students in other institutionally based programs and are centered in very basic academic and life requirements. Their needs with regards to learning to learn also differ from those of most other adults. The setting in which these students must be able to apply learning strategies is often in the noninstitutional, nonacademic areas of living. Applicable learning skills and strategies tend to be more of the generic type rather than subject- or context-specific. Perhaps it is these students who stand to benefit most from the development of process skills or strategies that would help them learn more effectively from nonschool environments.

Historically, basic education for adults reflected objectives identified in public school goal statements. More recently, numerous studies have been conducted to identify the needs of this population; the studies have focused on identifying the functional literacy needs of the adult within society. The objectives identified tend to include the ability to care for one's self effectively, to move successfully into regular occupational preparation programs, or to take advantage of further educational opportunities at the high school level. The focus of this chapter is on a recent study in Alberta that resulted in the identification of learning competencies and skills as an integral component of the basic education needs of adults. First, a brief overview of the nature and variety of adult basic education (ABE) institutions, programs, and learners is provided along with a discussion of the potential usefulness of concepts and strategies relevant to learning to learn. A description of the Alberta developmental project outlines the identification and refinement of needed learning-to-learn competencies and skills for ABE students. Finally, some reflections on the implementation of learning-to-learn skills and strategies within existing ABE programs are offered.

Context and Potential

A wide variety of institutions are involved in ABE programs but few are involved solely in the provision of these programs. Public schools, vocational schools, colleges, and technical institutes as well as private institutions offer academic upgrading, life skills, and job readiness programs to adults who have very low literacy levels. The Alberta Vocational Centres and Community Vocational Centres (AVCs/CVCs), which were central to this study, provide the focus for this chapter and consist of five adult education institutions within the province of Alberta whose mandate is to provide basic education and entry-level vocational and business programs to adults who in most cases have a history of unsuccessful learning in school. Two of the institutions are located within the large urban context and three are in rural settings, catering to a total of over twenty-five different communities and a significant proportion of native adult students (Burghardt, 1987).

Adult Basic Education generally encompasses academic upgrading programs from grades 0 to 9, as well as basic job and community readiness programs for the disadvantaged adult. Program goals include the development of functional literacy in the academic, occupational, and social sense. Instruction follows a wide variety of curricular and scheduling patterns. Attendance may be on a part-time or full-time, day or evening basis. Instruction may be in traditional classrooms, involve self-study, or be within a tutorial mode.

The Typical Learner. Thomas (1983) reports that close to one million Canadians lack the ability to read and write at the grade five level and a total of four million are termed "functionally illiterate" or unable to read and write at the grade nine level. (The estimated number of adults in Canada at that time was approximately fifteen million.) The ABE participant tends to come from a lower socioeconomic background and is often a member of a disadvantaged minority group. Either low academic abilities or lack of success in schooling for other reasons, such as incompatible learning styles or social problems, are usually found in the histories of the participants; and they often have problems fitting into the mainstream of society.

A document from Alberta Advanced Education (1985) describes typical ABE students: average age of thirty-two years, out of school almost twenty years, more women than men, history of sexual abuse or alcohol problems, poor and highly dependent on social assistance, single mothers with dependent children, low self-confidence and self-esteem, high dependency on authority figures, low level of resourcefulness in using community resources, high incidence of health problems, poorly developed interpersonal skills, and a significant incidence of learning disabilities. The personal goals of the ABE learner may include further education (for example, obtaining a high school qualification), but primarily they involve preparation for low-level occupations and for personal development. Few students complete their programs and fewer proceed to further educational opportunities (Fahy and Green, 1986).

Implications for Fostering Learner Confidence and Competence. The application of learning-to-learn concepts and principles in adult basic education has significant implications for both the individual and for society. The ABE participant, commonly saddled with a history of failure in school, is often the student who has had the most difficulty in developing the learning strategies required to meet the expectations and requirements of traditional institutional programs. Also these students usually have been unable to develop successful strategies for coping with adult life roles. Many have had difficulty taking their place in a production-oriented society.

It seems reasonable to assume that the above difficulties are at least in part the result of the failure of educational programs to emphasize the process skills inherent in approaches to learning to learn. Basic education programs that assist students in the development of learning strategies can prepare them for success in a variety of secondary and post-secondary education programs. Also, by focusing on learning strategies with applicability in the social and occupational context, opportunities for growth and success in nonacademic endeavors can be enhanced.

Very few adults enrolled in ABE programs continue for any length of time. Burghardt (1987) reports a dropout rate from 15 to 20 percent per quarter year and says that the majority of students either go on to low-level employment or enroll in skill courses not requiring high literacy levels. These people clearly require learning strategies that can be applied outside the formal learning situation. The potential benefits to society of enfranchising members who heretofore have had such difficulties are considerable.

In order to elucidate the needs of the ABE student with regard to learning to learn, the following section outlines a needs assessment project conducted in Alberta that led to the identification of a taxonomy of needed competencies and skills for participants in adult basic education.

The Alberta Project

Some learning-to-learn needs of functional illiterates and basic education students have been postulated, but apparently no systematic attempt has been made to establish a taxonomy of such needs except for the Alberta Study. Smith (1982) identified increased individual self-confidence in learning as perhaps the most critical need of this population. Mayes (1987) emphasized improved comprehension monitoring, memory recall, and the ability to raise questions, all subsumed under critical thinking. The United States Department of Defense's Job Skills Education Program, now being adapted to nonmilitary settings, aims at improving abilities in self-motivation, test taking, time management, and reading strategies, as well as in problem solving (Derry and Murphy, 1986). Leaders of Nicaragua's national literacy campaign sought to help participants to become better at "problem-posing, problem solving, and critical thinking; to become aware of contradictions and processes; to understand concepts and principles; to understand that knowledge can be created by nonexperts; to understand that the learner is the most important resource in the teaching transaction as well as the need to act after one gains new information" (Smith, 1988).

Collett, Deane, Kendal, and Brooks (1983) report on an extended ABE project conducted within the Alberta Vocational Centres and Community Vocational Centres (AVCs/CVCs) under the auspices of the provincial department of education and facilitated by the department of industrial and vocational education at the University of Alberta. The purpose of this project was to conduct a needs assessment of the Alberta ABE student and develop curricula to meet these needs. Since the development of the needs assessment included a heavy emphasis on occupational and social competencies and skills in addition to those of schooling, the expectations were that the results would be broader than if not different from needs assessment studies with a more academic focus. This assumption proved to be accurate. Following is a summary of this project, which identified those basic competencies that adults must possess in real-life situations and ultimately led to the development of a taxonomy of learning-to-learn competencies for the ABE participant.

Competency Identification and Validation. The objective of phase one of the project was the development of a general profile of competencies needed by adults living in Alberta. A team of ten profile participants (a diversified group of carefully selected competent adults) and two group facilitators engaged in a four-day brainstorming and developmental session to identify skills and abilities they felt were necessary to function adequately in society. A total of 103 competencies were identified and grouped.

The purpose of phase two was to validate the competencies identified in phase one. Personal interviews were conducted with 448 community representatives, a cross section of the population in the geographical areas served by the five vocational and community vocational centres. Respondents were members of the community who were functioning in a satisfactory manner, including businesspersons, various types of employees, homemakers, and ABE graduates. A stratified sampling procedure provided a balance of responses from the categories of age, gender, occupation, and educational attainment. In addition to this group, 101 staff members of the centres participated. The respondents were asked to rate the importance of the original competency statements on a five-point scale. Competencies were grouped together and ranked based on the information received. In addition to a ranking of the competencies, open-ended responses were solicited regarding competencies that perhaps should have been included. Many of the open-ended responses focused on learning, thinking, reasoning, and problem-solving strategies.

The analysis of results focused mainly on the responses of the community representatives, with the AVC/CVC staff responses used for comparison purposes only. In the first instance, demographic analysis of the data led to two important implications for phase three of the project. There was found to be little difference in types of responses received from the different centres; therefore, a province-wide ABE standard curriculum was considered feasible. Secondly, AVC/CVC staff members' responses were similar to those of the community-based respondents, suggesting that staff could be used as resource persons to verify and expand competencies on the profile.

Skills Identification and Cataloguing of Skills. The aim of phase three was to further develop each of the validated competency statements into sets of skills that would be detailed enough to allow subsequent construction of curricula for the ABE programs. AVC/CVC staff (eight groups of approximately eight members each) participated in the identification of specific skills needed for each competency. Each competency was then used as the title of a new profile for more specific development. A group technique similar to the one used in phase one was employed, producing more detailed and specific "miniprofiles."

There were two major components of phase four: the computer-based analysis of the miniprofile information and the review of analysis undertaken by instructors and administrators of each AVC/CVC. Computer-based analysis was used to eliminate redundancies (similar skills within categories) and identify commonalties (similar skills found in different categories). Then inspection for patterns of commonalties between the competency categories was made, which would point toward a model to help explain the relationships among the various skills and create a method of constructing an accessible catalogue of skills. "Learning How to Learn" emerged as one of the major categories of need. (See Table 10.1.)

Methods and results of analysis were presented for review to the AVC/CVC instructors and administrators at each of the five centres. In addition to the discussions that centered around the implications of the project findings for their programs, ideas for models to help explain the relationships among the various skills were discussed with AVC/CVC staff. A model was developed and described as the Cone of Adult Basic Skills, consisting of three major skill groups, labeled Context Skills, Interpersonal Skills, and Foundation Skills. Context skills included the following: Protect/Maintain Health and Safety of Self and Others, Earn a Living, Manage Home and Family Responsibilities, and Function as a Citizen. The interpersonal skills included two categories: Develop Self and Relate to Others. Foundation skills initially included four categories: Communicate, Use Mathematics, Reason, and Learn. Reason and Learn were later combined into Learn How to Learn. Phase four ended with the production of the *Catalogue of Adult Basic Skills,* containing a third draft of the profile, a keyword listing (including synonyms) of all 946 skills, a listing of interrelated skills, and matrices of interrelationships.

A Taxonomy of Learning Skills. During the early phases of the AVC/CVC project, validation instruments and developmental activities identified a significant need for additional efforts on behalf of the categories Reason and Learn. Indeed, some of the competencies listed had only recently been identified at the time the first edition of the *Catalogue of Adult Basic Skills* was issued. As a result, the project was extended (phase five) to permit the development of these two categories by means of two meetings: the profiling session—a two-and-one-half-day retreat for selected lay persons to initially identify skills within the two categories, and the workshop session—a two-day retreat for selected instructors from the centres to refine the product of the profiling session and incorporate it in the profile and *Catalogue of Adult Basic Skills.*

The purpose of the profiling session was to identify the skills used by an individual in the learning and thinking processes within the everyday life of the adult, breaking up the concepts of learning and thinking into unique and specific skill components. More specifically, activity focused on the identification-of-skill statements guided by two open-ended statements: (1) learning—"In learning new skills/knowledge/attitudes, I have found it helpful to be able to. . ."—and (2) thinking—"In thinking about issues/concerns/problems, I have found it helpful to be able to. . ."

A group of nine persons was selected to attend this session: individuals considered to have demonstrated some measure of success within their communities; individuals without theoretical background in the subject areas; representatives from each of the regions served by the centres; representatives from diverse academic, occupational, and cultural backgrounds; and a relative balance of males and females. The group first took up learning skills, then considered thinking and reasoning skills, and finally returned to further develop the learning skills. The result was a miniprofile of skills for each of these areas.

The purpose of the workshop session was to further expand the work of the profiling session by incorporating (where possible) current theoretical thinking and instructional experiences in order to form a highly comprehensive list of skills and subskills related to learning and thinking. It was also important to merge these skills, both conceptually and in written form, into the *Catalogue of Adult Basic Skills.*

Two instructional representatives were designated by each of the five centres to participate in the workshop. Large-group and small-group activities focused on the following: (1) a study of an overall structure and the interrelationships between the learning and thinking categories; (2) errors of omission in both learning and thinking categories; (3) structuring and incorporating skills and skill areas within one category, as decided by the group; (4) consideration of later implementation concerns and changes that might prove helpful; and (5) general polishing of skill and subskill statements.

The result of the workshop was a revised *Profile of Adult Basic Skills* with one of the seven categories of competencies entitled Learn How to Learn, which incorporated both the learning and thinking skills, and an addendum to the *Catalogue of Adult Basic Skills* listing the competencies, categories of skills, and basic skills that had been adopted by the group. The learn-how-to-learn skills were placed within competency areas entitled Understand Self as a Learner, Manage Self as a Learner, Understand the Learning Environment, Utilize Various Learning Methods, Practical Thinking, Recall and Apply Data to New Situations, and Apply Problem Solving Technique to Make Rational and Reasonable Decisions.

The competency area labeled Understand Self as a Learner encompassed skills with respect to self-confidence, goal setting, insight into one's learning style, and the acceptance of responsibility. The maintenance of a healthy mind and body, along with the management of learning time, were skill areas within Manage Self as a Learner. Understand the Learning Environment included skills related to the recognition and utilization of learning services and resources, the creation of a suitable home learning environment, and the ability to access other learning resources. Skills associated with learning as an individual, as a member of a group, by doing, and in a self-directed way were areas identified within Utilize Various Learning Methods. Practical Thinking involved the application of creative thinking, lateral/divergent thinking, convergent thinking, critical thinking, analytical thinking, and the application of logic or reason. The use of recall techniques and the application of knowledge to new situations are included in Recall and Apply Data to New Situations. Apply Problem-Solving Techniques to Make Rational and Reasonable Decisions included skills associated with identification of the problem, collection of information, establishment of decision-making parameters, generation of alternatives, evaluation of alternatives, as well as making decisions and evaluating those decisions. Each of the skills identified within these areas was identified as a requirement for functioning effectively in contemporary Western society. Table 10.1 presents the entire taxonomy of learning skills that emerged as the product of this phase of the project.

      The value of the taxonomy of learning-to-learn needs developed in Alberta derives from several factors. The comprehensiveness of the taxonomy (which may be forbidding to some persons seeking to apply it) should in the long term prove useful to curriculum developers and researchers who may use it as a model or a place to start experimenting with activities to strengthen the ABE curriculum. The taxonomy has legitimacy because it was largely developed by basic education personnel with a great deal of input from former ABE students and from "ordinary citizens." It is quite significant that the taxonomy did not arise out of a deliberate attempt to identify learning-to-learn needs but rather from the larger context of requirements for successful living, skills necessary to function adequately in society. Thus successful learning in school (in ABE programs) and successful learning outside of school are linked inseparably.

Moving Toward Implementation

Earlier in the chapter it was suggested that the needs of the ABE learner may well differ from those within the public school systems or those of the college or university student who has already demonstrated a minimum level of ability to learn. For the ABE learner there is a need for a much more basic and generic set of learning skills. The future learning situations for these adults will include a wide variety not only of subject areas but also of nonformal contexts in which effective learning will be perhaps even more important than in the classrooms of schools and colleges. Assuming that strategies fall into two categories, generic and context-specific, the focus of learning to learn for the ABE student must therefore be at the generic level with applicability to a wide variety of settings.

Sources of ideas, information, and intervention are numerous for assisting those coming into ABE programs to become more effective and efficient learners. Problem solving, basic thinking strategies, reading and listening skills, strategies for remembering, self-motivation and confidence building, transfer maximization, study skills, and other approaches are all useful skills and competencies to include in a learning-to-learn program at this level. However, the Alberta experience reveals that this breadth of need and these sources for program development can contribute to confusion among those seeking to mount learning-to-learn programs. Much more needs to be done on behalf of the integration of appropriate concepts and strategies into manageable, coherent programs.

Efforts to date on behalf of implementation by Alberta vocational centre staff members include the evaluation of an established learning-to-learn program that emphasizes thinking and problem solving, and the development and piloting of a forty-hour course for incoming students. At the Calgary centre, Feuerstein's Instrumental Enrichment Program, which addresses many of the competencies in the taxonomy of learning-to-learn skills found in Table 10.1, was taught to students in experimental and control groups in a forty-five-hour, semester-long course. The results were mixed. While the program did not produce significant improvement in academic performance nor in mental abilities (as measured on standardized tests), a majority of the students found it helpful. They reported gaining increased confidence with respect to asking questions and clar-

Table 10.1. Adult Basic Skills—Category G: Learn How to Learn

G1	Understand Self as a Learner
G1A	*Develop Confidence in One's Ability to Learn*
G1A1	Anticipate Success
G1A2	Capitalize Upon Previous Successes
G1A3	Accept a Challenge
G1A4	Accept Encouragement from Others
G1A5	Look to the Example of Respected Others
G1A6	Develop Enthusiasm
G1A7	Develop Curiosity
G1A8	Work at Achieving a Positive Self Image
G1B	*Establish Short-Term and Long-Term Learning Goals*
G1B1	Identify Purpose (While Maintaining Individuality)
G1B2	State Reasons or Values
G1B3	Recognize Limitations
G1B4	Predict Results
G1B5	Reevaluate Goals when Necessary
G1B6	Maintain Focus
G1B7	Recognize Results
G1C	*Develop Insight into Own Learning Style*
G1C1	State Strongest Sensory Mode
G1C2	Describe Preferred Amount of Personal Control over Learning
G1C3	State Preferred Frequency of Feedback
G1D	*Accept Responsibility*
G1D1	Accept Learning as a Personal Process
G1D2	Accept Teacher as Helper and Resource Person
G1D3	Relate to One's Own Environment (Physical, Cultural, Social)
G1D4	Recognize the Impact of What Is Learned on the Environment
G2	Manage Self as a Learner
G2A	*Maintain Health of Mind and Body*
G2A1	Maintain Emotional Well-Being
G2A2	Cope with Negative Feedback
G2A3	Develop a Feeling of Personal Control
G2A4	Seek a Positive Attitude
G2A5	Develop a Personal Point of View
G2A6	Relate Effects of Good Nutrition on Ability to Learn
G2A7	Relate Effects of Drug and Alcohol on Learning and Recall
G2A8	Allocate Time for Exercise
G2A9	Provide for Personal Rewards

Table 10.1. Adult Basic Skills — Category G: Learn How to Learn, Cont'd.

G2B	*Manage Time*
G2B1	Focus Study on One Subject at a Time
G2B2	Allocate Time for Rest and Relaxation
G2B3	Take Short Breaks from Study
G2B4	Plan for Regular Home Study
G2B5	Allow Time for Unforeseen Events
G3	Understand the Learning Environment
G3A	*Utilize the Complete Educational Environment*
G3A1	Recognize Availability of Support Services in the School
G3A2	Familiarize Self with School Policies and Regulations
G3A3	Utilize Library/Learning Resource Centre Fully
G3A4	Know Physical Layout of School
G3A5	Identify Transportation Alternatives
G3B	*Create a Home Environment Conducive to Learning*
G3B1	Organize a Suitable Time and Place for Study
G3B2	Share Learning Goals with Significant Others
G3B3	Plan, Schedule and/or Share Household and Family Responsibilities
G3C	*Learn to Access Other Learning Resources*
G3C1	Recognize Availability of Community Support Services
G3C2	Use Experience of Others
G3C3	Locate/Recognize Potential Consultants
G3C4	Recognize the Limitations of Consultants
G4	Utilize Various Learning Methods
G4A	*Learn as an Individual*
G4A1	Utilize Lectures/Demonstrations
G4A2	Utilize Visual Presentations (TV, Film, Graphics)
G4A3	Utilize Printed Materials
G4A4	Utilize Computers
G4A5	Write (Reports, Essays, Exams)
G4B	*Learn as a Member of a Group*
G4B1	Utilize Models for Emulation
G4B2	Utilize Group Participation
G4B3	Utilize Role Playing
G4B4	Utilize Peer Tutor Situation
G4B5	Utilize Discussion/Debate
G4B6	Utilize Peer Group Teaching

Table 10.1. Adult Basic Skills—Category G: Learn How to Learn, Cont'd.

G4C	*Learn by Doing*
G4C1	Utilize Experimental/Hands-On Approach
G4C2	Utilize Field Trips
G4C3	Utilize On-the-Job Training Programs
G4D	*Learn by Self-Direction*
G4D1	Plan Own Learning Project
G4D2	Set Objectives or Goals
G4D3	Organize Own Time
G4D4	Prepare Plan of Study/Approach
G4D5	Employ Self-Directed Learning in a Series of Steps
G4D6	Utilize Appropriate Resources
G4D7	Obtain Feedback
G5	Practical Thinking
G5A	*Apply Creative Thinking*
G5A1	Identify and Record Intuitive and Sub-Conscious Thought
G5A2	Consider Emotions
G5A3	Brainstorm for Ideas
G5A4	Imagine
G5A5	Look for New Patterns and Relationships
G5A6	Construct Diagram or Model
G5B	*Apply Lateral/Divergent Thinking*
G5B1	Generate Alternatives
G5B2	Seek Many Categories
G5B3	Explore Pros and Cons
G5B4	Propose Unconventional Methods
G5B5	Accept Alternatives
G5B6	Discuss and Share Ideas to Get Feedback
G5C	*Apply Convergent Thinking*
G5C1	Project Possible Alternatives
G5C2	Eliminate Inappropriate Ideas
G5C3	Choose a Solution
G5D	*Apply Critical Thinking*
G5D1	Gather Background Information
G5D2	Draw on Past Experience
G5D3	Determine the Relevant Standard
G5D4	Compare Data with Standard
G5E	*Apply Analytical Thinking*
G5E1	Recognize There Is a Problem
G5E2	Define the Problem and Establish the Key Points (Components)

Table 10.1. Adult Basic Skills—Category G: Learn How to Learn, Cont'd.

G5E3	Make Minor Decisions
G5E4	Construct Categories
G5F	*Apply Logic/Reason*
G5F1	Describe Situation
G5F2	Identify Facets
G5F3	Categorize Relevant and Irrelevant Facts
G5F4	Present Premises
G5F5	Formulate Assumptions
G5F6	Criticize Premises and Assumptions
G5F7	List Probable Conclusions
G5F8	Construct Deductive Arguments
G5F9	Construct Inductive Arguments
G5F10	Identify Faulty Logic
G5F11	Evaluate Process
G6	Recall and Apply Data to New Situations
G6A	*Employ Recall Techniques*
G6A1	Apply Rote Technique
G6A2	Apply Mnemonic Techniques
G6A3	Apply Note-Taking Techniques and Methods
G6A4	Apply Review Techniques
G6A5	Associate New Data with Prior Knowledge
G6A6	Apply Concentration Techniques
G6A7	Participate in Competition
G6A8	Apply Spaced and Massed Practice
G6B	*Apply Knowledge to New Situations*
G6B1	Extract Relevant Ideas
G6B2	Compare Old Knowledge to New Situations
G6B3	Study Related Fields
G6B4	Categorize New Knowledge into Appropriate Context
G6B5	Profit by Mistakes
G6B6	Evaluate the Design/Procedure
G7	Apply Problem-Solving Technique to Make Rational and Reasonable Decisions
G7A	*Identify Problem*
G7A1	Recognize Indications that Problems Exist
G7A2	Recognize Need to Make a Decision
G7A3	Determine if Change is Desired
G7A4	Accept Ownership of the Problems
G7A5	Analyze Consequences of Indecision and/or Impulsiveness
G7A6	Accept Associated Risks in Decision Making

Table 10.1. Adult Basic Skills—Category G: Learn How to Learn, Cont'd.

G7B	*Gather/Collect Information*
G7B1	Clarify All Aspects of Perceived Situation
G7B2	Determine Factors That May Have Contributed to a Problem Situation
G7B3	Access Appropriate Resources for Problem Solving
G7B4	Organize Incoming Information into Meaningful Pattern
G7B5	Prioritize Information
G7B6	Further Define Problem
G7C	*Establish Parameters for Decision to Be Made*
G7C1	Examine Constraints of Problems
G7C2	Consider Time Factor as a Constraint in Dealing with Problems
G7C3	Estimate Cost/Resource Factors in Dealing with Problems
G7C4	Calculate Risk Factors in Dealing with Problems
G7C5	Assess Impact of Others on Your Decision
G7C6	Assess Impact of Decision on Others
G7C7	Assess Impact of Circumstances and Conditions on Decisions to Be Made
G7C8	Define Absolute Limits on Decision
G7D	*Generate Alternatives*
G7D1	List All Possible Alternatives in Problem Solving
G7D2	Determine if Enough Information Has Been Gathered About Problem
G7D3	Consult Others for Additional Ideas on Problem Solving
G7D4	Determine Which Wants and Needs Have Highest Priority
G7E	*Evaluate Alternatives*
G7E1	Weigh Pros and Cons of Problem-Solving Alternatives
G7E2	Consider Criteria and Constraints of Problem-Solving Alternatives
G7E3	Speculate Possible Outcomes of Problem-Solving Alternatives
G7F	*Make Decision*
G7F1	Select Best Problem-Solving Alternative
G7F2	Carry Out Decision re Problem Solving
G7F3	Decide When and How to Evaluate Problems
G7G	*Evaluate Results of Decisions*
G7G1	Reflect on Consequences of Decision
G7G2	Accept Responsibility for Decision
G7G3	Relate Experience to Future Decisions

ifying the purposes of learning-related activities, as well as improvement in problem-solving skills (Rempel, 1986).

At the Lac La Biche Centre, learning-to-learn modules are now built in to both a human relations course designed to prepare students for academic success in postsecondary education and a community social services course for persons seeking employment as paraprofessionals in social work. The objectives of the learning-to-learn components include increased self-awareness and understanding of self-as-learner, improved interpersonal communication skills, and understanding of such matters as the theory of brain hemispheres, the need for active learning, and barriers to successful learning. Students are encouraged to get in touch with their thoughts and feelings as they seek to learn. Various practice activities involving self-disclosure and values clarification are conducted. Learning style profiling plays an important part in the design; several learning style instruments are administered, and staff members assist the students in clarifying implications for improved learning strategies and educational decisions.

Implementation of concepts and strategies into ongoing ABE programs may be approached from a variety of differing perspectives and in a number of different ways. Derry and Murphy (1986) discuss the advantages of embedded versus detached strategies. They identify the advantages of a realistic context to be associated with embedded strategies but they see transfer of skills to other settings or subjects as a major problem. Detached strategies provide for a much more generalized approach but do not address what they refer to as the executive function.

In discussing the direct teaching of learning strategies, McKeachie, Pintrich, and Lin (1985) outline three levels of possible instruction: knowledge of the specific learning skills for a specific course or subject, knowledge of generic process skills, and knowledge of when and why to employ a given learning skill. Similarly, Brown, Campione, and Day (1981) referred earlier to blind training, informed training, and training for self-control or monitoring of skills associated with learning from texts. They also found a need for explicit training for students with severe learning problems.

Clearly, for maximum benefit, a number of different opportunities to learn to learn need to be developed and structured within the ABE experience. Concepts and skills could reach the learner through (1) more appropriate teaching/learning strategies, (2) integration within specific subject courses, (3) direct instruction of skills and concepts in separately structured learning experiences, (4) counseling services, and (5) combinations of these approaches. Direct interventions can be most effective when accompanied by strategies within subject area courses to provide the application and practice of skills in new and different settings, as documented by Derry and Murphy (1986). Opportunities for the student to gain the benefits of new or improved learning strategies at the time of felt need can probably be best provided through counseling services.

The Implementation Challenge. The introduction of change into educational programs remains a slow and difficult process. Faculty and staff often lack a process orientation. Staff development activity is usually essential, and pilot programs are usually helpful. Other institutional change strategies will need to be activated. With the variety of training approaches available, implementation on an institution-wide basis can be very difficult. Instructor steering committees and extensive involvement from all areas of the institution are a necessity.

In Alberta, the materials made available to instructors, mainly through in-service training, focused on the potential of learning to learn. Teacher self-evaluation approaches believed to contribute significantly to the fostering of student learning strategies were also included. However, it is necessary to allocate more significant resources to learning-skills curriculum development projects, the products of which can be made available to other institutions and instructors for implementation.

A provincial implementation committee with membership from each of the five participating institutions is currently planning and guiding the implementation process in the province. The first major step has been the assembling and production of an instructor's manual entitled *The G Book* (Alberta Vocational Centres/Community Vocational Centres, 1987), which provides information concerning the purposes, objectives, and concept of learning to learn along with guidance and examples for implementation. At this writing it seems clear that many Alberta adult basic education personnel recognize the need for more emphasis on learning to learn, and the necessary competencies have been carefully identified. More support and initiative are needed now in order to translate taxonomies of skills into local programs, curricula, and teaching behavior.

References

Alberta Advanced Education. *Analysis: Field Services Division, Institutional Profiles.* Edmonton, Canada: Alberta Advanced Education, 1985.

Alberta Vocational Centres/Community Vocational Centres. *Adult Basic Education: The G Book.* Edmonton, Canada: Alberta Advanced Education, 1987.

Brown, A. L., Campione, J. C., and Day, J. D. "Learning to Learn: On Training Students to Learn from Texts." *Educational Researcher,* 1981, *10* (2), 14–21.

Burghardt, F. F. "Can the Problem of Illiteracy Be Solved? A View Based on AVC Edmonton's Adult Basic Education Program." Paper presented at Change: Implications for Adult Learning Conference, Regina, Saskatchewan, Canada, May 1987.

Collett, D. J., Deane, A. K., Kendal, G. D., and Brooks, T. *Catalogue of Adult Basic Skills.* Edmonton, Canada: Department of Industrial and Vocational Education, 1983.

Derry, S. J., and Murphy, D. A. "Designing Systems That Train Learning Ability: From Theory to Practice." *Review of Educational Research,* 1986, *56* (1), 1–39.

Fahy, P., and Green, W. *Student Characteristics from Student Information System Data.* Edmonton, Canada: Alberta Vocational Centre, 1986.

McKeachie, W. J., Pintrich, P. R., and Lin, Y. "Teaching Learning

Strategies." *Educational Psychologist,* 1985, *20* (3), 153–160.

Mayes, C. "Five Critical Thinking Strategies for Adult Basic Education Learners." *Lifelong Learning: An Omnibus of Practice and Research,* 1987, *10* (7), 11–13, 25.

Rempel, H. A. "Innovative Project Learning Skills Program: Final Report." Calgary, Canada: Alberta Vocational Centre, 1986.

Smith, R. M. *Learning How to Learn: Applied Theory for Adults.* New York: Cambridge Book Company, 1982.

Smith, R. M. *Theory Building for Learning How to Learn.* DeKalb, Ill.: Educational Studies Press, 1988.

Thomas, A. *Adult Illiteracy in Canada.* Ottawa: Canadian Commission for UNESCO, 1983.

❧ Chapter 11 ❧

Promoting
Active Learning
in the Workplace

Mark Cheren

There is growing acceptance that learning-to-learn competence represents essential workplace skills. This chapter examines how this newfound appreciation translates into an array of human resource development activities—some easy to identify, many a great deal less obvious. It explores ways that these efforts can be extended as workplace educators, educators in higher education, and consultants work together to bring about these improvements.

As in other contexts, the essence of learning to learn in the workplace is the fostering of learning that is more efficient and effective, more active and reflective (Cheren, 1983, 1987; Marsick, 1987; Smith, 1982, 1987). Enhancing basic learning skills and learning strategies to make learning more efficient and more effective involves such things as learning how to read, observe, listen, write, compute, or study more effectively. Fostering more *active* learning refers, among other things, to the practice of encouraging personnel at every level of the organization to initiate a greater number of learning efforts on their own. It also can mean encouraging people to take more initiative in tailoring and otherwise improving both organizationally sanctioned and self-initiated learning efforts.

Fostering more *reflective* learning in this context refers, among other things, to encouraging greater variety in the strategies and resources personnel use in their work-related learning. It involves enhancing the ability of members of an organization to make sound and imaginative choices about the learning strategies and learning resources they use, and to monitor the effectiveness of learning strategies and resources, making changes when and as these are needed or would be helpful. To the extent that people begin to take responsibility for such things themselves, they are learning to do what teachers, professors, and trainers have traditionally done for them in the past. What is significant is that in a very short time enhancing learning competence has come to be accepted as an important training function.

The American Society of Training and Development (ASTD) and the U.S. Department of Labor recently conducted a two-year study of basic workplace skills. The pace of change in technology and in markets, new demographics (fewer and generally less skilled workers), and the changing nature of work itself (less routine, more apt to involve workers in problem solving) have all contributed to sharply altered perceptions concerning what is *basic*. In an article summarizing the ASTD/Labor study (Carnevale and others, 1988) learning to learn is identified as the first of thirteen "new basics." The others are as follows: listening, oral communications, problem solving, creative thinking, self-esteem, goal setting/motivation, personal and career development skills, interpersonal skills, teamwork, negotiation, organizational effectiveness, and leadership. It will be noted that the latter twelve turn out to be indispensable to the first, and vice versa. The distinction between learning skills and work skills is disappearing. In the study, learning to learn was defined as the ability to acquire the knowledge and skills needed to learn effectively, no matter the situation.

There is now too much to learn and organizational resources are too scarce to expect organizations to provide all the training and development needed by their employees. Moreover, efficiency and effectiveness in learning and the application of what is learned on the job are issues of concern with respect to both organizationally sponsored and worker initiated learning. Human resource energy cannot be squandered in any function, certainly not training; margins are too tight. As a result, organizations are finding they can no longer afford to ignore issues of learning competence.

What this suggests is not only that learning to learn has become one of the new basic skills, but that an increasing percentage of the training dollar will be spent on the development of learning competence in the years ahead. This is particularly necessary since schooling at all levels does relatively little to prepare people to take initiative in or responsibility for their learning. There are exceptions, but these are few and far between. On the other hand, to imply as we have that many employers are doing more than schools and colleges in the way of research and innovation regarding learning—a contention buttressed by a Carnegie Foundation study (Eurich, 1985)—does not mean that workplace efforts to improve learning competence are always labeled as such. For example, many learning skill development activities are found under the heading of "career development," one of the above-cited workplace skills.

Organization-based trainers and consultants have often found it necessary to work more implicitly than explicitly to enhance learning competence. In the workplace, management wants help in getting the job done. Learning more effectively can be seen as a means to that end. But too much explicit attention to educational process can be seen as tangential, a diversion from bottom line priorities. When questions and reflection about learning become explicit, it is usually the tip of a rather large and extensive iceberg emerging above the seas of organizational activity here and there. As a result, skillful design is central to helping people to learn to learn more effectively in the workplace. Before describing some examples of both explicit and implicit efforts to enhance learning competence in the workplace, it might be helpful to consider some ways in which these efforts and the language used to describe them are evolving.

Learning Management

There is considerable agreement among workplace educators that it would be best if much current educational jargon could be left behind. The term *self-directed learning* offers an example. When equated with adult education, the term can set an inflexible and at times unworkable standard for organizational trainers to meet. More important, self-directed learning is not an accurate description of how people can or should operate as learners in organizations at all times. Negotiation and collaboration are consistently called for.

As efforts increase to institutionalize support for enhancing learning competence, more situationally responsive models and more neutral, accurate, and down-to-earth terms are being introduced. Among these is the idea of learning management skills. Learning and managing learning can usefully be understood as two separate if related groups of activities. Becoming more efficient in learning could involve learning to read more purposefully or memorize factual material related to work procedures. By contrast, managing learning equates closely with the more active and more reflective activities possible in a learning effort, as mentioned earlier. It may involve, for example, arranging for coaching from a colleague, negotiating something in the way of exchange for the service, and then incorporating the coaching into a learning plan previously prepared with the help of a supervisor.

Learning management conveys an essential flexibility in relating to expertise. The individual can direct, collaborate, confer, and request consultation, instruction, or coaching—in short, play a range of established management roles in the course of a learning or development effort. This flexibility is made more graphic by incorporating into the mix a situational learning model of learner and learning resource person interaction. Situational learning is closely analogous to the concepts of situational leadership and situational management, two names given to the management model most widely taught in U.S. corporations and universities. The situational learning model suggests the provision of varying amounts of external support, structure, control, and help with the performance of learning management functions. It calls for these variations not only between individuals, but from learning effort to learning effort, from one aspect of a learning effort to another, and from one phase of a learning effort to another. For example, for a staff member with good accounting skills, this could mean providing more help with designing a learning plan to improve negotiating skills than with a plan to learn about a new set of accounting procedures coming out of the central office. In the individual's efforts to learn negotiating skills, progressively less support will be required as implementation of the learning plan progresses. In the context of the interactive situational learning framework, learning management supports a particularly flexible and, as a result, a particularly powerful approach to learning (Cheren, 1987).

At the same time, helping personnel to manage their learning more effectively and to enhance and further develop these learning management skills complements well-established efforts in numerous organizations to help people manage their time more effectively. Also closely related is the concept of fostering stress management skills, which enjoys acceptance in the organizational setting. Subsuming both learning and learning management abilities under the single heading of learning management skills has the additional advantage of helping to put learners and educators on a more collaborative footing in the sense that they can both be seen to be managing learning. From this perspective, it is easier to see how they can and should collaborate to accomplish mutually negotiated learning and development objectives.

Some Workplace Examples

There is an increasing number of examples of educators and organizational trainers working to foster learning management skills. Sylvia Downs and her colleagues, in projects initially supported by Britain's Further Education Unit, set out to improve the learning skills of young working people and adults attending technical colleges. After carefully researching the process needs of low achievers, Downs and her colleagues took as a primary objective expanding the number and variety of skills people were using to learn in school and on the job. They also tried to increase the degree to which active rather than passive approaches were used and to help people overcome attitudinal blockages to learning. People were taught to assess which learning mode was the right tool for a particular task — using a construct called MUD: memorizing, understanding, and doing. The main intervention was to design, test, and evaluate a flexible short course (from two to five days depending on the amount of practice activity introduced). A train-the-trainer course was also developed. Downs considers the course successful but confesses that organizational inertia and instructors' ingrained tendencies to foster passivity represent a formidable "millstone of tradition" (Downs, 1987, p. 15).

Kenneth Carlisle developed a four-day study skills course to lead off a six-month educational program for entry-level technicians at a nuclear power station. The areas covered included short- and long-term memory, positive attitudes toward learning, greater self-awareness as one learns, characteristics of effective learners, a study system, a note-taking system, mnemonic devices, and other strategies for prompting recall of information. Activities included exercises to surface assumptions about satisfactory and unsatisfactory learning, personal goal setting and contracting to meet these goals during the ensuing six-month program, concept mapping, forming analogues and metaphors, and practice in writing various kinds of test questions. End-of-course evaluation by students and staff found that the learning management module made a significant contribution to the success of the course (Carlisle, 1985).

More typically, educators, consultants, and in-house human resource development professionals have been integrating the development of learning management skills into efforts on behalf of some more tangible objective than learning to learn. For example, many organizations, from the American Red Cross to Xerox Corporation, provide supervisors and managers with training for putting together personal development plans, which involves the exercise of a number of key learning management strategies (for example, locating and evaluating learning resources). Training is aimed both at enhancing supervisors' own skills in this area and the ability to foster learning management competence in those staff members they supervise.

In another example of building the development of learning management skills into supervisory training, consultant Vanda North was brought in to work with a group of Florida Department of Health and Rehabilitative Services personnel. The situation was fraught with difficult history and a number of thorny organizational development issues common to very large agencies. North's approach involved three activities: (1) working with the participant group as she would with any organizational development client, (2) providing supervisory training, and (3) applying Buzan's (1983) suggestions for accelerated learning techniques for learning skills enhancement. Some of the educational principles utilized in the latter were the following.

1. Accommodating different learning styles sequentially, and sometimes concurrently
2. Maximizing practice opportunities
3. Fully involving the total person
4. Creating an atmosphere of safety, emphasizing cooperation rather than competition
5. Paying attention to priorities
6. Making immediate application of what is learned
7. Reflecting on new learning and application by the learner and the instructor
8. Processing educational methods employed to encourage the learner to utilize them in future situations

Accelerated learning was implicitly incorporated throughout the supervisory training and explicitly presented as a reusable tool in its own right (conversation with Vanda North; Schuster and Gritton, 1985).

Most organizations have some form of orientation for new employees. John Redding, training and development manager for the Ball Seed Company, designed an orientation program that includes considerable emphasis on the development of learning management skills. The three-month process is viewed as socialization both to the organization and to learning in the organization. During the first few days on the job, the new staff member, his or her supervisor, a training department staff member, and a peer coach from the new staff member's department work together to develop an individual training plan for the new employee. Conversations include questions about past learning experiences, to identify how the individual learns best (methods, pace, and so on); key collaborators who should be interviewed; and skills that need to be mastered as soon as possible. A two-page written document, drafted by the training person or the supervisor, summarizes the discussions and the plan, including resources that are relevant and available to support the attainment of specific learning objectives.

Follow-up dates (progress check points) are indicated and the new staff member is asked to take control of those meetings. No matter how flexible the approach, workplace learning and other experiences during the orientation period are not to take a new staff member out of the office more than 50 percent of the time. To encourage diversity in learning modes, the training plan contains two columns, one for on-the-job and one for off-the-job activities. It has turned out to be important to keep the supervisor central to this process and to guard against too much responsibility coming back to the coach. When the process works well, the new staff member and the supervisor are learning to work in a new way as a team on personal development issues (conversations with John Redding). The American Red Cross chapter of greater Chicago, for example, established a six-month orientation program with many similarities in design and intent.

Problem-Based Learning. The work of Howard Barrows, associate dean of the Southern Illinois University School of Medicine is of particular relevance. Barrows (1985, 1986, 1988) has been one of the leaders in a current movement in medical (and continuing medical) education that has been strongly endorsed by the Association of American Medical Colleges. The association's

GPEP (General Professional Education of the Physician) report included a number of pertinent recommendations. Notably, it suggested that "medical faculties should offer educational experiences that require students to be active, independent learners and problem solvers, rather than passive recipients of information" (1984, p. 12). Barrows and his colleagues have devised an approach to the design of human, paper, and computer simulations and have combined this approach with a carefully orchestrated tutorial process. The resulting educational programming is referred to as "problem-based learning."

Though it is only one of several related educational processes that can be classified under this heading (it can also be termed *solution-oriented learning*), Barrows's version of problem-based learning has a number of characteristics that make it exceptional. A neurologist, Barrows undergirded this approach with research in the nature of expert clinical reasoning. Clinical problems are addressed in a way that (1) anchors new knowledge and skill in the context in which they will later be used (thereby facilitating recall), (2) tunes up professional reasoning and problem-solving skills, and (3) requires and fosters the use of skills essential to self-managed continuing professional development. In Barrows's process, as in North's work, competence in collaborative learning and problem solving is central. The approach also addresses listening and oral communication skills, creative thinking, goal setting/motivation, and interpersonal competence, several more of ASTD's basics. These abilities are certain to be useful in the innumerable diagnostic and treatment consultations and case conferences in which physicians participate (Barrows, 1986).

The number of key competencies addressed and the unusual power of this approach make it particularly promising. It has already been applied to several other fields, including training for sales personnel at Upjohn Company and management education at Ohio Bell Corporation through Capital University; faculty development at Sangamon State, DePaul, and Capital Universities; and a broad range of business, professional, and liberal arts courses at Capital, Sangamon State, DePaul, and Ohio University. The development of learning management competencies is skillfully woven into a larger learning process. On the surface, learning to learn represents a comparatively minor motif; but many critical learning and learning management elements pervade the infrastructure of the enterprise at deeper, less obvious levels. For example, all learning efforts are directed toward specific clinical or other work-related situations. Both the ASTD/Labor study cited above and an older study by Avice Saint (1974) have indicated that training is most productive when the instruction and learning are tied to action needed to meet work goals and solve organizational problems.

While the lesson of most of these examples points to the utility of unobtrusive designs when seeking to achieve improvement in learning management skills by the personnel of an organization, bolder strokes are possible. Malcolm Knowles, in a characteristically low-key piece of consulting for the DuPont Company, launched an entire audit of the organization as a learning environment. He asked two simple questions to a group that included high-level management personnel: What learning resources are you now using? How could these be better utilized?

The recommendations that resulted (most of which were implemented) were as follows:

Regularly Conducted Training Activities

1. Use a less pedagogical (and more "andragogical") design.
2. Provide instructor retraining.
3. Increase rewards for participating in these activities.

Line Managers and Supervisors as Resources for Learning

1. Change job descriptions to include teaching and learning activities.
2. Strengthen review system in relation to these functions.

Media Center

1. Encourage more people to use the center since technical staff are principal users.

Identify Other Individuals with Knowledge and Self-Perceived Interests and Needs

1. Survey all staff to find what knowledge they would be willing to share and would like to acquire.
2. Place the information in a data bank.

Community Resources

1. Establish an inventory of community resources, including retirees.
2. Update the inventory regularly (Cheren, 1987).

Learning Management Skills

It is possible to go further to apply an enhanced learning management standard to the human resource development procedures, programs, and systems within an organization. To do this requires reviewing all that an organization does to orient, educate, train, and develop its personnel. Orientations, workshops, courses, learning resource centers, assessment centers, supervisory training, management and executive development, educational reimbursement, and record keeping need to be examined. It is also appropriate to review organizational characteristics, including general operating procedures, leadership styles, policies, and norms, which combine to determine the climate for learning in the organization (Smith, 1987).

The objective of such a review would be to assess and, where necessary, make necessary changes to ensure that productive learning and development initiatives are strongly encouraged, to assess the extent to which people are helped to enhance the learning management skills necessary to succeed with these efforts, and to make on-the-job applications of what is learned. The desired result would be a situation characterized by (1) high-performance professional development activity on the part of most members of the organization; (2) a strong complement of metalevel components within the human resource development (HRD) system (that is to say, processes which in turn enhance learning and learning management processes); and (3) a high transference quotient, application of new learning to the job and to the demonstrated benefit of the organization. In what follows, several aspects of human resource development and organizational climate that offer potential for movement toward an enhanced learning management standard will be considered.

Orientation. All too often, orientation of new staff members takes place in several hours or several days (less frequently, several weeks) with a parade of organizational service providers and luminaries. For participants, it's sit and listen. But orientation can be turned into an active and useful process, lasting for up to a year, wherein people are challenged and helped to learn in a variety of the ways in which they will be expected to learn in the organization.

Activities, for the most part designed with input from the participants, could include the following: (1) a series of structured interviews and small-group discussions with people one will need to collaborate with; (2) some well-planned work experiences in relevant departments; (3) a modest initial career research project; (4) attractively packaged or electronic media presentations about one's unit, other organizational units, the history of the organization, and the industry; and (5) design of a comprehensive two-year job- and career-related development plan, which could serve as a tangible and appropriate capstone to this kind of orientation and provide for follow-up.

Each person's learning style should be assessed, interpreted to him or her, and taken into account in such activities. Participants can be encouraged to keep a lightly structured journal to record and reflect on their activities, their growing understanding of the organization, and questions they would like answered. A learning partner (trained for the role) can be assigned to each person to demonstrate the value of seeking out mentors and the variety of ways mentors can be of help in such matters as problem assessment, resource referral, and sponsoring contacts. In periodic meetings the new employee, a partner if one is involved, and the supervisor can meet to review progress and plan new activities.

Workshops, Courses, and Programs. Existing training and education programs can be modified and new programs designed to develop and encourage the use of learning and learning management skills. The possibilities here are limitless. Multiple options for learning the same content can be built in sequentially or concurrently to suit different learning styles and work styles at several points in each program. Self-instructional modules related to learning more actively can be included on a required or optional basis. It would be particularly useful to incorporate simulation processes dealing with actual organizational problems into the training. These can deal directly with difficult, perhaps critical situations and simultaneously sharpen reasoning and problem-solving skills. Self-managed learning excursions between meetings can be built into many program formats, routinely assessing the effects of various methods and resources whenever a group reconvenes following such an activity.

Courses and workshops can be dedicated exclusively to developing learning and learning management skills. The work of Downs and Carlisle was mentioned earlier, and Weinstein (1989) also described promising activity in this area, emphasizing the acquisition of learning strategies. Such courses can become a laboratory in which people are trained to take significant initiatives as a routine matter in all their learning activities, both formal and informal, to improve the quality of the experience and enlarge outcomes. This might be thought of as developing a new set of standard operating procedures for learning.

Modules on the use of libraries, resource centers, electronic data bases, learning strategies, content-appropriate study skills, and so on can be built into any staff development program and made available as separate modules in a self-paced, self-instructional format. Differentiated assessment of specific competencies at the beginning and end of each program can be supported with self-administered competency checklists, not only to support the identification of priorities and to assess progress but to promote ongoing development of competence in monitoring one's own performance and learning needs. External assessors and, where an assessment center exists, opportunities for self-initiated visits would also be helpful.

Specific Programs. Not all organizations will be ready to work toward meeting an enhanced learning management standard. At least in the short term, most organizations will stop short of the redesigning of all or most offerings. One answer may be producing or purchasing programs designed to enhance learning management skills in the process of addressing some other training need. In-house HRD specialists would want to design or choose programs that can successfully prepare people to use effectively the key elements in the organization's HRD system.

Supervisory Training. For a long time, supervisory training conducted by many organizations, university consultants, and vendors has included a picture of the supervisor's role with as much as one-third priority devoted to staff development (that is, the manager as teacher). Commitment to increased emphasis on development of learning management skills might suggest upgrading the quality of the staff development aspect of the supervisor's role to what in the current discussion might be described as enhanced development consulting. It is essential to begin to add metalevel development to this role as a deliberate and explicit objective.

To begin to move in this direction, consideration should be given to training supervisors and managers to become skilled and supportive in the encouragement of active and self-conscious learning by those they supervise. Such training can be included in supervisory and management training workshops, courses, and self-instructional modules. Much of what is recommended in this chapter for instructor training and some of what is recommended for learning resource center staff would be appropriate for supervisory training and management development programs. Several organizations, such as the Ball Seed Company and the American Red Cross, have begun to do so;

Ball Seed HRD staff members have found that direct involvement of supervisors in the company's individualized staff orientation program is particularly effective in developing competence in this area. Since supervisors play the primary role in helping staff members with personal development plans and since their control of staff time greatly impacts the individual's personal development efforts, the need for this involvement is apparent.

Preparation of Instructors. It is not enough to build the enhancement of learning competence into the design of programs. Those who present such programs must be prepared to cue, encourage, and respond positively and appropriately to a variety of learner initiatives. The objective here should be to foster a wide range of individualizing strategies. Instructors need to be able to work creatively with development program participants in order to focus the content more on their interests and needs, alter the activities so as to better suit some aspect of their learning styles, modify and/or enlarge the resources they use, change the timing to be responsive to their peak periods, emphasize application back on the job, and so on.

All of this needs to go on in a way that realistically balances the needs of the individual against the needs of the organization and the content of the presentations. Compensation, or time budgeted for instructors willing to put in the extra time such efforts require, needs to be appropriately adjusted; however, instructor creativity and imagination are at least as important as time expended.

The Learning Resource Center. Learning resource centers are essentially libraries in the workplace that have been expanded to include a wide range of media and materials to support the information and learning needs of organizational personnel. The shift in focus here would be from seeing staff primarily as curators of materials who sometimes play the role of reference librarians to seeing them primarily as educators, as learning and development consultants and resource brokers, skilled not only in supporting self-initiated learning but in the development of learning management skills as well.

Almost every aspect of a learning resource center might be enhanced from the perspective of the acquisition and effective use of learning management skills. Learning center staff need training to support the individualization of formal programs and the refinement of self-initiated and self-planned learning and development plans. While their level of competence in this area should be at least as great as that of instructors, it would be better if it were even greater so that they could function as master learning consultants. They should be skilled in matching the center's resources to the learning and cognitive styles of the client. Most important, they should be skilled in helping learners diagnose and overcome learning blocks that have slowed or stalled personal development efforts.

Center staff members should accumulate resources that are interactive or at least facilitate a certain amount of interaction. Simple aids that summarize the available self-instructional learning modules and the organization's formal training programs should be made available. Finally, the learning center should have resources that implicitly or explicitly address the enhancement or development of a wide range of learning and learning management skills. Such resources should ideally, like the computerized/videodisc interfaced CPR training developed by David Hahn of the American Heart Association, not only allow users to proceed at their own pace but as far as possible to pursue their own strategies, to jump out at any point and practice a skill with feedback, to review a section, to look up a term, to take an assessment test, all the while choosing from several levels of complexity (in the CPR training, all the way from layman to physician). It is difficult to see how an entire organization can move in this direction without at least one place to go for effective support for such efforts. A well-conceived, well-staffed, and well-stocked resource center is one logical choice. If this strategy were widely adopted as part of a commitment to the development of learning competence in the workplace, vendors would begin to develop the range and quality of needed materials.

Development Record Keeping. The manner in which training records are kept is particularly deserving of assessment from the perspective of learning management skills development. Most human resource record keeping is restricted to formal education and training or heavily biased to favor formal training activities. Some organizations record only the individual's participation in on-site training. All carefully planned, purposeful projects should be recorded if organizations wish to encourage a higher proportion of self-initiated development projects.

Both the initial development plan and a completed self-evaluation form should be inserted in the individual's personnel file or in a special set of development project files maintained in the learning resource center. A project would then be considered completed and logged into the individual's training record. Expert evaluations could be added as desired. If the files were located in the learning resource center, it might be relatively easy, with permission from the individual, to develop the portion of an organization-wide learning resource data base that deals with human resources.

Assessing the Entire Organization

Looking at the training and development function and the entire organization as a complex of systems, programs, policies, and procedures, it is possible to examine the extent to which each component encourages and reinforces active, self-conscious learning and a whole range of learner initiatives. Such evaluation holds promise of direct benefits for the individual and the organization. For example, if the only financial resources available for educational reimbursement are for college credit-bearing courses, the organization may well be forcing people to waste both time and money on an entire course when a short workshop or personal learning project would be adequate to satisfy a discrete job-related need. In reviewing organizational climate from this perspective, training managers and organizational executives will want to ask questions such as the following:

1. How well does the organizational climate support innovation?
2. Are supervisors evaluated and rewarded in regard to the support they provide for personal development planning and activities?
3. Are supervisors evaluated and rewarded for the fostering of learning and learning management competence in staff?
4. Is adequate time allowed for learning on the job?
5. Do organizational norms promote an atmosphere for working and learning that is predominantly collaborative or predominantly competitive?
6. To what extent are organizational development, human resource development, and market orientation integrated?
7. Does the chief executive provide a vision of the organization and set a tone and example by word and deed that encourages variety, quantity, and quality in continuing professional development?
8. Do senior managers and executives demonstrate willingness to commit resources to the enhancement of learning management skills in all staff?
9. To what extent does the organization encourage double-loop learning—learning from experience through the questioning and modification of existing norms, values, goals, policies, and procedures (Argyris and Schön, 1978)?
10. Is it assumed and made clear that primary responsibility for development lies with the individual staff member, and is initiative in this regard prized and rewarded?

An in-depth understanding of the learning climate of organizations probably lies ahead of us. Smith (1987) has pointed to a number of workplace and organizational characteristics that need to be explored. Marsick (1987) has suggested others.

The Role of Educators in Higher Education and Consultants

Educators (for example, university graduate faculty) and consultants can play a variety of roles in helping organizations move toward an enhanced learning management standard. The following chart identifies some of the possibilities and links them to workplace applications of learning to learn discussed in this chapter.

Organization's Response	*Educator-Consultant Role*
1. Build learning management skills (LMS) into employee orientation	1. Support design efforts
2. Design new content courses and modify existing courses and programs to enhance LMS	2. Educate organizations to include LMS development Collaborate with designers or provide designs
3. Provide specific courses and programs that develop LMS	3. Train trainers to handle LMS development specifically Provide trainers and train-the-trainer designs
4. Assess LMS development aspect of the entire organizational training (HRD) system	4. Train internal staff to assess the training and development program as an integrated system for LMS development
5. Prepare instructors of all organizational training programs to support LMS development	5. Serve as trainers or assist in redesign of instructor training
6. Incorporate LMS into all aspects of learning resource center functioning	6. Provide materials, training, and assessment of self-instructional resources
7. Train supervisors to help staff develop LMS	7. Provide training or train HRD staff to provide training

8. Provide record keeping that encourages staff-initiated as well as organizational sponsored personal development efforts	8. Audit record-keeping system and make recommendations Provide new system if appropriate
9. Enhance entire organization as a learning environment	9. Audit organization as a learning environment and make recommendations

These kinds of activities offer opportunities for far-sighted higher educators and competent consultant groups to do the kind of design science work that would establish for them a special and highly valued role in workplace education. The service is especially appropriate as a result of the inherent complexities in learning to learn and its application to the world of work.

Conclusion

Since today's workplace requires skilled, motivated learners, a range of efforts is underway to develop learning management competence in organizations, and many more are possible. Best results will usually be achieved when training and learning related to learning to learn are integrated with action in the solving of organizational problems. An unobtrusive approach coupled with an emphasis on metasystems design will be needed.

Activity in developing learning competence in organizations should itself begin to impact positively on the climate for learning in the workplace. New synergies of efficiency and effectiveness in learning should be possible. Workplace educators involved with the development of learning management skills will be giving to all members of the organization and the public at large skills and functions traditionally considered the province of educators. The role of educators should increasingly be to provide technical assistance and sophisticated consultation and to act as codesigners, collaborators, and supporters of detailed and differentiated assessment.

References

Argyris, C., and Schön, D. A. *Organizational Learning.* Reading, Mass.: Addison-Wesley, 1978.

Association of American Medical Colleges. *Physicians for the Twenty-First Century: The GPEP Report; Report of the Panel on the General Professional Education of the Physician and College Preparation for Medicine.* Washington, D.C.: Association of American Medical Colleges, 1984.

Barrows, H. S. *How to Design a Problem-Based Curriculum for the Preclinical Years.* New York: Springer, 1985.

Barrows, H. S. "A Taxonomy of Problem-Based Learning Methods." *Medical Education,* 1986, *20,* 481–486.

Barrows, H. S. *The Tutorial Process.* Springfield: University of Southern Illinois Press, 1988.

Buzan, T. *Use Both Sides of Your Brain.* New York: Dutton, 1983.

Carlisle, K. E. "Learning How to Learn." *Training and Development Journal,* 1985, *39* (3), 75–80.

Carnevale, A. P., and others. "Workplace Basics: The Skills Employers Want." *Training and Development Journal,* 1988, *41* (10), 22–30.

Cheren, M. E. "Helping Learners Achieve Greater Self-Direction." In R. M. Smith (ed.), *Helping Adults Learn How to Learn.* New Directions for Continuing Education, no. 19. San Francisco: Jossey-Bass, 1983.

Cheren, M. E. (ed.). *Learning Management: Emerging Directions for Learning to Learn in the Workplace.* Information Series no. 320. Columbus: National Center for Research in Vocational Education, Ohio State University, 1987.

Downs, S. "Developing Learning Skills." In M. E. Cheren (ed.), *Learning Management: Emerging Directions for Learning to Learn in the Workplace.* Information Series no. 320. Columbus: The National Center for Research in Vocational Education, Ohio State University, 1987.

Eurich, N. P. *Corporate Classrooms: The Learning Business.* Princeton, N.J.: Carnegie Foundation for the Advancement of Teaching, 1985.

Marsick, V. J. *Learning in the Workplace.* New York: Croom Helm, 1987.

Saint, A. *Learning at Work.* Chicago: Nelson Hall, 1974.

Schuster, D. H., and Gritton, C. E. *SALT: Suggestive Accelerative Learning Techniques: Theory and Applications.* Des Moines, Iowa: Des Moines Public Schools, 1985.

Smith, R. M. *Learning How to Learn: Applied Theory for Adults.* New York: Cambridge Book Company, 1982.

Smith, R. M. "Learning to Learn in the Workplace." In M. E. Cheren (ed.), *Learning Management: Emerging Directions for Learning to Learn in the Workplace.* Information Series no. 320. Columbus: National Center for Research in Vocational Education, Ohio State University, 1987.

Smith, R. M. *Theory Building for Learning How to Learn.* DeKalb, Ill.: Educational Studies Press, 1988.

Weinstein, C. E. "Why Knowing How to Learn Is Not Enough." Presentation at the National Conference on Higher Education, Valencia, California, 1989. (Available on AAHE-6 Mobiltape.)

Chapter 12

Encouraging
Self-Planned Learning

Allen Tough

Helping people of all ages develop better skills in planning and conducting their own learning is an exciting frontier in human learning. Benefits include improvement of speed and success in learning, growth in confidence, and willingness to tackle additional projects. Thus, in turn, people will gain knowledge and skill for their own fulfillment and to benefit their families, employers, and communities.

Indeed, in a rapidly changing world faced with severe global problems, the ability of citizens and politicians to learn about the environment, poverty, hunger, peace, and other societal issues is crucial. Most futurists agree that any successful path to a positive human future will require extraordinary changes in knowledge, understanding, attitudes, and behavior of people of all ages and in all walks of life. Widespread learning about global issues, potential futures, the consequences of today's policies, and their implications for each of us may lead to more enlightened decisions and behavior. Unless enough citizens are sufficiently informed and concerned, our society is unlikely to make the hard choices needed for a satisfactory future. Greater individual competence at self-planned learning, then, can pay off for all of human civilization and its future.

Adolescents and adults are already remarkably competent at planning and conducting their own learning projects, but they could become even more successful. The purpose of this chapter is to encourage educators and others to try various approaches to improving this sort of competence so that people of all ages can be highly skilled at planning and guiding their own learning.

During adulthood and even childhood, a considerable amount of learning occurs as a result of self-planned learning projects. Learning projects are highly intentional learning efforts with certain definite knowledge and skill as the goal. The planner is the person or program that does more than half of the detailed day-to-day planning in a learning project. It is quite common for the person himself or herself to plan what and how to learn during most of the learning episodes: this is called *self-planned learning*. Conceptually precise definitions of learning projects and the four types of planners are provided by Tough (1979, chaps. 2, 7, app. A).

Let us look at adults for a moment and then turn our attention to children and adolescents. About 90 percent of all adults conduct at least one learning project in any given year. Indeed, the median learner conducts five different major learning efforts in a year and spends an average of 100 hours on each one, a total of 500 hours per year at highly intentional learning. About 70 or 75 percent of these learning projects are planned largely by the learner and another 7 percent by peers or other amateurs, with the remainder planned by professionals. Originally presented by Tough (1979), these findings have been confirmed in more than 60 other studies by researchers in nine countries. A remarkably similar picture emerged from studies of the total range of intentional changes, including changes that result from major decisions and actions as well as from learning projects (Tough, 1982).

Children and adolescents also commonly conduct self-planned learning projects quite apart from their school-based education. These out-of-school learning efforts tend to be shorter than adult efforts but more numerous, since children have more to learn about a vast variety of topics (Tough, 1979, chap. 3). Self-planning is the most common approach for ten-year-olds and sixteen-year-olds (41 percent and 46 percent, respectively, in Tough, 1979, table 10). Learning in groups, however, is much more common than during adulthood and therefore the proportion of self-planned learning is lower than it is for adults.

It is clear, then, that planning and managing one's own learning efforts is a common human activity that occurs during childhood, adolescence, and adulthood in every population in every country that has been included in sixty different studies. (The one exception was a very old and ill population in a chronic care nursing home.) It occurs in homes and libraries, alone and with friends and with family members, on farms and in cities, at the workplace and in the wilderness. Most of us do it for an average of ten hours a week, yet we rarely think of ourselves as highly involved in self-planned learning.

How well do we do it? Could our competence and success at self-planned learning be improved?

How Competent?

Planning a personal learning effort can be a complex and difficult task, especially if a person is entering a new area of knowledge and skill. It is difficult to know what strategies, methods, and resources are likely to be effective in a new field. During self-planned learning, people handle these difficulties by seeking advice from various individuals and from printed materials and other nonhuman resources. As they proceed, they modify their strategies and paths after gaining further information and advice. In fact, a diagram of a self-planned learning project often resembles a zig-zag path or a path with many branches (and even dead ends), rather than a highway.

One study found that adults rated their self-planned learning higher than professionally planned learning on three variables: (1) the resulting amount of knowledge, skill, information, understanding, or change; (2) the enthusiasm the person has about this new knowledge and skill; and (3) the benefits to other people, such as family or employer (Tough, 1979, table 12).

The children and adolescents rated the two types of learning as approximately equal.

No doubt people vary in their level of competence at planning and managing a learning project; about 90 percent of learners achieve enough progress to make it worthwhile to continue. A few may be hopelessly inept but most are fairly successful. At the same time, there is little doubt in my mind that a large proportion of people, adults as well as children and adolescents, could improve their competence at choosing, planning, and guiding their various self-planned learning efforts. One must simultaneously keep in mind two facts that are not as contradictory as they may appear at first: (1) People are already competent and successful at planning and guiding their own learning, far more successful than they or we usually give them credit for. (2) Most of these same people, as well as the less successful learners, could become even more competent and successful.

Improving Competence in Planning and Managing Learning

There are four major strategies by which professional educators and writers can help learners improve their competence. Simultaneously facilitating all four is probably the most useful path to follow.

Help People Understand Self-Planned Learning. Many people lack understanding of their own learning efforts, let alone self-planned learning in general. They may even have false assumptions and beliefs that hinder their efforts. One useful strategy, then, is to provide them with information about the normal, natural process of self-planned learning. They will probably be quite surprised at how important and widespread self-planned learning is. They will be affirmed by the fact that their learning is mostly do-it-yourself, with help from friends and other nonprofessionals. It is also useful for people to gain accurate knowledge about their own learning by identifying their recent self-planned learning projects and then noting their methods, difficulties, and outcomes. As people come to see the variety of content and methods in their own self-planned learning, they regard these learning efforts more highly.

Many people believe they are strange and unique in how they learn. They believe they fail to correspond to some common pattern, even though they cannot articulate what that pattern is. They lack the raised consciousness that learning on your own, and learning with peers, is an effective and normal activity. As a result, they may not readily discuss their learning with other people as a natural topic of conversation and may miss out on hearing about the learning efforts of others.

It is time to correct the unbalanced picture of learning that is presented by many writers, educators, professional helpers, and television programs, which often depict learning either as unintentional or as professionally guided. Highly intentional, successful, self-guided learning with help from nonprofessionals is simply not portrayed very often in fiction, nonfiction, biographies, television programs, professional literature, and research literature. I do not believe that self-planned learning is somehow better than other kinds of learning, but I do believe that it has been neglected in the print and electronic media.

Let me hasten to point out that a few books have already presented a balanced picture of human learning, such as those of Gross (1977) and Rogers (1977). Indeed, even 170 years ago, at least one writer praised self-planned learning: "Glorious is the prospect, most fascinating the hope, held out by self-cultivation to those who . . . gather every day and every hour something that shall open the mind to yet greater improvement, prepare for further exertions, and ensure success in studies, and arts, and pursuits, of highest importance, through years long to come" (Taylor, 1820, pp. 87–88).

Help People Appreciate Their Competence, Power, and Success. In the first interviews that I conducted, I was surprised at the typical attitudes of people toward their own self-planned learning (Tough, 1967, pp. 39–40, 75, 77). When I stated at the beginning of the interview that I was interested in the person's recent learning, the initial response was often a self-deprecating remark. The initial perception of many interviewees was that they had not done any learning at all during the past year, or at least that their learning was unimportant or of low quality. Many said that their learning was very strange or offbeat, not at all like that of other people.

Although these initial self-deprecating comments were sincere, they were very unrealistic. By the end of most interviews it was evident that the person had learned a great deal, had spent a large amount of time doing so, and had used a variety of methods, with actual learning usually much greater than his or her initial attitude suggested. Interviewers in many studies since then have reported the same experiences. Even my graduate students in adult education at the Ontario Institute for Studies in Education, many of them experienced practitioners, are surprised during interviews to discover how much they underrate their own learning and that of others.

People simply are not in touch with the variety, competence, and success of their self-planned learning projects or their learning with friends and family, or with how thoughtful, active, and responsible they are during such learning. They often lack confidence in their ability to diagnose their learning needs, choose strategies, and evaluate the results. They may even feel powerless and incompetent at learning without the help of professionals. Some people have even reached the point of believing that if learning is not conducted or at least certified by a qualified educator, it simply is not legitimate, significant, or worthy.

A low self-image as a learner combined with exaggerated faith in the power of professionals can make the person less likely to take initiative and responsibility for learning, less confident at managing that learning, and less powerful and competent at achieving the desired knowledge and skill. A second important strategy, then, is to help people see as accurately as possible the effectiveness of their own natural learning efforts. If they examine their learning processes more thoughtfully, they should realize that they are remarkably capable, powerful, and successful at achieving serious learning objectives on their own. They may come to treasure their own change efforts and to see themselves less as pawns (De Charms, 1976).

Help People Improve Performance of Various Tasks. A third strategy is to help people become more effective at performing the various tasks involved in planning, conducting, and evaluating learning projects. Although many people are already performing these tasks reasonably well, some of them could benefit greatly by becoming even more competent, thoughtful, and assertive. Instead of hoarding our personal expertise, we can give it away to anyone who wants it. We have to be certain, though, that our principles and general suggestions really fit the learning process of most adults and are not simply reflections of our own styles or biased views.

The self-planner must have skill in diagnosing his or her own problems and needs and in deciding just which preparatory steps to perform at any given time. Learners also need competence in performing a wide variety of preparatory tasks such as setting objectives, choosing resources, finding or arranging a suitable environment, and deciding how to evaluate progress. Of course, competence at actually carrying out the learning project, not just in planning and arranging it, is also necessary. In almost any project, the learner needs certain minimum skills in listening, taking notes, reading, memorizing, or performing other comparable tasks. The increased efficiency that can result from a mastery of effective reading techniques, for instance, is very impressive.

As I think about the person who is highly competent at self-planned learning, I often picture a long-distance runner or a cross-country motorcycle rider. Confident, determined, proactive, the runner or rider faced with difficult terrain will surmount or bypass each object calmly and competently. In the future, more and more people may seriously consider a wide range of options before narrowing and choosing their learning goals. They may manage their learning and their lives with good cheer and easy flair. They may become remarkably thoughtful, reflective, insightful, self-directed, flexible, and joyful. Their learning may be not only sufficiently thoughtful and goal oriented, but also sufficiently loose and flowing and open to spontaneous opportunities.

Improve Effectiveness at Obtaining Appropriate Help. The fourth
strategy is to help people become more effective in getting
appropriate help when needed. People who are competent at
managing their learning have to sense when they would benefit
from help and when they can do without it. Then they have to
choose the most useful resources, whether a professional helper,
a friend or neighbor, a particular book, or a group. Most important, when faced with the resource the person must be proactive
and skillful in getting the needed help and information from it.

As people become more aware, thoughtful, and insightful
about their own change efforts, they may wish to use a greater
number of professional services and resources than previously.
If professionals and their materials are flexible enough to fit
emerging needs, the demand for them may double or triple as
people become more in touch with the difficulties and obstacles
in their learning efforts. It is also possible, of course, that the
opposite will happen — as people become more knowledgeable
and competent in managing their own learning, they may use
professionals even less. It is hard to predict which way this will
go, particularly because the outcome will be affected largely by
how rapidly and flexibly professionals develop materials, opportunities, and services that fit into people's ongoing natural
processes of learning.

Possibilities for Implementation

These four strategies for competence at self-planned learning
can be implemented with a wide range of populations and in a
wide range of settings. They can be implemented for the general
public, for the employees in an organization, for the members of
an occupation or profession, or for a neighbor. They can be
implemented by teachers and counselors in schools, colleges,
universities, and adult education agencies. Parents, libraries,
clubs, and employers can all play a role.

Three possibilities for implementation suggest themselves: printed and electronic materials, group activities, and
one-to-one situations. Printed materials, even a simple booklet
or magazine article, video cassette recordings, television, and

radio can be very useful, as well as computers, interactive two-way television, and other communications media. Courses, workshops, and other group situations for helping learners gain competence are easy to develop and reasonably inexpensive. Many people should be attracted to an educational opportunity entitled "How to Manage Your Own Learning." Smith (1982) presents a tested model for a workshop of twelve contact hours. One-to-one situations include information centers, counseling, and everyday conversations. The helper can be an educator, some other professional, a lay volunteer, or a friend. In Chapter Eleven of this book, Mark Cheren makes suggestions regarding how self-planned learning can be developed and supported in the workplace.

We need innovative programs that are oriented toward developing the learner's competence at self-planning. If many of us experiment with different approaches, we will eventually learn which approaches work best for which sorts of people. Feedback and evaluation should result in the development of even better approaches. As more and more people develop greater competence at planning and guiding their own learning, we will gradually understand just what sorts of improvement are possible, how many people are interested, and what stops others from being interested. This kind of activity will result in a much larger number of skillful learners—learners with a high degree of competence in diagnosing, planning, and arranging their learning; learners able to obtain appropriate help with a minimum of time and effort; learners who foresee the potential difficulties but strive to learn nonetheless; learners willing to surmount all sorts of obstacles with the ease and good humor of cross-country runners.

Some Encouraging Examples

The aim of this chapter is to encourage educators, writers, and others to experiment with a diversity of approaches to helping people of all ages improve their competence at planning and guiding their own learning. With the possible exception of Robert Smith's workshops (Smith, 1982), I am aware of no approach that has yet been refined enough to serve as a single model for others to imitate. Instead, at this stage, there is plenty of opportunity in this area for experimentation, innovation, and primitive, naive, early-stage efforts.

Fortunately, a few pioneering efforts have been described in print, which encourage us to develop our own approaches or to replicate and modify the efforts of others. The beginning attempts can be organized into four clusters: (1) books and other printed materials, (2) a repertoire of possible techniques, (3) workshops and courses that aim directly at improving competence, and (4) courses that provide experience with self-planned learning. Additional ideas have been presented by Brookfield (1985, 1986, chap. 4), Cheren (1983), Hiemstra (1988), and Smith (1982, 1983, 1988).

The first approach is the development of printed materials that help people examine and improve their self-planned learning projects, such as a checklist, a two-page summary of basic principles, a lively booklet, or an entire book. Two books by Gross (1977, 1982) have been outstanding in helping people gain insights into themselves as potentially powerful learners and improve their ability to find appropriate resources. Copies could be prominently displayed in libraries, classrooms, and bookstores. A slim book called *Expand Your Life* (Tough, 1980) grew out of my major project on helping people become more effective in their learning, especially in choosing significant learning goals and broad strategies. During evaluation interviews, many people reported to us that the panorama of possibilities in this book had greatly widened their horizons about learning opportunities and had stimulated them to consider several new learning projects.

Within the field of behavior modification, some practitioners are moving toward self-managed change or behavioral self-management. As Coates and Thoresen (1977, p. x) put it, "These procedures are designed to teach persons the skills necessary for them to reach personally meaningful and important goals." Rather than insist that all readers follow the same advice, the authors encourage the reader to become "a personal scientist," to study and monitor his or her own situation, and to choose and evaluate the strategies most likely to be personally useful. A popular book in the Soviet Union describes self-education, suggests strategies and resources for carrying it out, and encourages increased self-directedness (Ruvinsky, 1986).

A second approach is to help people develop a rich repertoire of possible techniques and exercises from which they can choose at various times during their learning endeavors or when faced with a problem. The range of techniques for controlling and healing one's body has been expanding during recent years, for example, imaging and relaxation exercises. Within the human growth movement, these include dream work, journal writing, informal peer counseling, imaginary dialogues, self-guided fantasies, cathartic emotional expression, and several other therapeutic techniques (Lande, 1976; Matson, 1977).

Workshops and courses provide a third approach to helping people become more competent and confident at self-planned learning. John Loughary and T. Ripley, for example, developed a workshop for increasing one's planning skills and self-empowerment (Bramucci, 1977, app. I). Doug Scott (1981) developed a workshop to help school administrators become competent at choosing goals and learning strategies within the human relations area. Margaret Nacke (1979) studied the effects of a workshop designed to enhance competence at learning and change related to one's life work and spiritual activities.

Keith Sehnert, a physician, experimented with the teaching of courses to produce knowledgeable, capable, and activated patients. As a result of his self-empowerment efforts, he states as follows: "Many of my patients already are their own doctors—sometimes. They've learned to handle minor illnesses and emergencies without help, and major ones without panic. They have 'black bags' of their own, with everything from stethoscope to sphygmomanometer in them. They examine their youngsters' ears with otoscopes when they complain of earaches. . . . They are members of that brand-new breed, the Activated Patient—a kind of hearty hybrid who is three-quarters patient and one-quarter physician. They've learned to speak the doctor's own language, and ask questions rather than passively sit, honor and obey" (Sehnert, 1975, p. 3).

Robert Smith, the editor of this volume, has been an outstanding pioneer in the development of courses and workshops on learning to learn, including the improvement of competence at self-planned learning. He conducted a six-hour workshop for public library patrons to acquaint them with library resources and the principles of successful self-planned learning. He was involved in a project that encouraged and helped teachers undertake self-planned professional improvement efforts. For many years, Smith has devoted part of a graduate course in learning to learn to increasing competence in self-planned learning and assisting others to do so. Students in this course read and hear about self-planned learning, analyze their self-planned learning projects, and practice gaining help from a resource person. His significant vision, workshop designs, and rich details can be found in several publications (Smith, 1982, 1983, 1988).

A fourth approach is more indirect and possibly less powerful, but, because it is widespread, it may in fact affect large numbers of people. This is simply to give students more freedom and help in courses and classes so that they can experience self-planned learning *within* an educational institution.

Let me use my own graduate teaching as an example. Because I was originally trained as a school teacher, I assumed that the teacher should be responsible for virtually all decisions about what and how to learn. Later, however, as I listened to people telling me about their highly successful self-planned learning, I began to question my own teaching approach. As a result, I developed an approach that emphasizes three components (Tough, 1982). First, it provides the students with some minimum structure, requirements, and boundaries. I retain some control (as little as possible) over what and how students learn. Second, as long as they stay within the prescribed structure, students have complete freedom of what and how to learn. Each student in the course develops an individual learning path. I urge them not to plan too far ahead because their interests and questions are bound to change as they gain new ideas early in the course. Class sessions open up topics for students, provide support for their individual learning paths, and provide a safe haven for discussing their adventures and difficulties. The third component is access to plenty of help and resources. This help is not compulsory and has no strings attached. Useful resources include books, class sessions, individuals in the class (including the instructor), and learning partners.

This approach unleashes a surprising amount of energy, enthusiasm, social interaction, creativity, and diversity. The majority of students report that they read and learn more than in traditional courses. They employ an amazing variety of methods and activities—far more than I could ever have suggested to them. Presumably many of the students also become more competent at planning and conducting their own self-planned learning, at least within an educational institution.

The Future

Maurice Gibbons and Gary Phillips (1982) have been very active in helping students become more competent at self-directed and independent learning. They have developed a perceptive set of guidelines and principles that can be used by parents as well as elementary and secondary school teachers. These authors concluded that humankind can learn to make the future what we will: "Our future begins with a shared vision [of] a world which has learned to use technology for humanizing purposes, in which the needs of people are met without violating the needs of the environment, the purposes of nations are secondary to the purposes of humanity as a whole, and education and community are committed to the individual's discovery of how well he can learn, relate, and act throughout his lifetime" (p. 85).

Children, adolescents, and adults plan and manage a large portion of their intentional learning projects. The planning and conducting of many learning efforts is a do-it-yourself venture with help from family, acquaintances, co-workers, professionals, books, and other materials. These learning projects tend to be reasonably successful, but many people would benefit from additional help and competence. In recent years, a few pioneers have experimented with ways of providing better help and enhancing competence, and in the future even more educators will experiment with an exciting variety of formats, content, opportunities, and settings. If these innovations are sensitively based on people's natural ongoing processes of planning and learning, they may lead to a higher level of competence among learners than we can imagine at the present time.

References

Bramucci, R. J. "A Factoral Examination of the Self-Empowerment Construct." Doctoral dissertation, University of Oregon, 1977. *Dissertation Abstracts International,* 1978, *38,* 5087B. (University Microfilms no. 78-2507.)

Brookfield, S. (ed.). *Self-Directed Learning: From Theory to Practice.* New Directions for Continuing Education, no. 25. San Francisco: Jossey-Bass, 1985.

Brookfield, S. D. *Understanding and Facilitating Adult Learning: A Comprehensive Analysis of Principles and Effective Practices.* San Francisco: Jossey-Bass, 1986.

Cheren, M. E. "Helping Learners Achieve Greater Self-Direction." In R. M. Smith (ed.), *Helping Adults Learn How to Learn.* New Directions for Continuing Education, no. 19. San Francisco: Jossey-Bass, 1983.

Coates, P. J., and Thoresen, C. E. *How to Sleep Better: A Drug-Free Program for Overcoming Insomnia.* Englewood Cliffs, N.J.: Prentice-Hall, 1977.

De Charms, R. *Enhancing Motivation: Change in the Classroom.* New York: Irvington, 1976.

Gibbons, M., and Phillips, G. "Self-Education: The Process of Lifelong Learning." *Canadian Journal of Education,* 1982, 7 (4), 67–86.

Gross, R. *The Lifelong Learner.* New York: Simon & Schuster, 1977.

Gross, R. *The Independent Scholar's Handbook.* Reading, Mass.: Addison-Wesley, 1982.

Hiemstra, R. "Self-Directed Learning: Individualizing Instruction." In H. B. Long and Associates, *Self-Directed Learning: Application and Theory.* Athens: Adult Education Department, University of Georgia, 1988.

Lande, N. *Mindstyles Lifestyles: A Comprehensive Overview of Today's*

Life-Changing Philosophies. Los Angeles: Price/Stern/Sloan, 1976.

Matson, K. *The Psychology Today Omnibook of Personal Development.* New York: Morrow, 1977.

Nacke, M. "Life After the Workshop: Effects of the Survey of Resources for the Development in Ministry Workshop." Unpublished doctoral dissertation, Ontario Institute for Studies in Education, University of Toronto, Canada, 1979.

Rogers, C. *Carl Rogers on Personal Power.* New York: Delacorte, 1977.

Ruvinsky, L. I. *Activeness and Self-Education.* Moscow: Progress Publishers, 1986.

Scott, D. "Developing Learning Projects to Improve Interpersonal Skills: A Workshop and Helping Resources for Educational Administrators." Unpublished doctoral dissertation, Ontario Institute for Studies in Education, University of Toronto, Canada, 1981.

Sehnert, K. W. *How to Be Your Own Doctor — Sometimes.* New York: Grosset & Dunlap, 1975.

Smith, R. M. *Learning How to Learn: Applied Theory for Adults.* New York: Cambridge Book Company, 1982.

Smith, R. M. (ed.). *Helping Adults Learn How to Learn.* New Directions for Continuing Education, no. 19. San Francisco: Jossey-Bass, 1983.

Smith, R. M. "Improving Dissemination of Knowledge About Self-Directedness in Education." In H. B. Long and Associates, *Self-Directed Learning: Application and Theory.* Athens: Department of Education, University of Georgia, 1988.

Taylor, I. *Self-Cultivation Recommended, or Hints to a Youth Leaving School.* Boston: Wells & Lilly, 1820.

Tough, A. *Learning Without a Teacher: A Study of Tasks and Assistance During Adult Self-Teaching Projects.* No. 2030095-00067. Ann Arbor, Mich.: Books on Demand, University Microfilms International, 1967.

Tough, A. *The Adult's Learning Projects: A Fresh Approach to Theory and Practice in Adult Learning.* (2nd ed.) No. 2029355. Ann Arbor, Mich.: Books on Demand, University Microfilms International, 1979.

Tough, A. *Expand Your Life.* New York: College Board, 1980.

Tough, A. *Intentional Changes: A Fresh Approach to Helping People Change.* New York: Cambridge Book Company, 1982. (Available from the author.)

PART THREE

Challenges
and Opportunities

Chapter 13

Changing
the Way We Live and Learn
in the Information Age

Dennis D. Gooler

Many kinds of developments in technology have been thrust upon us in unprecedented magnitude, and with those developments have come changes in our society, culture, and personal lives that can only be described as profound and fundamental. We may be excited or dismayed, but one fact seems inescapable: we ignore profound changes wrought by technology at our own peril. As one writer puts it, "Once a new technology rolls over you, if you're not part of the steamroller, you're part of the road" (Brand, 1987, p. 9). And, for better or worse, we are likely to see many more technological developments whose characteristics and consequences we at best grasp vaguely.

What is the nature of these changes, and what have the changes to do with learning and learning to learn? This broad question frames the inquiry in this chapter. First, a sampling is provided of some perspectives on technological developments and the changes accompanying those developments. Next, an overview of learning in an age of information technologies is offered, followed by considerations of learning to learn.

Technological Developments and Change

In his treatise on technology and the character of contemporary life, Borgmann (1984, p. 1) observes: "The modern world and contemporary life particularly...have been shaped by technology, which has stamped them with a peculiar pattern and so given them their character. But although our world bears the imprint of technology, the pattern of technology is neither obvious nor exclusively dominant." The theme of the intertwining of technology and the character of life has repeated itself through many generations, and through the writings of countless authors. Science in general and technology in particular have meant change, sometimes in ways we value, other times in ways we neither like nor understand. Technology has been viewed as the most visible and perhaps most powerful artifact of what we know, the most concrete expression of our collective body of knowledge. What we say we know (as through our technologies) keeps changing: "Today we live according to the latest version of how the universe functions. This view affects our behaviour and thought, just as previous versions affected those who lived with them. Like the people of the past, we disregard phenomena which do not fit our view because they are 'wrong' or outdated. Like our ancestors, we know the real truth" (Burke, 1985, p. 9).

Society has always been in a state of change, and presumably always will be. What concerns many people today are the particular *kinds* of changes, the *fundamentalness* of the changes, and the *rate* at which they seem to be occurring. Some argue that the kinds and rate of change today are more dramatic than ever before, and that the implications of current changes for the conduct of our individual and collective lives are staggering. Asimov, a keen observer of social change, states that "some things can't be predicted, depending as they do upon the chance mixing of genes that contribute to the talents of a particular human being or to the infectiousness of a particular microorganism. But then changes like these are not truly important. Conquerors, plagues, and natural disasters make themselves deeply felt in the history books, but they are not permanent; they go away. And once they are gone, the survivors pick up the pieces and life goes on as before. There are some events, how-ever, that produce permanent changes with consequences that are never undone. In almost all cases, such changes are tech-nological in nature" (1986, p. 10). What are some of these changes being stimulated by contemporary technologies?

For many people, historically reliable and familiar guideposts for defining reality itself are changing. That is, the traditional means we have used to define what is *real,* or what our world consists of, are no longer as clear or reliable as we once thought. An instance of this concerns photography. Most of us trust photographs. We tend to believe that what we see in a photograph represents a real state of affairs; we shape much of our understanding of reality through visual images captured in photographs. But do photographs in fact capture or reflect reality? Not necessarily. Consider the emerging technology of digital retouching. Using computers, pictures can be rearranged or retouched in ways that make detection of the changes nearly impossible. Brand (1987) illustrates: "There has been almost no press about the coming of digital retouching, perhaps because the press itself is implicated. In 1985 Kevin Kelly and I did a cover story on the subject for *Whole Earth Review* which turned up the following, randomly collected. *Popular Science* used the technique to put an airplane from one photograph on the background from another photograph for a cover. *World Tennis* had Bjorn Borg and John McEnroe back to back in dueling costumes on its cover, apparently in one photo together but actually joined by digital retouching from two photos taken on separate occasions. In a book of photographs called *Idylls of France,* by Proctor Jones, prominent telephone poles and lines were surgically removed from one picture of a Basque shepherd, and litter in a stream has disappeared from another picture" (p. 220).

The last photograph that you saw: was it a representation of reality, or the work of a creative digital technician? How can we decide? What, in fact, is real? That which can be done to still photographs also can be done to video images. Many of us form our sense or outline of the world through news and other kinds of programs on television. How do we know that what we see is what exists? How will we form our sense of reality in the future as technological developments of this kind become commonly used, often without our knowing? The processes available through modern photography/computer interfaces represent but one of many changes that impact our construction of personal reality, which in turn profoundly influences our hopes, fears, aspirations, and actions.

The means by which individuals sustain themselves or, indeed, simply survive are undergoing change. Most notable here are changes in the nature of work and the character of the workplace. While consensus has not yet been reached about the amount and kind of impacts technological developments have on the skills required to hold jobs, there is at least a conventional wisdom that technology *is* changing the nature of work, and thus skill requirements for workers. Rumberger (1987, p. 74) comments on the issue: "New technological innovations, spurred by the revolution in microelectronics, are yielding an increasing array of new consumer products and altering the way virtually all products and services are produced and delivered in our society. Perhaps the single most influential product is the micro-computer. As these machines become smaller, cheaper, and more powerful, they are increasingly being used in a wide variety of jobs throughout the economy. New technologies are expected to have a profound and widespread impact on many aspects of society. Probably the most important impact from an educational perspective concerns the effects of technological change on the skill requirements of jobs."

Rumberger and others wonder about the nature of the relationship between technologies and job skill requirements. All the evidence is not in, but it does appear that almost all people will be affected in some way by technology as they seek to survive economically in tomorrow's society. For some people, changes in specific job skill requirements will impact their lives. For others, the impacts of technology may be felt less directly through changes in specific job skill requirements than by how work is distributed throughout the society. In either case, individuals may experience change in how they compete in the marketplace and thus how they fare economically.

Developments in technology are bringing about changes in perspectives on place—transportation and communications technologies are especially influential here. Our sense of geographic and personal place is irreversibly changed when we travel by air to locations we have not been before, particularly to places we have heretofore thought far beyond our reach. For some of us, that means travel to another state, while others have made the entire world their backyard. For a very few individuals, the earth itself is no longer the only place people have walked. When one can leave Chicago and in a matter of twenty to thirty hours be halfway around the world, one's sense of the world community changes. And when one uses on a daily basis products produced in nations whose names are but vaguely familiar, one begins to understand the changing nature of the world community and to feel uncertain about one's own personal place and space in that community.

Time also means something different now. Satellite technologies make it possible for us to communicate in seconds with others around the globe. We transmit monies electronically throughout the world in microseconds, raising major questions about the nature of money itself. We are told that nuclear holocaust is always technically but a matter of minutes away, and we fear that the political processes that govern us (and that, in turn, are influenced by technology developments) will go awry. For many people, daily life is increasingly dictated by minutely measured and specified passages of time; for some, a high price is paid for the loss of control and spontaneity that results. The first great discovery was time, as Boorstin (1983) puts it, and, while "communities of time would bring the first communities of knowledge, ways to share discovery, a common frontier on the unknown" (p. 1), that frontier has itself been altered by our emerging technologies.

There is another way in which life is changing for many people. Technological developments have made it increasingly difficult for a person to know how things work, or how to *make*

things work. That is, the individual has grown ever more dependent on someone else to maintain the essentials of life; self-
reliance or independence in many aspects of our lives (with all
due respect to Emerson) is virtually a thing of the past. Not many
years ago, for example, many people maintained and when
necessary repaired their own automobiles; today, even trained
mechanics have problems fixing cars produced by complex new
technologies. Simply maintaining a house presents challenges
few people can master on their own. We are rapidly coming to a
position of not understanding our own relatively simple technologies, to say nothing of the complex technology systems we
have created, and we are therefore by and large at the mercy of
the specialist. Whether this is a good or bad situation is a matter
of individual judgment, but the fact of new forms of dependence
seems undeniable.

There are other changes in the lives of individuals, of
course. Technology has changed the way we think about our
bodies and our longevity. Genetic engineering and medical
technology have raised fundamental questions about the definition of life, and about the rights and responsibilities of individuals with regard to their health and their very existence.
Technology has changed our daily methods of organizing ourselves, such as the way we do our banking, shopping, and countless other tasks. And technology has changed the way we seek
and use information, the way we learn, and the way we share
what we know.

Changes in the lives of individuals brought about by
technology are writ more broadly but similarly in the institutions, agencies, and businesses of society. Technology is changing the way things are produced, how we govern ourselves, how
we communicate, and how we determine the value of things.
Technology is, in short, inseparable from the essential fabric of
our individual and collective lives. Faced with the centrality of
technology and change, we must reasonably and urgently ask
about the implications of technological developments for the
acts of teaching and learning.

Learning in an Age of Information Technologies

Against a general backdrop of technological developments and social change, it is useful to examine more closely some emerging technologies that probably will have particular impact on how (and why) people go about learning in the coming decades. The technologies and systems described below may be grouped under the broad label *information technologies.*

Emerging Information Technologies. Information technology systems generally consist of combinations of computers, video, and telecommunications carefully integrated to provide users with access to vast amounts of information, processes and programs to act on that information, and means of communicating information among users on the system. Hawkridge (1983) presents a comprehensive description of information systems and their possible uses in education. Forester (1985) edited an extensive collection of papers under the title *The Information Technology Revolution.* The range of technologies can be seen in the table of contents of the Forester volume, which includes such topics as artificial intelligence, the intelligent network, cellular radio, videotex, computers, and others. Inose and Pierce (1984, p. x) describe the power of information technologies: "Current advances in information technology have become more than extensions of the information technologies of the past. Information technologies are rapidly merging into one common digital electronic art of tremendous power and impact. The power of this art is so great that the changes it is working and will work in our civilization are qualitative as well as quantitative."

Literature on information, information technologies, information societies, and related topics has burgeoned, indicating the perceived importance and potential social impacts of growth in information technology capacity. Writing in the early 1970s, Sackman (1971) described mass information utilities and considered some of the social and personal implications of such utilities. Gooler (1986) describes a concrete manifestation of the idea of a utility expressly designed to promote educational uses of information technology systems. Finnegan, Salaman, and Thompson (1987) provide a volume of papers focused on some of the social issues raised by the growth of information technologies. Cleveland (1985) describes what he believes are the kinds of individuals who will provide leadership in an information society dominated by information technologies. Beniger (1986) attempts to trace the origins of the information society.

There are strong and vocal advocates for continued development and uses of information technologies, and at the same time there are voices raising concerns and expressing cautions about the long- and short-term implications of further developments of information technologies. There is, of course, an enormous literature available on the specific individual technologies or systems that are often lumped under the term information technologies: telecommunications, microcomputers, artificial intelligence, video technologies, and so forth. Confronted with all this information, how does one draw conclusions about implications for teaching, learning, and learning to learn?

The following points are likely to be included in most summaries of the possible implications of the development and uses of information technologies. (For a more detailed analysis of these kinds of implications, see Marien, 1987.)

The development of computer technology is certainly central to the character of information technologies. The increasing power, storage capacity, and flexibility of computers, together with decreasing physical sizes and costs, make computing more accessible to more people, and with a greater range of functionality, than has ever been possible. Developments in computer hardware and software, coupled with an increase in the kinds of information that can be manipulated by computers (primarily through digitization), are expanding the potential uses of computers on almost a daily basis.

Telecommunications capacities continue to increase, making new and more extensive avenues of communication ever more available. Miniature satellite receiving equipment provides telecommunications opportunities in areas where it was not possible in the past. New forms of wiring, such as fiber optics, provide opportunities for new communications patterns. Work in progress at places such as the Massachusetts Institute of Technology's Media Lab features explorations in making mass broadcasting more responsive to individual learner control; or developing technologies that can "read" lips; or creating entire offices that respond to voice commands. Highly interactive systems are within practical sight, making possible patterns of communications that were once the province of science fiction writers alone.

Interconnecting technologies makes developments in computer and telecommunications technologies all the more powerful. Integrated information technology systems are upon us, raising new issues that provide fascinating prospects. Interconnection microcomputers and video brings us learning programs of mind-boggling characteristics, such as those suggested by Johnson (1987). Networking computers in a local environment, and, further, interconnecting computers through modems from any point on the globe, offer opportunities for communications and collaborative work of an unprecedented nature. Combining television, computers, and fax machines permits "classes" scattered geographically to come together electronically so that teachers and students physically remote from each other can interact as though they were in a single classroom. In the past, teachers and learners have had access to video, or computers, or radio, or whatever; they have seldom had access to video *and* computers *and* telecommunications, all working together to serve a common purpose.

The interconnectedness described here is not a figment of a futurist's imagination but in many areas is a present reality. It should be pointed out, however, that while it is a reality in at least some places, the interconnected technology system is not yet fully understood. "While computers probe and imitate the 'society of mind,' they are also shaping the mind of society. Computers and communications have already blended so far that they are one activity, still without a verb to express what it does. We don't even have a word for the nervous activity in the body—it's not 'thinking,' 'sensing,' or 'talking.' All the chemical and energy activities in a body (or a society) have a word for their sum action—'metabolism'—but there's no equivalent word for the sum of communications in a system. The lack of a word signals a deeper ignorance. We don't know what constitutes healthy communications" (Brand, 1987, p. 228).

Important changes are also occurring in the way that information is organized or designed. Given the tools now available, and an ever-expanding information base, it is important to pursue new ways of thinking about how to use the tools to organize, analyze, and access information resources. Digitization has clearly impacted how we think about organizing information, and how we can gain access to that information. The idea of a CD-ROM (Compact Disc—Read Only Memory), and the many variations on the idea (such as Compact Disc—Interactive), represents a new approach to organizing, storing, and accessing information. A single disc can hold 54,000 individual frames of information, each of which is directly "addressable." The library of CD-ROMs is expanding rapidly, making information available to more people, and in new ways.

The new tools have stimulated numerous creative approaches to information organization and access. Hypermedia, for example, enables a user to access information bases in more flexible ways than is usually possible, permitting new approaches to learning material. Locatis (1987) describes hypermedia as but one of a number of instructional designs that take advantage of the capacities of new information technology systems and call for new conceptions of how to organize and present information for users. Literature coming from instructional psychology, information sciences, and related fields foretells a new generation of thought about the design and organization of information.

These, then, are but four outcomes of the development of information technologies that influence learning in an information age. The developments in information technologies alone are rapid, comprehensive, and simultaneously exciting and frightening—it is difficult for any individual to stay abreast of developments. There are, of course, many sources of relevant information about information technologies. For people working in education and training, trade journals—such as *Educational Technology Electronic, T.H.E.*, and other such vehicles—regularly contain descriptions of new applications of technology systems. Commercial and government-sponsored data bases are good sources of information—systems such as ERIC, BRS, and DIALOG. The literature contains case studies of technology systems applications, such as that by Gooler and Roth (forthcoming). Professional associations seek to monitor technological developments and to share that information with constituents. There is a play-within-a-play here: people involved in education at all levels need information systems that permit access to information about information systems. Such is the essence of the emerging information society.

Information about the design, development, uses, and consequences of information technologies is growing exponentially; yet, as we have suggested, in many respects we still do not comprehend what is really going on, or what might go on. The stage is too vast to take in at a glance, or even with a long look. But given the collective experience thus far, the following observations can be made about the character of learning in the rapidly emerging age of information technologies.

Implications for Learning. Psychologists, sociologists, information scientists, educators, and others have been working to understand the relationship between how people learn and the possible applications of tools represented by information technologies. Work has included both narrowly focused experimental studies and broad, social, policy-oriented case studies. From this work, and from an examination of the character of the technologies currently emerging, it is possible to suggest four ways in which the activities of learning might be shaped in the future.

We can expect *access* to more and different kinds of information for an increasing number of people. What an individual learns is determined in part by the kinds and amount of information available to him or her. Information, in whatever forms it takes, constitutes the substance of learning activities. For some, access to information is extremely limited, while others can gain access to vast amounts and kinds of information with relative ease. To the extent that information is power in future societies, having access to information is likely to be a significant determiner of one's ability to obtain personal and social benefits.

As the invention of printing made certain kinds of information available to more than an elite few, so too do information technologies promise to expand even further the circle of people who can avail themselves of opportunities to access all kinds of information. Of course, there will inevitably be some people who, by virtue of having more power, money, or influence, will have access to just a bit more information, or perhaps information of different kinds, than do the masses. But the masses of people will in the future have access to unprecedented amounts of information.

What are the implications for learning? Quite frankly, no one knows for sure. Some individuals may find that their learning efforts are substantially enriched because they have available a greater amount of information germane to their learning goals; an information-rich environment will be a very positive thing for these people. Other individuals may become immobilized by the existence of more information than they can usefully handle, and so learning activities will become exercises in frustration and anxiety. For most people, however, having access to greater amounts and kinds of information resources will mean that new kinds of searching, categorizing, analyzing, and interpreting skills will be needed. There will be more about this later.

People will have greater choices in the future about the learning *modalities* with which they accomplish their learning tasks. It is something of a truism to suggest that different people appear to learn more, or more effectively, through some learning modalities or strategies than through others. For example, interactive computer/video systems will permit learners to engage in powerful simulation experiences never before possible, and for some learners, engaging in such simulations provides an approach that is exceptionally effective. Advances in the ways certain video technology is used may enhance the learning strategies of others, while communications via a teleconferencing system should prove effective for still other learners.

It is not that such systems have been totally unavailable in the past. The significant factor for the future may well be that more learners in more situations will be able to take advantage of a variety of kinds of learning tools. In some respects, this is an access issue again, but in this case access is obtained not only to information resources but to tools that permit a range of operations to be performed on that information. In the future, learners may not be as restricted as now in how they can accomplish their learning goals but will rather be faced with understanding *which* tools of learning seem to work best for them, in which kinds of settings. These are problems (or challenges) of a rather different order than most learners face today.

Learners in the future will exercise far greater *control* over how they learn. Even with access to a large amount of information resources through mass media, computers, and the like, most learners today remain at the mercy of the machines that deliver the information. Television, for example, delivers an enormous amount of information to the home (forgetting for the moment questions of quality), but those who access that information do so in a passive form. What is coming, however, is release from the "tyranny" of the machine. In his book describing activities at the MIT Media Lab, Brand (1987) outlines experiments taking place related to *interactivity*, that is, the capacity of users to interact in various ways with technologies. The entire book is in some respects a testimony to the kinds of technological developments that promise to enhance learner control over the means of delivering (or receiving) information: personal television, personal computers, and so forth. At one point in the book (p. 255), Brand suggests a direction the technology is heading: "The Media Lab is committed to making the individual the driver of new information technology rather than the driven. It does so by focusing on 'idosyncratic systems' that adapt to the user, by encouraging computation in real time and communication out of real time. Computation in real time means the human can interact live, 'converse' with the machine, oblige it to function in human terms. Thus the push at the Lab for real-time computer animation, holography, and speech interpretation. Communication out of real time, as with Personal

Television and the Conversational Desktop and Electronic Publishing, means the individual human schedule prevails over the institutional. 'Prime time becomes my time.'" In the land of new information technologies, the learner determines the what, when, and, in many cases, the how of learning.

Opportunities for *cooperative learning* will greatly increase. So far, information technologies have been largely described as making possible new avenues for individuals to learn. As the new technologies appear to make individual pursuit of learning a more reasonable, manageable, and feasible enterprise, they also make possible new ways in which individuals can work together with other individuals in the pursuit of learning goals.

Take electronic mail and teleconferencing, for instance. As microcomputers have proliferated, interest or user groups have formed, comprising people who share common interests who get together electronically to pursue those interests. With emerging technology systems, people who are geographically separated can work together on projects or problems in ways that have simply not been feasible before. To be sure, people at a distance have found ways to work together in the past, but the new technologies not only support such collaborative work, they encourage collaborative enterprises. They make it possible to move files among users, to connect people with others who can make contributions to the pursuit of a learning goal but who in the past would have been both unknown and unconnected. The prospects for collaborative undertakings are substantial. The long-range consequences of an increase in collaborative learning are largely unknown, but some speculate that such collaborative work, undertaken on a regular and "business as usual" basis, could dramatically alter our sense of community and the role of collaboration versus competition in learning.

This review of possible implications of emerging information technologies has of necessity been brief but should suggest the kinds of changes in learning strategies and patterns that are possible. Opinions differ as to whether these changes are positive or negative, but it is probably fair to say that the processes of teaching and learning are likely to be shaped in major ways by the infusion into society of new information technologies. It is interesting to wonder if such technologies will alter our present theories of learning, or our notions of how to facilitate learning in positive ways. Suppose approaches to learning are impacted by the tools called information technologies. Further suppose that these tools become commonplace, so that they become largely "invisible" or "transparent" to the average citizen and are readily accessible to all peoples. What might these developments mean for learning to learn?

Learning to Learn in an Age of Information

As described throughout this book, learning to learn implies not only that individuals gain certain skills but also that they develop attitudes or proclivities toward learning, and toward their own capacities to learn. The kinds of societal changes outlined in this chapter, together with the character of emerging information technologies and their potential impact on strategies of learning, argue for a careful examination of what it will mean in the future to learn to learn.

One of the most pervasive implications of technological developments and social change is that needs for learning and motivations to learn may be heightened. More specifically, individuals may need to engage in a lifetime of learning not as a matter of choice but as a matter of survival. In the future, individuals may lack the option to choose *not* to engage in learning activities over the lifespan. Their capacity to function in the workplace, the home, or the community in general may require that they constantly access and process information, develop new occupational and personal skills, and generally cope with rapid change driven by technology developments. Cleveland (1985, p. 190) captures the essence of this idea: "But to two predictions I would assign a high probability value. People who do not educate themselves, and keep reeducating themselves, to participate in the new knowledge environment will be the peas-. ants of the information society. And societies that do not give *all* their people a chance at a relevant education, and also periodic opportunities to tune up their knowledge and their insights, will be left in the jetstream of history by those that do." Beyond survival, the people who *prosper* will be those who learn to deal with an expanding knowledge base: "There is ample evidence that those who learn how to achieve access to the bath of knowledge that already envelops the world will be the future's aristocrats of achievement, and that they will be far more numerous than any aristocracy in history" (Cleveland, 1985, p. xviii).

Learning to learn in the future will thus require a certain kind of orientation toward knowledge and information, a sense of the importance of learning, and a commitment to the pursuit of knowledge as an ordinary and necessary aspect of daily life. This precondition for the pursuit of individual freedom and achievement can be understood as the very cornerstone of the matter. For many people, developing such an orientation toward learning will need substantial changes in perspective from those they hold today.

What of the skills of learning? Emerging information technologies will probably require people to obtain certain kinds of skills that are not presently so essential, among them the following.

Locating and Accessing Information Resources. People will need to develop sophisticated skills in identifying sources of relevant information, and then gaining access to the information from those sources. The mere existence of information does not mean that everyone who may have use of the information instinctively knows that it exists, or knows how to get at the information. If access to information is increasingly critical for most people, then developing skills to gain access is also critical.

For example, people will need to learn about and use electronic data base systems and services. Numerous companies offering data base services (such as The Source, CompuServe, DIALOG, and others) have already recognized the future importance of access to information and have devised means of gathering, organizing, and making available to people various kinds of information. It is expected that such services will increase as new data bases are created and as people begin to demand access to information on an expanding number of topics. Until common user interfaces (and friendly ones) are devised, it will take a fairly high level of skill to obtain access to these services, just as today a person cannot necessarily operate all word processing programs simply because he or she is familiar with one such program; standardization has not become a reality. People need to learn how to work the systems; such knowledge will become a basic or fundamental skill of the future.

Organizing Information. Individual users will need to become adept at categorizing and organizing information for their particular purposes and goals if they are not to become hopelessly mired in a sea of information. The problem is complicated by the fact that learners will find themselves utilizing numerous sources of information, as well as a variety of tools for acting on that information. It is one thing to be able to analyze information from a single source, but quite another to know what to do with information coming from a variety of sources, through a variety of delivery mechanisms, often in seemingly incompatible formats. The capacity to organize intellectually and search through disparate sources and kinds of information will therefore become increasingly important.

Self-Diagnoses and Assessments. To the extent that new information technologies expand the amount of control an individual exercises over his or her learning activities, learners will need to develop or refine their skills at self-diagnosis and assessment. Learners will be required to exercise more skill in determining *what* they need to learn, *how* to learn it, and *how well* they have learned what they attempted.

Everyone has some skills in this arena, of course, but the kinds of technologies available to us in the future are likely to demand even more refined skills in self-assessment. We will all have access to more information resources than ever, but each of us will need to understand ourselves and our own needs well enough to know which of those resources are most relevant to what we are trying to get done. We must each refine our sense of what works for us and seek a match between our styles of learning and the characteristics of the technologies of information delivery available to us. Most will need help to gain this understanding.

The Skills of Collaboration. After a long history of learning being basically a competitive and often isolating enterprise, many people do not appreciate or possess the necessary skills for collaboration. If technologically based collaborative learning projects are more common in the future, individuals will need to develop skills to support such activity. It is hard to know at this point just what those skills are, but we must seek to identify, describe, and foster them.

Already, we are seeing evidence of some of the kinds of strains that emerge in various collaborative undertakings. Perhaps the most simplistic, yet important, examples of such difficulties can be found in debate about how to behave in entries on electronic bulletin boards. Beyond the predictable instances of certain people using abusive, sexist, racist, or other forms of objectionable language in bulletin board communications, there are questions about how to facilitate the needs of the many people who hook into a network. How do you present one person from dominating the network? How are individuals to gain equitable opportunities to direct the attention of others on the network to topics of interest to him or her? These are minor examples, but the point is that the collaborative projects made possible by information technologies will become realities only when the collaborators learn how to use the technology and interact appropriately.

Conclusion

Technological developments, and the social changes resulting from those developments, have moved the importance of learning to a new level. In the future, learning and learning to learn will be both necessitated and complicated by the existence of dramatic kinds of information technologies. Some have argued that what is ahead is not merely another incremental social change, not an evolution, but rather a revolution of far-reaching consequences. Such claims may be hyperbole, but we have evidence at hand that new technologies are presenting bold new possibilities and complicated challenges to educators, administrators, and individual learners. We need not wait for a distant future to feel the impacts of new technologies, for we are already living with those impacts. We cannot afford to wait to see where the world is going before we move to examine how we are educating people to function in tomorrow's world. Learning to learn is clearly central to what will happen to us as a people. We will all need new orientations and skills if we are not only to cope with new information, but also to direct those technologies to ends we value.

References

Asimov, I. *Living in the Future.* New York: Beaufort Books, 1986.

Beniger, J. *The Control Revolution: Technological and Economic Origins of the Information Society.* Cambridge, Mass.: Harvard University Press, 1986.

Boorstin, D. *The Discoverers: A History of Man's Search to Know His World and Himself.* New York: Random House, 1983.

Borgmann, A. *Technology and the Character of Contemporary Life.* Chicago: University of Chicago Press, 1984.

Brand, S. *The Media Lab: Inventing the Future at MIT.* New York: Viking, 1987.

Burke, J. *The Day the Universe Changed.* Boston: Little, Brown, 1985.

Cleveland, H. *The Knowledge Executive: Leadership in an Information Society.* New York: Truman Talley Books, Dutton, 1985.

Finnegan, R., Salaman, G., and Thompson, K. (eds.). *Information Technology: Social Issues.* Milton Keynes, England: Open University Press, 1987.

Forester, T. (ed.). *The Information Technology Revolution.* Cambridge, Mass.: MIT Press, 1985.

Gooler, D. *The Education Utility: The Power to Revitalize Education and Society.* Englewood Cliffs, N.J.: Educational Technology Publications, 1986.

Gooler, D., and Roth, G. *Instructional Technology Applications in*

Vocational Education: A Notebook of Cases. Springfield, Ill.: Illinois State Board of Education, forthcoming.

Hawkridge, D. *New Information Technology in Education.* Baltimore, Md.: Johns Hopkins University Press, 1983.

Inose, H., and Pierce, J. *Information Technology and Civilization.* New York: Freeman, 1984.

Johnson, K. "Interactive Video: The Present and the Promise." In J. A. Niemi and D. D. Gooler (eds.), *Technologies for Learning Outside the Classroom.* New Directions for Continuing Education, no. 34. San Francisco: Jossey-Bass, 1987.

Jones, Proctor. *Idylls of France.* San Francisco: Proctor Jones, 1982.

Lewis, L. H. "Adults and Computer Anxiety: Fact or Fiction." *Lifelong Learning: An Omnibus of Practice and Research,* 1988, *11* (8), 5–8, 12.

Locatis, C. "Instructional Design and New Technologies." In J. A. Niemi and D. D. Gooler (eds.), *Technologies for Learning Outside the Classroom.* New Directions for Continuing Education, no. 34. San Francisco: Jossey-Bass, 1987.

Marien, M. (ed.). *Future Survey Annual: 1986.* Bethesda, Md.: World Future Society, 1987.

Rumberger, R. W. "The Potential Impact of Technology on the Skill Requirements of Future Jobs in the United States." In G. Burke and R. W. Rumberger (eds.), *The Future Impact of Technology on Work and Education.* London: Falmer Press, 1987.

Sackman, H. *Mass Information Utilities and Social Excellence.* Princeton, N.J.: Auerbach, 1971.

Chapter 14

Expanding
Knowledge About
How We Learn

Stephen D. Brookfield

The attempt to understand learners' phenomenological worlds was proposed by Lindeman as the purpose of adult education. To him, education was "a co-operative venture in non-authoritarian, informal learning, the chief purpose of which is to discover the meaning of experience; a quest of the mind which digs down to the roots of the preconceptions which formulate our conduct" (1925, p. 3). It represented "a new technique for learning. . . a process by which the adult learns to become aware of and to evaluate his experience" (p. 3). Ascribing to education the necessity of furthering the discovery of the meaning of experience, assisting in the critical evaluation of such experience, and attempting to understand the preconceptions underlying behavior are themes which find a ready echo in the writings of contemporary theorists of learning.

Mezirow (1981) characterizes the educational process as one in which educators work toward "bringing psycho-cultural assumptions into critical consciousness to help a person understand how he or she has come into possession of conceptual categories, rules, tactics and criteria for judging [that are] implicit in habits of perception, thought and behavior" (p. 20).

Becoming self-consciously aware of such cognitive and cultural processes is central to learners' developing an understanding of how they learn and to researchers' understanding how they can be helped to learn more effectively. Kitchener (1983, 1986) describes this as epistemic cognition; that is, "knowledge of whether our cognitive strategies are sometimes limited, in what ways solutions can be true, and whether reasoning correctly about a problem necessarily leads to an absolutely correct solution" (1983, p. 226). Epistemic cognition "includes the individual's assumptions about what can be known and what cannot (such as, our knowledge of some things is ultimately uncertain), how we can know (such as, by observing what exists; via authority), and how certain we can be in knowing (such as, absolutely, probabilistically). Following from each form of knowing is an understanding of how beliefs may be justified in light of the characteristics of the knowing process" (Kitchener, 1986, p. 76). Kitchener has developed the reflective judgment model to measure the development of epistemic cognition in learners.

Empirical studies of learning to learn tend to exhibit a phenomenological orientation. Entwistle and Hounsell (1979) advocate studying learning in its natural setting. The research undertaken by Marton and others at the University of Göteborg in Sweden employs a phenomenological perspective (Marton, 1981; Marton and Säljö, 1976a, 1976b, 1984). As noted by Gibbs, Morgan, and Taylor (1982), the Göteborg studies underscore the importance of encouraging learners to be introspective about their learning experiences. In contrast to more positively derived research approaches, learners in the Göteberg studies are encouraged to identify what is idiosyncratic in their experience as much as what is generic. These studies embody the phenomenological assumption that accounts of the specific often have the generic embedded within them. Put another way, these studies of learning are idiographic rather than nomothetic; they seek to highlight what is particular, concrete, and contextually specific about a learner's experiences, rather than to try constantly to find generalizable aspects in each person's testimony. A group of studies at the Ontario Institute for Studies in Education in Toronto, Canada, also focuses on people's perceptions of their learning experiences (Bates, 1979; Denis, 1979; Taylor, 1979). The recent anthology by Boud and Griffin (1987) contains colorful descriptions of learning from learners' perspectives.

The assumption in all the studies cited is that generic features are frequently embedded in richly descriptive accounts of specific events. For example, Stanage (1986) argues that by studying individual accounts of how people have learned how to learn we can discover one or more essential structures in the process of learning to learn. Researchers can undertake a "phenomenological auditing of the ways through which a person knows that s(he) learns" (p. 267) by encouraging that person to identify the "reflective moves" made during various learning projects. He writes that "a phenomenological description of the stages through which this process moves is both an identification and a description of additional *essential structures* of phenomena and clusters of phenomena relevant in any understanding of learning how to learn" (p. 270). These essential structures in learning to learn will be discovered through encouraging learners to undertake retrospective descriptions of how they came to learn that they knew something.

Seen from these perspectives, research in learning to learn entails studying the reflective domain of learning. This means exploring how people self-consciously reflect on the way they assign meaning to new experiences, filter and code new stimuli, process new information, become aware of outmoded and unworkable assumptions, and make changes in their ways of perceiving and interpreting the world. How is this reflective domain investigated? In this chapter a number of methods are proposed: interviews, critical incidents, life histories, and the use of such unobtrusive measures as the analyzing of learning journals. This cluster of methodologies can be characterized as a phenomenological approach.

Applying Phenomenological Approaches

In this chapter, it is maintained that phenomenological research approaches are the most appropriate for studying how learners become aware of how they learn and learn to learn. The basic tenet of phenomenological research is that "meaningful interpretation of human experience can only come from those persons who have thoroughly immersed themselves in the phenomenon they wish to interpret and understand" (Denzin, 1983, p. 133). Phenomenological research into learning to learn seeks to enter the existential reality of learners so that the assumptions, reasoning processes, and belief systems informing their perceptions of the world can be appreciated and understood. Research methods generate analytical categories and concepts grounded in these perceptions rather than imposing them from without. The purpose is to enter another's frame of reference in such a way that the learner's structures of understanding and interpretation, and the perceptual filters through which the learner apprehends reality, can be experienced and understood by the researcher as closely as possible to the ways they are experienced and understood by the learner. Researchers become explorers of the topographies of learners' perceptual and interpretive terrains. This is described by Mahrer (1983) as a form of existential therapy in which the researcher's aim is "being in touch with the actual form and shape of the patient's phenomenological world, and being in touch with the deeper experiencings in that world" (p. 282).

Phenomenology is not so much a method as an epistemological orientation, a way of thinking about how we come to know and construct our realities. The phenomenologist investigates the meaning of events or actions to the people experiencing these and seeks to apprehend or intuit these events and actions in the way their subjects do. Morgan (1983, p. 25) summarizes the phenomenological orientation as follows: "Human beings construct and organize their everyday life through intertwined streams of consciousness—phenomenological and interactional. Humans are seen as reflexive, intentional actors, constructing and reconstructing a world rich in meaning, motive, emotion, and feeling through interaction with others." Phenomenologists study consciousness and the nature and meaning of experience. This activity is described as phenomenological reduction and is accomplished through intuiting one's experiences; that is, reflecting on the essence of people's subjective experiences.

When are phenomenological approaches particularly useful in studying learning to learn? First, they must be used in studies that are trying to enter people's interpretive frames of reference and to explore their structures of understanding. Something as complex and sophisticated as understanding someone else's meaning schemes and meaning perspectives can be accomplished only through talking to them intensively and at length, through watching them closely, and through reading their personal jottings—in other words, through interviews, observations, critical incidents, and unobtrusive measures such as analyzing learning journals. Second, phenomenological methods are particularly suited to scene-setting studies in which researchers are investigating an area of concern where no accepted and established research paradigm exists, as is the case with learning to learn. (A research paradigm is defined as the collection of organizing concepts, predominant hypotheses, substantive concerns, methods of data collection, and classificatory typologies that prevail in an area of investigation.) In a research area where there are only the beginnings of a body of literature, a paucity of easily replicable data collection instruments that have been tested for reliability and validity, and few concepts that are generally agreed upon as informing discussion and analysis in the area, phenomenological approaches are particularly appropriate.

Because phenomenological approaches have built into them a certain flexibility and adaptability, they can accommodate researchers' immersing themselves in a problem area as they try to discern some central themes for investigation. When researchers are studying phenomena that no one else has studied, there are no convenient methodological maps to guide their efforts. They have to try different approaches, expect frequent blockages, anticipate that confusion and ambiguity will alternate with clarity and insight, and be able to change their methodological tack as readily as possible. Given that learning to learn is a relatively recent focus for educational research, phenomenological studies fit very well.

Three Methods for Investigating Learning to Learn

Three investigative methods show promise with regard to phenomenological investigation in the area of learning to learn: interviewing, the developing of critical incidents, and the analyzing of written autobiographical materials.

Interviewing. The most frequently used research method employed in exploring learners' phenomenological worlds is the interview method. Longitudinal studies of British Open University students' orientations to learning (Morgan, Taylor, and Gibbs, 1982; Taylor, Morgan, and Gibbs, 1981) use in-depth interviews to document learners' biographies. In exploring the concept of "self-organized learning," Harri-Augstein and Thomas (1984) employ the "learning conversation" to help people understand their learning processes. The conversation is "a dialogue on the process of learning: the learner reflects on his or her learning with the assistance of a teacher or tutor" (Candy, Harri-Augstein, and Thomas, 1985, p. 102). In a study of reflective learning that attempts to discover the kinds of essential structures discussed by Stanage (1986), Boyd and Fales (1983) used interviews to explore how people became aware of their own reflective learning patterns and how they decided consciously to use these. Boyd and Fales use the phrase "reflecting on reflection" to describe the focus of their interviews, and it is clear that this self-conscious attempt by learners to reflect upon their own reflective patterns involves the same kind of psychological processes as learning to learn.

The literature of organizational psychology contains interview-based studies of how workers have learned to learn, though this term is not generally used. However, in Schön's (1983) descriptions of "problem setting" and "reflection in action," we see how practitioners in a range of settings develop a self-conscious awareness of the strategies they have evolved for problem solving. In the development of "theories in use"—those apparently intuitive ways of responding to specific situations, which are actually grounded in a careful and repeated testing against experience—workers apparently become aware of how

they typically and most effectively deal with very different problems and crises. "Double-loop learning" (Argyris and Schön,
1978) — learning through which people become aware of implicit organizational norms and begin to challenge their effectiveness — entails a process of becoming aware of one's typical
style, its shortcomings, and its possible alternatives. Argyris
(1976) has used interviews and critical incidents to help executives become aware of "nested paradoxes" in their reasoning,
that is, forms of reasoning that are productive in the short term
and disastrous in the long term. Closely related to this is the
action science approach (Argyris, Putnam, and Smith, 1985), in
which individual interviews and group encounters are tran-
scribed and crucial conversations reconstructed to help people
become aware of the interpretive frames of references within
which they are learning.

Within the developmental psychology tradition, people's
development of cognitive and ethical capacities has been investigated mostly through forms of interviewing. Dialectical thinking schemata have been identified by Basseches (1984) after
extensive in-depth interviews with his subjects. Perry's (1970)
stages of intellectual and ethical development were inductively
derived from interviews with Harvard freshmen. Levinson
(1978) and Gilligan (1982) explored men's and women's patterns
of moral reasoning through interviews. Kitchener (1986) and
King (1978) measure the development of reflective judgment
through the "reflective judgment interview," in which people are
presented with four ill-structured problems, called dilemmas,
drawn from physics, social science, biology, and history. They
are then asked to explain and defend their judgments on the
issues and how they have come to know their beliefs as true.

There are also problems accompanying the use of the
interview method. Briggs (1986) contends that researchers have
traditionally misused the method because they are not "her-
meneutically sophisticated." By this he means that interviews
often interpret subjects' perceptions from within the researchers' frames of reference. He argues strongly that the most
important interviewing skill is that of metacommunicative competence, in which researchers become alert to the symbolic

significance to learners of analogies, images, and metaphors that are voiced by them.

Used sensitively, the interview method provides for an interactive exchange of perceptions between researchers and learners. In becoming familiar with each others' phenomenological terrain, both parties to the interview can call for clarification, elaboration, and explanation. They can build upon already elaborated ideas and refer back to components of the shared experience. Ideally, the interview becomes the occasion for sustained and sophisticated exploration of learners' perceptions and recollections of learning to learn. Unfortunately, the culture-specific associations surrounding the term *interview* mean that in everyday discourse the word calls to mind television confrontations in which a detached questioner elicits information from a knowledgeable and articulate subject, often in a more or less hostile manner. The term is likely to be associated in most people's minds with interrogation, since the only other common usage is in the context of the competitive and anxiety-provoking job interview. Such approaches are very far from the subtle and sensitive exploration of learners' phenomenological worlds needed in research on learning to learn; indeed, television and job interviews are not real interviews at all, because the purpose of the protagonists is not to seek a genuine exchange and exploration of contrary opinions.

One of the sources of advice on how to overcome the mistrust and artificiality generated by the term *interview* is Zweig in "The Art and Technique of Interviewing" (1965). Zweig spent many years interviewing blue-collar workers about their work, leisure activities, political attitudes, and familial relationships. He regarded interviewing as "a branch of a larger art, the art of conversation" (p. 245). Following an interview schedule rigidly in a research project and asking the same questions in the same order and with the same vocal inflections is hardly conducive to a genuine exchange of views. The interview schedule can easily become a monolith, which reduces the interviewer to a mere appendage of methodology, a functionary whose task is to administer the interview schedule rigidly and record the subsequent responses. Zweig believed that if interviewers ask people to reveal their perceptions of activities that have great personal significance for them, then interviewers must be prepared to express their own enthusiasm, pleasures, and anxieties. His advice was summarized as follows: "The act of interviewing does not need to sink to the level of mechanicalness. It can be a graceful and joyful act, enjoyed by the two sides and suffered by neither. What is more, my contention is that unless it becomes such an act it will only fail in its main function. One cannot conduct an interview by bombarding one's victims with a barrage of questions, which is only tiresome and tiring for both sides. The only way is to make an interview an enjoyable social act, both for the interviewer and the respondent, a two-way traffic, so that the respondent feels not a 'victim' but a true partner, a true conversationalist" (p. 245).

Interviews, then, are not interrogations—they are reciprocal and involving, with an interchange of views. "Interviews," quite literally, are encounters where two or more people explore each others' perceptions and where they seriously consider views, ideas, and perceptions contrary to their own. A guiding principle to keep in mind in framing questions for such a reciprocal, interactive encounter is that such questions should be invitational. Invitational questions are open-ended and provocative and encourage subjects to talk freely and spontaneously about their feelings and concerns. Invitational questions do not contain within them clear cues regarding the desired response; they are easily interpreted by the subject on the basis of his or her own experiences. Invitational questions convey to subjects that the purpose of the interview is to encourage them to express to a sympathetic responder some of their concerns and thoughts. An important criterion by which the success of a phenomenological interview can be judged is the extent to which subjects feel they have gained some increased insight into their own actions as a result of participating in the interview. Gaining familiarity with the experiential terrain of their phenomenological worlds is an important aspect of the interview for both interviewer and subject.

Critical Incidents. Critical incidents have been used for over thirty years in the social sciences and education, ever since Flanagan's (1954) initial formulation of the technique. Flanagan describes the procedures as follows: "The critical incident technique consists of a set of procedures for collecting direct observations of human behavior in such a way as to facilitate their potential usefulness in solving practical problems and developing broad psychological principles. The critical incident outlines procedures for collecting observed incidents having special significance and meeting systematically defined criteria. By *incident* is meant any observable human activity that is sufficiently complete in itself to permit inferences and predictions to be made about the person performing the act. To be *critical,* an incident must occur in a situation where the purpose or intent of the act seems fairly clear to the observer and where its consequences are sufficiently definite to leave little doubt concerning the effect" (p. 327).

Many researchers choose to integrate critical incidents into interviewing or observation, and to obtain data about significant events by these means. In other words, researchers ask subjects in interviews to speak about critical incidents, or they observe people's actions with the intention of recognizing important turning points in their behaviors. However, this approach overlooks the particular advantage of the method, which lies in the securing of written testimonies from subjects. Ideally, in my opinion, critical incidents should be written accounts by subjects of events that have particular significance to them.

Critical incidents are incontrovertible sources of data in the sense that no researcher stands between the subject and the data collected. Researchers do, of course, write the critical incident instructions, administer them to subjects, and code the responses. However, the responses stand alone as primary data sources—written accounts, by the people concerned, of situations and happenings in which they are actually involved. Since they are usually completed in private by subjects, neither researchers nor fellow subjects distort the responses to the incident instructions. Critical incident responses also have the great virtue of being short and manageable for coding. One does not have to wade through page upon page of interview transcript before noticing common themes among subjects' responses. One might spend weeks in naturalistic participant observation in a factory, school, or street gang, trying to learn internal norms and to understand the symbolic significance of certain critical events to workers, students, or gang members. By asking people to provide brief (one or two paragraphs) descriptions of past events that were somehow of significance to them, researchers can quickly assemble a collection of interesting vignettes of actions and situations. If the instructions are written carefully, the written responses can quickly give researchers a sense of the informal culture of the population under study.

Critical incident responses should not generally be used as the sole data source in studies of learning to learn. They are too abbreviated, too truncated, to provide the richness and fullness of descriptions that can be obtained through interview and observation. As with all research, methodological plurality is the cardinal virtue. How can critical incidents be best used in studies of learning how to learn? They can be principally administered to subjects at two points. At the outset of a study, they provide a way of identifying themes and categories—the "essential structures" described by Stanage (1986)—which might profitably be explored further through interviews, observations, and other methods. They are thus useful in suggesting fruitful areas for more focused exploration. The critical incident paragraphs completed by learners provide us with hunches as to what are the most significant concerns and assumptions of respondents. Moreover, these concerns and assumptions are framed within directly observable happenings, rather than in vague generalizations.

At the conclusion of a study, critical incidents are administered as a validity check. After conducting interviews and making observations, we use critical incidents as another means of data collection to tell us the accuracy of the data collected through other methods. By comparing the subjects' spoken comments in interviews to their written comments in reply to critical incident instructions, researchers gain important insights and a clearer picture of how unequivocal or ambiguous their responses have been. If the critical incident responses are consistent with those given in interviews, then we can claim with some degree of certainty that we have accurately relayed the subjects' perceptions. If the responses contradict those given in interviews, we can point to these contradictions as ambiguous findings that might provide a focus for future research.

Analysis of Written Autobiographical Material. Life histories, learning journals, and other forms of written autobiographical analysis are very effective methods for understanding how people learn to learn. The life history method elicits from learners a linear account of marker events in their learning activities. Jones (1983) states that it "offers an interpretative framework through which the meaning of human experience is revealed in personal accounts, in a way that gives priority to individual explanations of actions rather than to methods that filter and sort responses into predetermined conceptual categories" (p. 147). The method provides a means to explore how people interpret and define their actions and the meanings they attribute to them. As with critical incidents, life histories can be written or verbal, but applications in adult education have concentrated on the former (Warren, 1979, 1981). My own doctoral research explored independent learners' life histories through in-depth interviewing by encouraging them to re-create the origins of their learning activities, their most significant learning episodes, the transformational turning points in their learning projects, and their plans for the future. Since the mean length of learning activities (as defined by the learners themselves) was twenty-two years, a life history method was particularly appropriate. Finger (1986) has used this method to help adult educators develop a self-conscious awareness of the reasoning and circumstances that caused them to enter their work setting.

Employing such unobtrusive measures as analysis of learning journals provides a useful approach to understanding learning to learn. In their discussion of documentary sources in adult learning research, Merriam and Jones (1983, p. 55) state that "in an area such as adult development and learning, the researcher cannot make judgments about relevance until the phenomenon is encountered in the actual environment in which it exists." Given that cognitive activities can be apprehended only at one or more stages removed from the actual phenomenon (we can never know something, or realize an insight, in exactly the manner in which the learner did), journals provide an immediate and relatively direct recounting of the experience of learning by learners themselves. For example, Fingeret's (1982) description of the culture shock of a practitioner entering graduate school, and the resulting intellectual journey, is probably the closest we can get to how she experienced this reality. We cannot, of course, claim that the writers of learning journals possess full knowledge of all aspects of a process in which they are involved. Neither can we assume that their perceptions of their experiences are wholly inclusive and authentic in terms of integrating all possible perspectives on the situation. Nonetheless, as outlined in Cell (1984), asking people to keep a learning journal in which they document their activities, their emotions during the different phases of these activities, their interpretation of the meaning and significance, and their discernment of overall patterns and interrelations can be valuable research strategy, as well as an intervention strategy to aid in more effective learning.

In addition to highly systematic research, there are many uses to which life histories, learning journals, and other autobiographical analyses of learning to learn can be put. Christensen (1981) describes how diaries and learning journals can be used as planning and evaluating tools for personal learning projects and for fostering creativity in learning. Written autobiographical accounts can be used to develop curricula for training educators; only if we know how educators learn to do their work in the contexts in which this work actually occurs can we develop meaningful training curricula which have any grounding in the reality of practice. Brookfield (1988) advocates the use of critical incidents in this regard, while Finger (1986) records his use of group analysis of participants' written accounts. Powell (1985) documents a number of experiments in autobiographical analysis, including his own attempt to encourage learners to write about particularly significant learning experiences they had had within educational institutions. Abbs (1974) and Dow (1979) use group analysis of individual participants' written learning autobiographies in teacher training.

Barnes (1981) describes a British Open University course, "Education Through Autobiography," in which students complete educational autobiographies in reply to various questions. The written autobiographies are then analyzed by these learners as a way of fostering a self-conscious awareness of how different learning experiences contributed to their personal development. All these initiatives share a similar orientation to understanding how people learn to learn. In Powell's terms, the fundamental purpose is that of "encouraging students to explore the nature of their own learning experiences and thus deepen their understanding of themselves as learners" (1984, p. 50).

Conclusion

Research in the reflective domain and helping learners to understand their personal styles and patterns of learning is one of the most important, though least immediately tangible, ways in which people can be helped to become critically sophisticated. Bowers (1984, p. 87) writes that "if the teacher understands how the phenomenological world of the student is constituted, it is then possible to make explicit important elements of the students' tacit knowledge." Awareness of how we learn is a form of tacit knowledge—we have naturally evolved ways of discovering meaning in the events of our lives, yet we are often unaware of these processes. Learning can be regarded as the attempt by learners to construct, interpret, and ascribe meaning to their actions and experiences. Though the psychological terrain of this voyage of discovery is of crucial significance to the learner, it frequently remains relatively ignored by those teachers and facilitators who view learning as the achievement of high scores on standardized tests.

Yet the ability to reflect consciously on one's learning activities, and on how one has come to know what one regards as obvious, common sense, and taken for granted, is a crucial element in developing self-knowledge regarding one's critical thinking. Many interesting problems and questions suggest themselves. How do learners develop and maintain the motivation for various learning ventures? To what extent are extrinsic motives (social contact, job advancement, ego aggrandizement, reinforcement of self-image) and intrinsic motives (innate fascination with learning, being tantalized by problem solving, intrigue with perceived ambiguities, anomalies, and contradictions) interrelated? How do learners integrate new ideas and insights into their existing analytical and interpretive frameworks? What general approaches (trial and error, problem solving, careful planning of short-, intermediate-, and long-term goals) do learners take toward exploring new areas of knowledge? To what extent do previous experiences act as a hindrance or stimulus to the acquisition and integration of various learning styles? In what ways do people feel most comfortable entering the new and potentially frightening intellectual terrains represented by critical thought and analysis? How are new meanings constructed and, being constructed, how do we change our meaning schemes and perspectives?

Answers to these questions will help teachers, counselors, trainers, and other professionals to assist people to reflect on their learning and take greater control over this crucial aspect of their lives. When people become aware of how they learn and learn to learn, they can choose from among strategies which they know will be most effective. They can make informed choices regarding mentors and teachers whose personal and pedagogic styles match their own. They can anticipate and adjust for the fear, pain, anxiety, or distress we all experience as we learn. Becoming aware of how we learn and learning how to adjust for weaknesses and to emphasize strengths is not a pedagogic exercise. It is a fundamentally liberating way to rid ourselves of tendencies and inclinations that act to prevent us from entering the uncharted intellectual, personal, and political waters represented in critical thinking.

References

Abbs, P. *Autobiography in Education.* London: Heinemann, 1974.

Argyris, C. "Increasing Leadership Effectiveness." New York: Wiley, 1976.

Argyris, C., Putnam, R., and Smith, D. M. *Action Science: Concepts,*

Methods, and Skills for Research and Intervention. San Francisco: Jossey-Bass, 1985.

Argyris, C., and Schön, D. A. *Organizational Learning: A Theory of Action Perspective.* Reading, Mass.: Addison-Wesley, 1978.

Barnes, P. *Education Through Autobiography.* Milton Keynes, England: Open University Press, 1981.

Basseches, M. *Dialectical Thinking and Adult Development.* Norwood, N.J.: Ablex, 1984.

Bates, H. M. "A Phenomenological Study of Adult Learners: Participants' Experiences of a Learner-Centered Approach." Unpublished doctoral dissertation, Department of Adult Education, Ontario Institute for Studies in Education, Toronto, Canada, 1979.

Berger, P. L., and Luckmann, T. *The Social Construction of Knowledge.* New York: Doubleday, 1967.

Boud, D. J., and Griffin, V. *Appreciating Adults Learning: From the Learners' Perspective.* Toronto, Canada: Ontario Institute for Studies in Education, 1987.

Bowers, C. A. *The Promise of Theory: Education and the Politics of Cultural Change.* New York: Longman, 1984.

Boyd, E. M., and Fales, A. W. "Reflective Learning: Key to Learning from Experience." *Journal of Humanistic Psychology,* 1983, *23* (2), 99–117.

Briggs, C. *Learning How to Ask.* New York: Cambridge University Press, 1986.

Brookfield, S. D. "Developing Critically Reflective Practitioners: A Critical Rationale for Graduate Adult Education." In S. D. Brookfield (ed.), *Training Educators of Adults: The Theory and Practice of Graduate Adult Education in the United States.* London: Croom Helm, 1988.

Candy, P. C., Harri-Augstein, E. S., and Thomas, L. F. "Reflection and the Self-Organized Learner: A Model of Learning Conversations." In D. J. Boud, R. Keogh, and D. Walker (eds.), *Reflection: Turning Experience into Learning.* London: Kogan Page, 1985.

Cell, E. *Learning to Learn from Experience.* Albany: State University of New York Press, 1984.

Christensen, R. S. "Dear Diary: A Learning Tool for Adults." *Lifelong Learning,* 1981, *5* (2), 4–5, 31.

Denis, M. M. "Toward the Development of a Theory of Intuitive Learning in Adults Based on a Descriptive Analysis." Unpublished doctoral dissertation, Ontario Institute for Studies in Education, Toronto, Canada, 1979.

Denzin, N. K. *The Research Act.* New York: McGraw-Hill, 1978.

Dow, G. M. *Learning to Teach: Teaching to Learn.* London: Routledge and Kegan Paul, 1979.

Entwistle, N. J., and Hounsell, D. "Student Learning in Its Natural Setting." *Higher Education,* 1979, *8* (4), 359–363.

Finger, M. "La Formation Enjou de la Recherche Sociale." Unpublished doctoral dissertation, Department of Educational Psychology, University of Geneva, 1986.

Fingeret, A. "Culture Shock: Practitioners Returning to Graduate School." *Lifelong Learning,* 1982, *51* (4), 327–358.

Flanagan, J. C. "The Critical Incident Technique." *Psychological Bulletin,* 1954, *54* (4), 327–358.

Gibbs, G., Morgan, A. R., and Taylor, E. "A Review of the Research of Ference Marton and the Göteborg Group: A Phenomenological Research Perspective on Learning." *Higher Education,* 1982, *11* (2), 123–145.

Gilligan, C. *In a Different Voice: Psychological Theory and Women's Development.* Cambridge, Mass.: Harvard University Press, 1982.

Grumet, M. R. "Restitution and Reconstruction of Educational Experience: An Autobiographical Method for Curriculum Theory." In M. Lawn and L. Barton (eds.), *Rethinking Curriculum Studies.* London: Croom Helm, 1981.

Harri-Augstein, E. S., and Thomas, L. F. *Self-Organised Learning.* London: Routledge and Kegan Paul, 1984.

Jones, G. R. "Life History Methodology." In G. Morgan (ed.), *Beyond Method: Strategies for Social Research.* Newbury Park, Calif.: Sage, 1983.

King, P. M. "The Development of Reflective Judgment and Formal Operational Thinking in Adolescents and Young Adults."

Unpublished doctoral dissertation, Department of Psychology, University of Minnesota, 1978.

Kitchener, K. S. "Cognition, Metacognition and Epistemic Cognition: A Three-Level Model of Cognitive Process." *Human Development*, 1983, *4*, 222–232.

Kitchener, K. S. "The Reflective Judgment Model: Characteristics, Evidence and Measurement." In R. A. Mines and K. S. Kitchener (eds.), *Adult Cognitive Development: Methods and Models*. New York: Praeger, 1986.

Levinson, D. J. *The Seasons of a Man's Life*. New York: Knopf, 1978.

Lindeman, E.C.L. "What Is Adult Education?" Unpublished manuscript, Lindeman Archive, Butler Library, Columbia University, 1925.

Mahrer, A. R. *Experiential Psychotherapy: Basic Practices*. New York: Brunner/Mazel, 1983.

Marton, F. "Phenomenography—Describing Conceptions of the World Around Us." *Instructional Science*, 1981, *10*, 177–200.

Marton, F., and Säljö, R. "On Qualitative Differences in Learning: Outcome and Process." *British Journal of Educational Psychology*, 1976a, *46* (1), 4–11.

Marton, F., and Säljö, R. "On Qualitative Differences in Learning: Outcome as a Function of the Learner's Conception of the Task." *British Journal of Educational Technology*, 1976b, *46* (2), 115–127.

Marton, F., and Säljö, R. "Approaches to Learning." In F. Marton, D. Hounsell, and N. Entwistle (eds.). *The Experience of Learning*. Edinburgh: Scottish Academic Press, 1984.

Merriam, S. B., and Jones, E. "The Use of Documentary Sources in Adult Learning and Development Research." *Adult Education*, 1983, *34* (1), 54–59.

Mezirow, J. "A Critical Theory of Adult Learning and Education." *Adult Education*, 1981, *32* (1), 3–27.

Morgan, A. R., Taylor, E., and Gibbs, G. "Variations in Students' Approaches to Studying." *British Journal of Educational Technology*, 1982, *13* (2), 107–113.

Morgan, G. (ed.). *Beyond Method*. Newbury Park, Calif.: Sage, 1983.

Perry, W. G. *Forms of Intellectual and Ethical Development in the*

College Years: A Scheme. New York: Holt, Rinehart & Winston, 1970.

Powell, J. P. "Autobiographical Learning." In D. J. Boud, R. Keogh, and D. Walker (eds.), *Turning Reflection into Learning.* London: Kogan Page, 1985.

Schön, D. A. *The Reflective Practitioner.* New York: Basic Books, 1983.

Smith, R. M. *Learning How to Learn: Applied Theory for Adults.* New York: Cambridge Book Company, 1982.

Stanage, S. "Learning How to Learn: A Phenomenological Analysis of Adult 'Eductive' Learning." *Proceedings of the Adult Education Research Conference,* no. 27. Syracuse, N.Y.: Syracuse University, 1986.

Stanage, S. *Adult Education and Phenomenological Research: New Directions for Theory, Practice and Research.* Malabar, Fla.: Krieger, 1987.

Taylor, E., Morgan, A. R., and Gibbs, G. "The Orientations of Open University Students to Their Studies." *Teaching at a Distance,* 1981, *20* (1), 3–12.

Taylor, M. "Adult Learning in an Emergent Learning Group: Toward a Theory of Learning from the Learning Perspective." Unpublished doctoral dissertation, Ontario Institute for Studies in Education, Toronto, Canada, 1979.

Warren, C. E. *Perceptions of Achievement: A Study of Women in Two Occupations in England and Canada.* London: University of London, 1979.

Warren, C. E. "Using the Life History as a Prime Research Tool." Adult Education Research Conference Proceedings, no. 21. Vancouver, Canada: University of British Columbia, 1980.

Warren, C. E. "Using the Written Life History for Program Evaluation." *Canadian Journal of University Continuing Education,* 1981, *8* (2), 10–14.

Warren, C. E. "The Written Life History as a Prime Research Tool in Adult Education." *Adult Education,* 1982, *32* (4), 214–228.

Zweig, F. *In Quest of Fellowship.* London: Heinemann, 1965.

Chapter 15

Disseminating
Current Knowledge
About Learning to Learn

Robert M. Smith

Directing education largely to the imparting and acquiring of subject matter has proved inadequate and unrealistic. The learning-to-learn idea has long been proposed as a viable alternative by a few visionaries, and recent research and development provide promising concepts, tools, and rationales for implementation. How can the vision be more fully realized and the momentum be sustained? This chapter suggests four strategies: stimulate more instruction and programming from a learning-to-learn perspective; encourage appropriate preservice education and staff development; support research-to-practice endeavors; and make the dissemination of learning-to-learn information more systematic. The chapter is directed primarily to those who wish to act on the implications of what has gone before.

Some Implications for Program Development
and Management

Once learning to learn is seriously endorsed as an educational goal, program development is seen from new perspectives. Administrators, program developers, and curriculum specialists find themselves confronting these kinds of questions:

1. How well prepared are the participants to learn from the methods and task requirements they will encounter in this program?
2. What provision should be made to assist the participants to learn effectively in this program?
3. What can be built into the program to enhance or maintain such generic learning-to-learn competencies as self-awareness, reflection, and understanding the structures of subject matter?
4. Can we highlight our concern with learning to learn in program promotion activity?
5. How can the program's learning-to-learn outcomes and shortcomings be ascertained?
6. How well equipped are the instructional and support staff to implement the learning-to-learn requirements and activities of the program? What are the implications for faculty and staff development?

Paying attention to these questions enables programmers and curriculum developers to become sensitive to the learning-to-learn aspects of what they do. They watch for symptoms that might call for a learning-to-learn response: high dropout rates, frequent complaints about a method or an instructor, low student morale, a high cancellation rate for noncredit offerings. An instructor receiving poor ratings may need to change his methods (group discussion, simulation, out-of-class projects) *or* be encouraged to provide students with support in the use of a method.

Educational needs analysis comes to be seen in a different light. Assessing people's process needs often becomes as important as assessing their content needs, and the two kinds of needs may well require different programmatic responses. Organizational mission statements and program objectives will begin to reflect greater concern with such outcomes as motivation and readiness for further learning, confidence in learning, comfort with a new educational methodology, and acquisition of learning strategies. Accordingly, new focuses emerge for program evaluation, and it no longer suffices to evaluate solely on the bases of program processes and products, of content acquisition, or even of content acquired and applied. Programmatic effects on the participants *as learners* come under review and such questions as these become relevant: Does the program diminish, maintain, or enhance the disposition and ability of the participants to take control of learning-related activity? Does it encourage and reward meaningful learning, as opposed to the rote acquisition of undigested information? Does it adequately prepare the participant for the next level of education or life phase? (This question might be asked, for example, about the curriculum of the final year of elementary or secondary school or college.)

Agencies that conduct open programming, such as the continuing education arms of colleges, universities, and educational companies, can consider adding a learning-to-learn line to their offerings. A few possibilities for courses and workshops come readily to mind: the learning-to-learn aspects of parenting; learning to learn holistically; how to learn through mentoring; collaborative problem solving; understanding and negotiating the world of higher education.

Optimum occasions for major programmatic initiatives in learning to learn include when people are new to an organization, when a degree or certificate program is getting under way, and when people near the end of a program. Models for informing an entire curriculum or organization with a learning-to-learn dimension have been proposed by Gibbons and Phillips (1982) and Lindsey (1988) for elementary-secondary education; by Schlossberg, Lynch and Chickering (1989) for higher education; and by Cheren (1987) for human resource development.

Teaching from a Learning-to-Learn Perspective

To teach is to be automatically involved in learning to learn—by design or default—because teaching, learning, and learning to learn are reciprocally and synergistically related. On the positive side, according to McKeachie, Pintrich, and Lin, "When students are learning, they are not only learning facts, principles, and relationships, they also learn something about how to learn" (1985, p. 602). On the negative side, students may be learning to dislike the subject, to fear examinations, or to understand learning as a passive process.

Good teaching supports learning to learn, but good teaching from a learning-to-learn perspective does even more. Effective teaching is associated with setting an effective climate, clearly communicating objectives and goals, selecting and using appropriate methods and procedures, providing useful feedback, and supporting the application of what has been learned. The recipient of such teaching can be expected to come away with new knowledge and positive feelings toward the experience. But the person who receives good teaching grounded in a learning-to-learn perspective will have gained considerably more.

It may be useful here to keep a model of the ideal learner in mind. She has been described in this book as an active, confident, reflective, self-aware learner — one who learns effectively for a variety of purposes in a variety of contexts. This paragon demonstrates flexibility, knowing when to take and when to relinquish control, and when to modify plans when the unexpected transpires. She employs a broad repertoire of learning skills and strategies. She learns holistically, sensing or knowing the limitations of the rational mode. She tends to be open to new experience and unfamiliar ideas. She can identify and evaluate the personal rules that govern her attitudes toward learning and learning-related behavior. She knows her rights as a consumer of education. She negotiates educational bureaucracies smoothly and sometimes advocates institutional reform.

Modifying Instructional Design. One way to bring a learning-to-learn emphasis to instruction is to modify an approach that is already employed. Schmitt and Newby (1986) describe a modification of a methodology commonly used to teach work skills. The traditional four-part approach entails communicating or arranging for (1) declarative knowledge (*what*)—for example, what the person is expected to learn; (2) procedural knowledge (*how*)—for example, how to carry out the requisite tasks; (3) practice activity; and (4) provision of feedback.

The learning-to-learn modification of the method consists of the insertion of two components that provide "conditional" knowledge. The first component comes between steps number one and two and deals with *why* the skill is important and *when* to use it. The second involves not only practice of the task (in step three) but also practice pertaining to when and why to use the skill. Justification for this change in format comes from research demonstrating that instruction that includes the rationale, significance, and utility of the skills to be imparted improves performance *and* the maintenance of performance in appropriate situations.

Teaching Interactively. One-way communication—from teacher to learner—usually contributes little to the enhancement of learning competence. Aristotle may have been the first to warn us that the only way to be is to become, and it should be obvious that "telling" seldom changes behavior. Interactive teaching challenges both student and teacher to raise questions, to examine purposes and assumptions, to problem pose and problem solve, and to accept mutual responsibility for the learning-teaching transaction. Diagnosis, negotiation, and collaboration come into play. The teacher is called upon to provide an environment with a "judicious mixture of compatible and conflicting experience" (Brown, 1987, p. 108); the student is called upon to learn actively and reflectively.

Interactive teaching focuses on meaning and understanding. The teacher tries to lead the learner to the limits of his understanding and to help him find aspects of the subject that are especially interesting and meaningful (everyone can be an expert in at least one area). The teacher helps the student to understand the structures of knowledge, to interact with it, and to anchor new knowledge in prior knowledge; the student may be invited to entertain more sophisticated conceptions of what knowledge is, and its constructivist nature should be revealed to him. The teaching and learning of concepts, principles, and relationships (the making of connections) and the examination of critical issues become very important; and learning facts becomes of less consequence than learning where and how to access them. Feedback and assessment are directed not only to the amount but also to the quality of knowledge attained, as well as readiness for further learning and the improvement of learning and teaching.

This kind of teaching is oriented to process as well as content. It is directed toward increases in self-awareness and reflection in learning. People are helped to understand what was termed in Chapter One their personal learning contexts — the values, goals, and assumptions they bring to educational settings as well as their learning styles and repertoires of strategies. They are encouraged to "reflect on the learning process rather than concentrate on the finished product" (Nisbet and Shucksmith, 1986, p. 77), to make mental processes visible. They are helped to acquire both context-specific and generic strategies and to use them in other in-school and out-of-school situations. Teachers use a variety of models and methods, chosen both to impart knowledge and for their nurturant effects (Joyce and Weil, 1986). Teachers employ such activities as learning style profiling, student logs and journals, concept mapping, and group exercises for reflecting on learning. They may encourage the use of self-questioning, rehearsal, visual imagery, and relaxation strategies. They may model or demonstrate various tasks — examining an unfamiliar text, planning an essay, active reading, or active listening — or improvise ways to keep learning processes, problems, and strategies on the agenda.

With regard to self-directedness, instructors should avoid doing for learners what learners can do for themselves and support movement toward increased responsibility for learning. People need to learn to take, or try to take, varying amounts of control in learning situations; they usually need help in understanding the advantages of doing so and in establishing meaningful criteria for assuming and relinquishing control. Students can develop questions to inform their reading or to be included in an examination, but they need to feel that such activity is worthwhile and know the characteristics of useful questions. When they encounter a course format or teaching style that calls for unusual amounts of self-direction, they are entitled to initial orientation and later support as needed.

Here are some principles and questions to guide teaching from a learning-to-learn perspective:

Principles

1. The learning-to-learn aspect latent or manifest in most teaching decisions, activities, and outcomes is usually there to be found and taken into account.
2. The learning-to-learn concept is best implemented through a combination of indirect and direct methods.
3. Both contextual and generic learning competencies and strategies can be cultivated.
4. Since learning to learn usually requires changes of ingrained assumptions and habits by learner and teacher, it helps to think big, begin small, and be grateful for modest gains.

Questions

1. To what extent does current instructional practice reflect a learning-to-learn perspective?
2. What additions or adjustments appear appropriate to experiment with?
3. What are some potential rewards for teacher and learner?
4. What support is available from administrators, program coordinators, or peers? What resistance may be encountered?
5. What is needed in order to get started?
6. How will progress be evaluated?

Implications for Preservice Education and Staff Development

Widespread implementation of the learning-to-learn concept will entail helping facilitators and putative facilitators to understand themselves as learners who have much in common with clients, whom they can help to learn more effectively. Teacher education programs will need to foster participants' understanding of teaching and learning as a transaction — a process in which learning-to-learn potentialities and effects are embedded. Emphasis on teaching interactively and strategically is in order. The program should demonstrate the utility of such techniques as self-questioning, mental rehearsal, concept mapping, and personal goal setting, as well as provide supervised practice opportunities. Learning *about* learning-to-learn philosophy, resources, and strategies will not suffice: preservice teachers will need to acquire personally meaningful ways of operationalizing the concepts and the disposition to apply them. This may require the support of university faculty members who themselves have gone through similar experiences.

Neely (1986) investigated the effects of training in cognitive monitoring on the lesson planning and implementation activities of preservice teachers. Training focused on forming more elaborate mental images of the lessons planned and self-interrogation (What do I know about this topic?). Training activities included modeling, rehearsal, self-probes, and thinking aloud. All subjects planned and carried out two lessons during field experience. Prospective teachers who received training were significantly more effective in developing and implementing their plans, as well as better able to identify goals, predict outcomes, establish alternate plans, and remain sensitive to student needs. She concludes that the study suggests that good teaching requires that the teacher be a self-aware, self-monitoring, reflective learner and problem solver.

Cruickshank (1986) calls for educators of teachers to foster "wisdom" — the "ability to have and use good habits of thought" — by providing valid situations that provoke reflection, in order that the teachers in turn will be able to do likewise for those they teach. He states that wise teachers have greater awareness of the conscious and unconscious determinants of behavior, greater open-mindedness, less naivete in thinking, and more appropriate instructional goals and activities. They are more likely to "seek out, examine, and use information about

teaching in general and their own teaching habits in particular."
Central to the process of fostering wisdom in teachers are curricula and staff development programs that balance the provision of teaching situations and experiences with opportunities
to reflect on them (p. 21).

Similar considerations obtain with regard to the practicing teacher. Writing of reform to change schools from places
where children recite to "environments in which they are assisted to perform," Tharp and Gallimore (1989) challenge teachers to accept responsibility for professional development involving "long and sometimes painful self examination." Inservice
education must go beyond merely making information available
to bring about the intellectual growth of teachers (p. 52). Adey
and Shayer (1988) conclude that "radically improved methods of
in-service teacher education" will be needed if proven strategies
for metalearning (strategies for teaching difficult concepts, for
example) are to be implemented in science instruction (p. 104).

A Case in Point. An example of experienced teachers accepting
responsibility for their own intellectual growth and that of their
students was found in the PEEL Project, a long-term experiment
carried out in a state-supported secondary school in a working-
class community in Australia (Baird and Mitchell, 1987). PEEL
stands for Project for Enhancing Effective Learning. The aims
of PEEL were (1) to improve the quality of school learning and
teaching and (2) to help students become more willing and able
to accept responsibility for their learning. Students were expected to increase their knowledge of what learning is and how
it works, gain greater awareness of learning process and outcome, and improve their control of learning through more
purposeful decision making. The ten participating teachers
(volunteers) agreed to direct instruction toward changes in student attitudes and behaviors that would promote "enhanced
metacognition." They also agreed to support the action research
component of the project through such activity as keeping
personal diaries. Each teacher also contributed a chapter to the
ensuing publication, *Improving the Quality of Teaching and Learning: An Australian Case Study,* which was edited by project leaders

John Baird and Ian Mitchell. This book is rich in details of the day-to-day problems, setbacks, triumphs, frustrations, and activities of a cohesive group of experienced faculty members discovering ways to teach from a learning-to-learn perspective. It sheds light on the process of the development of effective strategies and of solid commitment by both teacher and student. It presents the multiple reactions and views of students, teachers, administrators, outside observers, and consultants. The description and analysis take place in the contexts of action research and change theory. The implications for preservice and inservice education warrant a close look at PEEL.

At the end of its first year, a consensus evaluation by project staff, participating teachers, and students determined that PEEL had made modest but significant gains and was well worth continuing. Several additional teachers joined the project, while only one dropped out. Major benefits to students were described by one as understanding that learning is "many things, from asking questions and taking part in discussion, to understanding what you are doing and why," and the acquisition of such habits as questioning others' statements and differing answers, "picking up on what others are saying," and reflecting on one's notes. Students and teachers felt that students had come to ask better questions and participate more actively, and that prospects were good for many of the newly established habits to continue in use.

Students encountered many unsettling experiences on first entering the project, without the option to withdraw and the mutual support system that buoyed up the teachers. They lacked confidence in their ability to monitor, reflect on, and control learning. They exhibited restricted, conservative views of what constitutes learning and appropriate student/teacher classroom behaviors. ("All this thinking is interfering with our work.") Active learning represented for most a novel and tiring experience difficult to deal with early in the project. Peers played a central role in students' responses to efforts to modify their approaches to learning.

Critical factors in motivation to get wholeheartedly behind change efforts and to persist in them were different for students and teachers. Students tended to resist until they came to see "personal costs flowing from inadequate learning behaviors." Student resistance declined, however, when teachers eventually learned to design and facilitate the use of fruitful, context-specific procedures with clear, short-term goals and rewards. Teachers had entered the project because the idea had appeal, a challenge was involved, new techniques and strategies could be acquired, and student learning was perceived by them as largely passive, superficial, and lacking in transference. Teachers remained in PEEL, despite the considerable demands and many frustrations, because they came to value highly their new perspectives on learning and teaching and to view the overall experience as authentic professional development: "In PEEL we set out to change the learning styles of secondary school students, and found that it was not a simple matter of practising them in a few easily acquired skills. We also found that we had changed ourselves" (Baird and Mitchell, 1987, p. 230).

As with most successful efforts to implement the learning-to-learn concept, the PEEL Project leaders were sensitive to issues of change: overcoming resistance, planning for change, creating a climate for change, assessing for change. In a concluding chapter entitled "Reflections on the Nature of Change," John Baird presents a model of personal development that takes the form of a pinwheel with three colors—attitudes, conceptions, and behaviors: "The basis of the model is that each of these features of an individual grow, develop, and expand together as a result of the wind of experience. . . . The model emphasizes the interdependence of attitudes, conceptions, and behaviors for personal development. . . [and at] any given time each person has a unique combination of the three" (pp. 255–256). Baird goes on to interpret the significant changes and processes in PEEL students and teachers with models, including a three-stage adoption model and one that sets forth three requirements for a person to accept a concept. One is reminded of the importance of change theory to researchers and writers who have dealt with learning to learn in and through laboratory learning and participation training (Bradford, 1964; Bergevin and McKinley, 1965; Smith, 1976).

What are some implications of PEEL for preservice and inservice activity concerning learning to learn? One lesson is that significant educational change is a long-term process involving a multitude of person-specific and context-specific changes. Both teachers and students will change to different extents, at varying rates, and in different ways. Attitudes, conceptions, and behaviors change together, combining in reciprocal, interdependent fashion for personal development. Change cannot go smoothly; the inevitable mistakes and reversals need to be reflected on in order to minimize their effects and go forward. A pivotal insight for PEEL teachers, for example, came with recognition of the gulfs between their own and students' perceptions of learning purposes, tasks, assignments, and so forth.

Resistance is normal and to be expected. In order for a person to understand and accept a concept (active learning, reflection in learning), it needs to be (1) intelligible (related to other knowledge), (2) plausible (consistent with other knowledge), and (3) fruitful (perceived as potentially beneficial). PEEL students had more difficulties accepting the plausibility and benefits of metacognition than did their teachers. For both, understanding came in piecemeal fashion, and teachers shared with students the difficulties in recognizing and acknowledging changes in themselves.

Short-term rewards and recognition are important in major change efforts; without them, initial enthusiasms wither. PEEL teachers found rewarding the administration's efforts to cooperate in class scheduling and enabling project staff meetings to be held regularly and for significant amounts of time. The presence of a nonthreatening consultant and two outside observers lent support. A major source of recognition was the decision (late in the year) of all project participants to collaborate in an effort to produce a book. Rewards in a project of this kind tend to be intrinsic in the early stages, but some eventual extrinsic rewards are necessary for optimum results.

Teachers found facilitative strategies to be more useful when they focused on specific (inadequate) learning behaviors and promoted positive alternate behaviors, noting that each topic and subject has different requirements. Teachers found metacognitive concepts difficult to grasp until a substantial reservoir of relevant experience was acquired. For both teachers and students, changes in behavior tended to precede changes in conceptions, attitudes, and dispositions.

Some Principles. In summary, preservice and inservice education concerning learning to learn will probably be successful if these guidelines are followed.

1. Direct instruction to self-examine assumptions and to reflect upon practice by the participants.
2. Maintain an orientation to learning to learn as a change process, involving learner change, staff change, and organizational change.
3. Recognize that both facilitator and client need experiences that confirm the utility of learning-to-learn activity.
4. Enable the participants to acquire contextually appropriate procedures and strategies.
5. Provide organizational support and rewards to participants as they make applications of their newly acquired knowledge.

Making Dissemination More Systematic

Knowledge about learning to learn is now extensive and much of it is potentially useful, despite the fact that it is scattered through various fields of inquiry and practice. While knowledge production has been accelerating, dissemination has neither kept pace nor been approached systematically. Some of the obstacles are discussed by Hounsell (1979), Novak and Gowin (1984), Merriam (1986), and Smith (1988). Educational innovations have seldom received what dissemination experts term "early adoption." (It took about fifty years for the kindergarten to gain nationwide acceptance.) Practitioners tend to be skeptical of research findings and to lack external incentives to implement them. Researchers often write for their colleagues' approval and confront institutional reward systems ill suited to applied research. Recommendations for bridging the research-to-practice gap include (1) persuading researchers to pay more attention to practical applications when designing their studies, (2) encouraging the production of more process materials for learners and facilitators, and (3) establishing dissemination centers.

University faculty members are well positioned today to conduct and encourage collaborative research with practitioners in pre- and postsecondary education. The PEEL Project, led by a professor of educational psychology, represents an excellent example in which the method (action research) also proved to be a felicitous choice. Until recently, however, educational research in universities was dominated by the experimental paradigm. A variety of paradigms are now acceptable, including the phenomenological orientation and interactive approaches advocated by Stephen Brookfield in Chapter Fourteen.

Learning-to-learn knowledge has not always proven easy to package or disseminate. It stems from research and experience in a variety of academic disciplines and is anchored in various settings and contexts (school, workplace, math and science, therapy, remediation, adults returning to college). It involves processes, metaprocesses, and clear thinking about such multiple realities as are inherent in these questions: How can teachers be taught to help students examine the personal rules and purposes that inform their learning? What activities will help people to understand the difference between process and content? How can facilitators assist learners to externalize their thinking and problem-solving processes?

The skeptical may well question the utility of stepping up and systematizing dissemination efforts in behalf of a complex subject short on both prescriptive knowledge and thoroughly tested procedures. A great deal has been learned since research on the following questions was proposed over two decades ago:

1. What is the nature of the learning-to-learn concept?
2. What are the conditions under which one learns to learn?

3. What methods and techniques interfere with the learning-to-learn concept?
4. Does learning to learn follow a different development pattern in youth than in adulthood?
5. To what extent has the high school or college graduate learned to learn?
6. What "educational ingredients" encourage learning to learn in adults? (Kreitlow, 1968)

Nor will the present knowledge keep well, unlike "a historical film secure in a container until the market seems right"; and the information is undergoing dissemination now, however inefficient the processes (Smith, 1988, p. 151). Making these processes more effective will require experimentation.

Dissemination Centers and Models. Gunter and Brady (1984) point to the need for research to develop and examine effective dissemination models for educational knowledge. They suggest the maximizing of user choices and the minimizing of cost as two criteria for such models. The dissemination literature divides established approaches into (1) the diffusion model, (2) the research-development-dissemination model, (3) the problem-solving model, and (4) the linkage model. The diffusion model (which describes the present situation with regard to learning-to-learn) delineates an unplanned spread of information through networks of practitioners by way of conversation, publications, and meetings. The research-development-dissemination model involves well-organized effort with responsibility shared among research and development people, disseminators, and practitioners; it clearly fits the Cooperative Extension movement and its legendary impact on rural life in the United States through massive government funding. With the problem-solving model, people seek new knowledge in order to solve self-perceived problems that clearly relate to their existing resources. The linkage model seeks to "stimulate consumption" through new resources and better utilization of existing local resources and fostering of networks (Hoyle, 1985).

    The establishment of one or more dissemination centers

for learning-to-learn knowledge applications emerges as an appealing goal. Such a center could serve as a demonstration project for the development of an appropriate dissemination model. It could establish an electronic data base of information on learning to learn and provide an information clearinghouse. It could evaluate emerging materials, encourage research and development, and put researchers and practitioners in touch with each other. It could sponsor workshops and conferences on such topics as electronic media applications of learning to learn and the production and marketing of learning-to-learn materials. Technical assistance could be provided for staff development and the establishment of a learning resource center.

If such a dissemination center were located in a university, faculty and graduate students from various academic disciplines could be involved and research could be stimulated. Maintaining a *dissemination focus,* however, might be difficult because of the faculty reward system and multiple demands on faculty time and energy. The survival of an independent center established through external funding would probably require making services cost effective, which raises the issue of equity. A university-based program might succeed by combining an acceptable amount of dollar return with demonstrable payoff in the form of student internship opportunities, in-house services to students, institutional image, and contributions to knowledge about processes and procedures for disseminating educational knowledge (Smith, 1988, pp. 161–162).

Other means of dissemination might include sections or columns on learning to learn incorporated into existing periodicals. A generic society or professional association might be established, along with special-interest sections in such existing bodies as the Association for Supervision and Curriculum Development, the American Association for Adult and Continuing Education, and the American Society for Training and Development, as well as their state and regional affiliates.

In short, more active, systematic dissemination makes sense and appears feasible. For those who would further this process, there is a role for the researcher, the concerned research-to-practice advocate, and the materials developer, as well as for universities, funding agencies, professional associations, and local providers of education. Dissemination should be directed toward programming and instruction from a learning-to-learn perspective and supported by pre- and inservice education that is grounded in experience and focused on change processes.

References

Adey, P., and Shayer, M. "Strategies for Meta-Learning in Physics." *Physics Education,* 1988, *23* (2), 97–104.

Baird, J. R., and Mitchell, I. J. *Improving the Quality of Teaching and Learning: An Australian Case Study — The PEEL Project.* Melbourne, Australia: Monash University Printery, 1987.

Bergevin, P. E., and McKinley, J. *Participation Training for Adult Education.* St. Louis, Mo.: Bethany Press, 1965.

Bradford, L. P., and others (eds.). *T-Group Theory and Laboratory Method.* New York: Wiley, 1964.

Brown, A. "Metacognition, Executive Control, Self-Regulation and Other More Mysterious Mechanisms." In F. E. Weinert and R. H. Kluwe (eds.), *Metacognition, Motivation and Understanding.* Hillsdale, N.J.: Erlbaum, 1987.

Cheren, M. E. (ed.). *Learning Management: Emerging Directions for Learning to Learn in the Workplace.* Information Series no. 320. Columbus: National Center for Research in Vocational Education, Ohio State University, 1987.

Cruickshank, D. R. "Helping Teachers Achieve Wisdom." *Texas Tech Journal of Education,* 1986, *13* (1), 21–27.

Gibbons, M., and Phillips, G. "Self-Education: The Process of Lifelong Learning." *Canadian Journal of Education,* 1982, 7 (4), 67–86.

Gunter, P., and Brady, M. "Increasing the Practitioner's Utilization of Research." *Education,* 1984, *105,* 92–98.

Hounsell, D. "Learning to Learn: Research and Development in Student Learning." *Higher Education,* 1979, *8* (4), 453–469.

Hoyle, E. "Educational Research: Dissemination, Participation, Negotiation." In J. Nisbet (ed.), *World Yearbook of Education*

1985: Research, Policy, and Practice. New York: Columbia University Teachers College, 1985.

Joyce, B., and Weil, M. *Models of Teaching.* (3rd ed.) Englewood Cliffs, N.J.: Prentice-Hall, 1986.

Kreitlow, B. "Educating the Adult Educator: Taxonomy of Needed Research." Madison: University of Wisconsin Center for Cognitive Learning, Part II, 1968. (ED 023 031)

Lindsey, C. W., Jr. *Teaching Students to Teach Themselves.* New York: Nichols, 1988.

McKeachie, W. J., Pintrich, P. R., and Lin, Y. "Learning to Learn." In G. d'Ydewalle (ed.), *Cognition, Information Processing, and Motivation.* Amsterdam, The Netherlands: North Holland, 1985.

Merriam, S. "The Research to Practice Dilemma." *Lifelong Learning: An Omnibus of Practice and Research,* 1986, *10,* 4–6, 24.

Neely, A. M. "Planning and Problem Solving in Teacher Education." *Journal of Teacher Education,* 1986, *37* (3), 29–33.

Nisbet, J., and Shucksmith, J. *Learning Strategies.* New York: Routledge, 1986.

Novak, J. D., and Gowin, D. B. *Learning How to Learn.* New York: Cambridge University Press, 1984.

Schlossberg, N. K., Lynch, A. Q., and Chickering, A. W. *Improving Higher Education Environments for Adults: Responsive Programs and Services from Entry to Departure.* San Francisco: Jossey-Bass, 1989.

Schmitt, M. C., and Newby, T. J. "Metacognition: Relevance to Instructional Design." *Journal of Instructional Development,* 1986, *9* (1), 29–33.

Smith, R. M. *Learning How to Learn in Adult Education.* DeKalb, Ill.: ERIC Clearinghouse in Career Education. Information Series no. 10, 1976. (ED 132 245)

Smith, R. M. "Improving Dissemination of Knowledge About Self-Directedness in Education." In H. B. Long and Associates, *Self-Directed Learning: Application and Theory.* Athens: Adult Education Department, University of Georgia, 1988.

Tharp, R. G., and Gallimore, R. "Rousing Schools to Life." *American Educator,* 1989, *13* (2), 20–25, 46–52.

Name Index

Subject Index